Preface

This book has been written specifically for the NCC Joint Diploma syllabus of Computerised Accounts. However, it is also suitable for a wide range of computer studies courses that include an accounting element.

Most computer studies courses will include some form of accounting – it is clearly important that students studying for a career in the computing industry should have some insight into the purpose and function of accounting in the modern organisation.

The object of the book is not to provide instructions on the *how* of accounting but rather the *why*. Computer studies students at any level are not likely to be accoun- tants, but require some knowledge of the importance of accounting since a large proportion of their time as analysts, programmers or operators will be spent on handling tasks or data which form part of the accounting system.

One major difference between this book and other standard accounting texts is that this one places greater emphasis on modern practices and styles of presentation as opposed to accepted theory. This approach has been adopted as some knowledge of general accounting theory is essential in order to understand computerised systems – but by explaining theory in a more modern style students should be able to understand the link between accounting theory and computerised systems much more easily.

Consequently, the main purpose of this book is to explain why accounting is necessary and why particular methods are used. There are a large number of examples and exercises which ask you fairly standard accounting calculations. I include these not to train you as a bookkeeper but to ensure that you understand the principles involved so that you will eventually be able to design or program accounting systems.

As the book is principally for use by NCC Joint Diploma students there are examination questions at the end of most sections. Also, the new edition includes answers for some questions so that you can check on your progress.

P.H. Bassett

Contents

1   The basic concepts of accounting

INTRODUCTION

This section aims to provide you with an awareness of why accounting is important in the modern business. The chapter gives an appreciation of why accounting has developed in its present form, and explains the need to maintain accounting records as well as the uses different groups make of accounting information.

OBJECTIVES

The object of this chapter is to outline the reasoning behind accounts and explain why they are so important. It will begin by giving a short history of accounting and then explain why accounts are so important in the present day. Finally, it will demonstrate some of the accepted rules which all accountants must follow.

At the end of this section you should be able to:

— explain why organisations maintain accounting records

— define the basic rules applicable to accounting records (especially the accounting concepts and conventions)

— identify the various groups who make use of accounts, and the reasons for their interest

— explain the accounting equation and its implications for the programmer

— define the various categories of assets and liabilities used in accounting statements.

1.1   THE SEPARATION OF OWNERSHIP AND CONTROL

The first thing that the beginner needs to understand about accounts is not an "accounting" concept but a general business concept known as the "separation of ownership and control". Prior to the Industrial Revolution most societies were based on agriculture as the main means of production. Also, in these societies most of the land farmed was owned by a relatively small group of people who employed other people to work on their land. However, a situation common in most of these societies was that the "owners" owned land in more than one place. This situation became more common in the United Kingdom (and elsewhere)

1

as the owners' families intermarried or perhaps even physically took over someone else's land.

As this practice continued, the owners were presented with a problem: when they were living on one of their estates they could control what went on and decide what crops to plant, where to plant them, when to plant them, etc, but with estates scattered all over the country it was obviously impossible to have complete control over each individual estate. The solution to this problem was to appoint people that they could trust as "stewards".

The job of the steward was to manage the estate on behalf of the owner whilst the owner was staying at one of his other estates. This would involve the steward making all of the decisions relating to which crops to plant and also handling the storing the cash received from the sale of produce, paying the workers, buying feed for the animals, etc. However, the majority of owners were sensible enough to require the steward to keep written records of all transactions which the steward had entered into and all activities that he had sanctioned. For whilst the owner might trust the steward sufficiently to delegate responsibility to him, he would also require evidence of how the steward had been managing his property. This practice is often referred to as the "concept of stewardship" and effectively lays the foundation for present day accounting practices.

Whilst the most common means of production is no longer based on agriculture, the principles developed during this period are still relevant. These principles are:

— As businesses get larger it becomes impossible for the owner to carry out all the tasks needed to run the business.

— The owner has to employ trusted stewards to help him carry out these tasks. Stewards nowadays are more commonly known as managers.

— The owner will insist that the managers keep full records of everything they have done so that he can check they have been managing his business correctly.

— Most of the decisions made by the managers will involve money, and as money is what owners are especially concerned with, then most of the records will relate to financial transactions.

— To ensure that the managers keep proper records, a procedure has been developed to ensure that records are accurate. This is known as double-entry accounting, which was originally developed hundreds of years ago, and was used by the original stewards.

The list above defines the various points associated with the concept of stewardship. The situation in many modern firms is very similar but in larger firms it has become even more accentuated.

In very large firms the situation still exists where one person owns the firm and others manage it, but the owner is in fact a very large number of people who all own a "share" in the business. These people are called "shareholders". As there is often a very large number of shareholders owning a firm, it becomes unrealistic to expect them all to assist in running the business. These shareholders appoint

Figure 1.1 The separation of ownership and control

directors to run the business on their behalf (with the assistance of managers) but will still want to see, at least once a year, written records of what has been done with their money. In other words:

— There is often a separation of ownership and control: managers work at the firm every day, whereas many shareholders will never have seen the firm's works. This fact creates various possible problems but they are not strictly relevant to accounting.

— The need for good records becomes even more important to enable shareholders to see what has happened to their money. Therefore they will want to see the accounts of the firm at least once a year.

The true meaning of the word "account" is to give a history of something, which is essentially what the estate stewards originally did and what managers today are doing. They are giving a history to the owners of what they have been doing with the owners' money and belongings. This concept is illustrated in Figure 1.1.

Exercises

All questions ending in A do not have answers supplied.

1   What is the concept of stewardship?

2A   How is the modern day manager similar to the medieval steward?

3A   Why is it that shareholders do not run the businesses that they own?

1.2   THE USERS OF ACCOUNTS

Once it became common practice to produce accounts of a firm's activities for a yearly period, various other groups decided that they could also make use of some of the information contained in them. These groups are as follows:

Shareholders/owners

This group has already been partly discussed. Their interest in accounts lies in the fact that it is their money which is invested in the firm. They will examine the accounts to ensure that they are getting a good return on their investment: this is assessed by how much profit the firm is making and whether their investment is increasing in value (ie is the firm expanding?). If the firm is making good profits then they will get a good dividend (sharing out profits amongst the shareholders) and, if the firm is expanding, the value of shares will usually increase and the shareholders can make a profit by selling their shares at a higher price than they originally paid for those shares.

Directors

The directors of a firm are appointed to safeguard the interests of the shareholders and to ensure that the policies of the firm are carried out by the managers. They will also be responsible for deciding how much of the profit can be paid out as dividends and how much should be retained to finance further expansion.

Therefore they are concerned with ensuring that an adequate profit is made and that managers are doing their job properly.

Managers

The job of the manager is to carry out the policies decided by the shareholders and directors. Managers' interest in the accounts lies in whether the firm makes a good profit, which would normally result in their receiving a bonus or pay rise. However, one of the facts that has emerged from studies of management and the concept of the separation of ownership and control is that there is sometimes a difference between management objectives and shareholder objectives. As previously mentioned, shareholders want to see larger profits and a growing business as this means more money for them. On the other hand, although managers will often gain some financial reward from increased profits, many managers have realised that the quickest way to increase salaries is to increase the size of the manager's department. Clearly, a personnel manager who doubles the number of staff in his department has double the responsibility and therefore deserves more money in respect of the extra responsibility. It is far easier for a personnel manager to double the size of his department than it is for him to double the firm's profit!

Banks/loan companies

This group may be approached by the firm if it is in need of additional funds to acquire new equipment, for instance. Whilst lenders like to see if the firm is making a profit, their main interest will be as to whether or not the firm is capable of repaying the loan. This will depend on cash flow (this is different to profit) and also on how much the firm owns. If the firm is unable to make the repayments on the loan, then the bank will require the firm to sell some of its belongings in order to pay back the money owed.

Employees

Employees will feel that it is their efforts that have created the profit and will therefore want to see how much profit has been made, and also what proportion was paid to the shareholders. This information will be used to support their pay claim.

Suppliers/customers

Most firms operate on a credit basis: goods are ordered and delivered in one month and payment is usually made in the following month. There are a variety of reasons for this but one very obvious one is that most firms do not want to entrust delivery staff with the responsibility of carrying and collecting very large sums of money. However, because of this method of trading, suppliers will want to be reasonably confident of eventually receiving payment. Their interest in the firm's accounts will therefore be similar to that of the banks and loan companies (ie has the firm sufficient funds to pay its debts?).

Although customers will owe the firm money, they will often have the same concerns as suppliers. This is because a customer may be dependent on the firm for its raw materials and if the firm goes out of business, the customer may be forced out of business as well, as it is unable to obtain raw materials for its products. Therefore, customers will want to ensure that the firm is in a position to pay all of its debts and continue trading for some time.

Stockbrokers/future investors

This group will either be advising investors or investing in the firm itself, and so will want to be sure that the firm is likely to continue paying out good dividends, and that the value of its shares will rise in the future.

Government

Various government departments will be interested in a firm's accounts for the variety of reasons listed below:

— *Taxation*	Firms will have to pay tax on profits.
— *Employment*	Failing firms will affect unemployment figures; the government may take steps to help the firm.
— *Pollution*	Some firms' effluent will affect the environment. The government may insist on preventative measures.
— *Social Security*	The firm may have to pay social security costs on behalf of its employees.
— *Industry*	The government will try to encourage investment in industry, often in research into new products.
— *Inflation*	Some governments have tried to stop firms increasing prices/wages as a means of controlling inflation.
— *Free Trade*	Most governments have some policies to stop the formation of monopolies.

Figure 1.2 gives just a sample of some of the uses to which the accounts of a firm can be put, but clearly they have come a long way from simply explaining to the landowner what the steward has done since his last visit!

There are, however, two points that apply regardless of who is using the accounts:

— The basic method used to record the accounting transactions is the same for all firms.

— Firms are only allowed to present one set of accounts for each year. The reason for this is that there should only be one set if the accounts are correct, and it removes the temptation to falsify accounts so that one set would suit shareholders, another set would suit banks, yet another would suit the government for tax purposes, etc. Therefore the accounts need to be presented in a standard way that would be of use to all users (whilst unfortunately not entirely satisfying any of them) and still be an accurate reflection of the firm's performance and possessions.

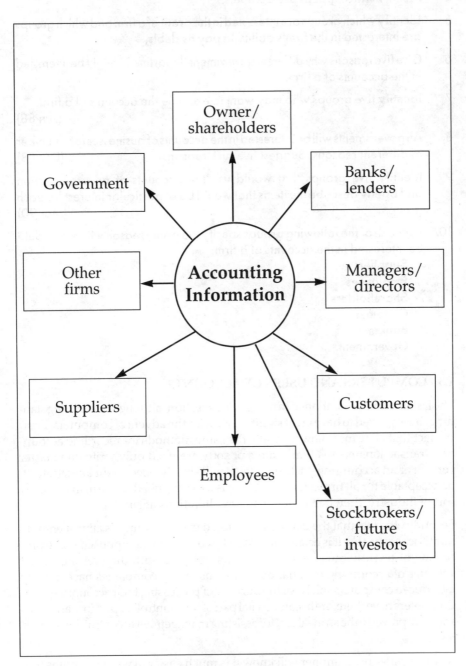

Figure 1.2 The users of accounts

Exercises

4   Identify which groups use accounts.

5   Identify which groups are interested in the profit of a firm and which groups are interested in the firm's ability to pay its debts.

6   Give five reasons why different government departments might be interested in the accounts of a firm.

7   Identify five groups who may want to examine the accounts of a firm.

(Jun 88)

8   All governments will be interested in the accounts of businesses for a number of different reasons. Suggest five such reasons.   (Dec 88)

9   Identify five groups that would use the accounts of an organisation and briefly describe the items that would be of particular interest for each group.   (Mar 90)

10A For each of the following groups specify the prime reason why they would be interested in the accounts of a firm:
    Suppliers
    Employees
    Shareholders
    Customers
    Banks
    Government

1.3 COMPUTERS AND USERS OF ACCOUNTS

The last two points mentioned in the previous section, although of very long standing, have proved to have great significance with the advent of computers. First, the fact that all firms follow basically the same methods for recording accounting transactions means that writers of software need only write one master version of an accounting package, which will simply need slight alterations to be acceptable for all firms. If the software is to be supplied to a firm in the same sort of industry, then it may not need any alterations at all.

Secondly, the fact that the data being handled in the accounts is almost entirely numeric means that it is easily processed by computers (as opposed to the processing of text). Because of these reasons, coupled with the ever increasing volumes of accounting data handled by firms, many companies have initially introduced computers solely for the purpose of processing their accounting data. Computers have therefore become a vital part of the "control" aspect in many firms and have proved to be an ideal tool for assisting management to control the owners' resources.

Any computer programmer will know it is much easier to write programs that will be handling numerical data than it is to write a program which will have to handle text strings. The quantity of text required in an accounts program is always a small quantity and, by careful use of codes to describe different items, it is

Possible to reduce the need for text-handling even further. Section 1.7 demonstrates how codes can be used to limit the quantity of text within a program.

Exercises

11A Explain why computers are better able to handle and process numeric data as opposed to text.

12A Consider the requirements of the users of accounts and for each category devise a list of requirement under the headings of "Textual Data" and "Numeric Data".

1.4 ACCOUNTING CONCEPTS AND CONVENTIONS

Having considered the reasons for producing accounts, we now need to consider some of the rules that relate to the ways in which accounts should be prepared. The accounting concepts and conventions are well- accepted "rules" governing how accounts should be prepared.

The reason for having these rules is connected with the fact that different groups may make use of the accounts and these groups all need to be convinced that the accounts presented by a firm are an accurate reflection of that business. The problem is that the different groups are all interested in slightly different aspects of the accounts, and the accounts produced must contain figures that all groups can agree on. Furthermore, it is also essential that the different groups examining the accounts can be assured that the figures contained have been arrived at by using the same methods as those applied by all other firms. In this way it is possible for potential investors or suppliers to make comparisons between different firms, safe in the knowledge that all of the accounts have been drawn up using the same methods.

1.4.1 Concepts

The cost concept

This concept states that the figures shown in the accounts must be valued at a figure that all parties can agree on. This may sound simple, but it is difficult in practice because all parties would use the item involved in a different way. For example, if the firm owned some goods for resale to customers, then customers would place a higher value on those goods than a supplier, because the customer would expect to buy them at retail price whereas the supplier would expect to sell them at wholesale price. The bank would consider how much the firm would get for the goods if they had to be sold quickly to pay off debts; the only way to sell off large quantities of goods quickly is to sell them at a sale price, which would be less than retail price but still above wholesale price.

This same dispute over the correct "value" applies with every item that a firm owns and the cost concept states that the correct value to record items at is the only value to which all users would agree, ie the amount paid for them, or initial cost of the item.

The money measurement concept

This concept is concerned with which items should be recorded in the accounts. All items that have been bought are included because it is easy to determine their cost price. But, there are a number of items that most firms possess for which there is no initial cost price, or for which the cost price is clearly incorrect.

Examples of such items which have no clear value are factors such as the skill of management, the effect of new products currently being developed, threatened strike action, the beneficial effect of a works' canteen, etc. The problem with these items is that they will all have some effect upon the performance and profit of a firm but they can be allocated no value to which all parties agree. Therefore the money measurement concept states that only those items that have a clear monetary value can be included in the accounts; all other items must be ignored.

In practice large firms add copious notes to their accounts and often mention facts such as new products about to be launched, but they cannot alter the accounting figures to include any predicted increase in profit. Also, in recent years some firms have used a method of accounting known as "human asset accounting" which is a form of accounting designed to include the value of trained and experienced staff. Unfortunately, this method has not received widespread support and is therefore unacceptable in accounts intended to be shown to the various user groups, but it can be used internally or within the group if the firm forms part of a larger group of companies.

The business entity concept

This concept states that the accounts should only contain items that relate to the business and not to the personal transactions of the owner. This business is a completely separate entity to the owner and the only items that should be recorded that relate to the owner will be details of how much money the owner has invested in the firm and how much money he has taken out from profits. Clearly, it is irrelevant from the business point of view whether the owner has bought, for example, a new television, and not only is it incorrect to record this in the firm's accounts, but in most countries it would be bordering on the illegal, as it would be seen as an attempt to defraud the taxation department.

Furthermore, if the accounts of a small firm were allowed to show all of the personal transactions of the owner, the same principle would have to be applied to all firms, including limited companies with over 100,000 shareholders; the accounts would become so complex as to be meaningless.

The going concern concept

The cost concept states that all items are to be valued at their original cost price. This is because everyone should agree with the valuation so long as the firm is a healthy organisation. However, if the firm should announce that it is going to cease trading then it would be necessary to revalue all of the items at current selling price rather than cost price as this would be a more realistic valuation and would be a truer reflection of the firm's accounts. In practice most firms assume that they will continue to operate for the foreseeable future and in these cases the cost concept can be applied — this is known as the going concern concept. It is only where firms know that they are going to cease trading that they would have to revalue items at their current price.

The realisation concept

All firms prepare their accounts once a year. If they operate on a credit basis (selling goods in one month and receiving payment in the next), there will occasionally be transactions that spread over more than one year.

Example: A firm prepares its accounts each year on 30 June. In the current year it received an order for goods from a customer on 25 June; the goods were delivered on 29 June and payment for the goods was received on 21 July.

Order received	25 June
Goods delivered	29 June
....	Accounts year ends 30 June
Payment received	21 July

The difficulty lies in deciding in which year the transaction falls. This is important as the sale (and profit) will be included in that year. The realisation concept states that profit is deemed to have arisen at the point at which the goods change hands. In the above example the profit on the sale arises on 29 June when the goods are delivered. The transaction would therefore be included in the first year's accounts.

The dual aspect concept

This is the most frequently applied of all the concepts and states that every transaction will affect two items. This concept applies the accounting equation, which is:

Assets = Capital + Liabilities

This is the most important factor in recording transactions and will be discussed in full later in this chapter. For the moment, it is sufficient to remember the golden rule that every transaction will affect two items in the accounts. This is vitally important when recording transactions or devising computer programs.

The accruals concept

This concept is almost the opposite of the realisation concept. Just as profit is measured when the goods change hands and not when payment is received, it should equally apply that when a firm is buying goods or paying items such as rent, insurance, etc, these items should be recorded when the item changes hands, not when it is paid for. This is the accruals concept. The concept is primarily concerned with the difference between cash receipts and cash expenditure (the recording of items when ownership changes hands). In short the accruals concept states that items should be recorded when used and not when paid for.

1.4.2 Conventions

The problem with the above concepts is that they were first developed when accounting was much simpler and consequently they are too vague for modern use. To overcome this vagueness the accounting conventions have been developed as a means of interpreting the concepts and applying them in practice.

The materiality convention

This convention can be applied in two different ways but the convention, in essence, is that it is not worth spending hours or a great deal of effort over small amounts. The effort is only worthwhile if the item is of a reasonable (material) value.

One of the common circumstances where this will apply is in the tracing of errors, either by the firm's own staff or by the auditor. For example, if an amount of £50 is "missing" from the accounts, a small firm would consider this a substantial amount and would take steps to trace the error. However, if the firm was a multinational with an annual profit in excess of £50 million then it is clearly not a sum to get too upset about and it would probably be stored in a separate account until the reason for the error came to light.

The "materiality" of items also determines how they will be recorded. Items of considerable value are called assets and are recorded in the accounts for a number of years. Items that are only of low value will be written off as expenses in the year in which they were bought. A small firm may decide that £50 is material and record the item as an asset; however, if the multinational bought the same item for £50 it would probably decide that the item was not material and write it off as an expense. Therefore, it should be clear that to a certain extent the firm can be its own judge as to what is to be classed as a material amount.

The prudence convention

This convention is often referred to as the conservatism convention. The basic principle is that if the accountant is faced with a choice of figures to include for one item, he should use the figure which is most likely to produce a lower profit. The feeling behind this convention is that it is better to be prudent and underestimate profits now rather than overestimate profits with possibly disastrous effects in the future. This is not just because accountants are conservative but because managers and directors use the profit figure as a means of financing reinvestment. If the profit figure is higher than it should be, then any reinvestment may be higher than the firm could really afford.

The consistency convention

This convention is applied in similar circumstances to the prudence convention in that it arises where there is a choice of figures to use. In this case, however, it applies where the accountant has a choice of methods to use in preparing the accounts. These different methods will be considered later in the book where it will also be proved that different methods can produce different profits. In most cases firms may make the choice of which method to use.

The problem arises if firms decide to change their method. By careful selection of when to change the method, it is possible to create a very false impression of profits over a period of four to five years. Therefore, this convention states that for profits to be meaningful the firm should consistently apply the same method. If, for some unavoidable reason, the method has to be changed, there should be a distinct note in the firm's accounts pointing this out so that users are aware of the reason for the change in profit levels.

These are the basic rules that apply in the preparation of all accounts. They are of importance to computer programmers since they should be catered for in any program that will be used to process accounting data. However, the drawback of the concepts and conventions is that they are too vague for modern businesses and in order to ensure that all firms prepare accounts in a standard manner the professional accounting bodies of most countries have developed other rules to indicate to accountants how certain specific items should be dealt with. In the United Kingdom these rules are known as "Statements of Standard Accounting Practice" and all accountants belonging to the professional bodies are expected to understand them and apply them in their particular firms. The rules will vary from country to country but will generally run on similar lines.

1.4.3   Other accounting rules

The concepts and conventions stated are accepted and used internationally. However, as organisations have become more complex and diverse in their activities most countries have realised that some additional, and more specific, rules are necessary. This is particularly true for large organisations such as Limited Companies which frequently own additional, smaller companies not only in their country of origin but throughout the world.

In order to ensure that there are still similarities between organisations trading in very different products/services and even different countries, most countries have devised additional rules for accountants to follow when preparing accounts.

These rules will often come from two sources:

— Government legislation: This will involve laws that determine the content of accounting records; these are especially common for Limited Companies as most governments have considered it necessary to introduce laws to protect the interests of shareholders.

— Professional Accounting bodies: These organisations exist in all countries and they will devise rules by which all of their members are expected to abide. These rules are usually more detailed interpretations of the accounting concepts and conventions to provide guidelines on how to treat accounting data relating to specific areas. The UK accounting bodies' "Statements of Standard Accounting Practice" (SSAPs for short) give details as to how accountants should deal with specific topics such as the valuation of stock, depreciation, goodwill, long term contracts, research and development costs, etc.

Exercises

13   What are the accounting concepts and conventions, and why are they important to computer programmers?

14   State which Accounting Concept or Convention has been used in each of the following transactions.

  (i)   A Provision for Bad Debts has been created.
  (ii) A wheelbarrow for use on site costing $25 has been recorded as an expense item.
  (iii) The firm have not included any value to reflect the benefits expected from new Production procedures.
  (iv) The owner of the firm has just bought a new house but this has not been recorded in the accounts.
  (v)   Wages paid have been recorded in both the Wages and the Cash Accounts.

  (5 marks)
  (Mar 91)

15A Identify which Accounting Concept or Convention is being observed in the following instances:

  (i)   The accounts of the firm are adjusted to allow for invoices not yet received.
  (ii)   The amount recorded in the books for an expense is recorded at the invoiced amount rather than the value to the firm of that item.
  (iii) Provisions for depreciation are created.
  (iv)   Only the financial affairs of the company are being considered in the records.
  (v)   A stock value is placed on unsold goods but not on unused stationery.
  (vi)   The local currency is used as a yardstick of performance.
  (vii) A firm assumes that its profit on a transaction is accruing from the DATE of the SALES INVOICE.
  (viii) The firm employs a double-entry book-keeping system.
  (ix)   Stock is valued by the firm as though it would be sold in the normal course of events and not at its liquidation value.
  (x)   The LIFO system of stock costing is NOT changed to AVCO.

  (Dec 89)

16   The Accounting Conventions are often said to be the practical application of the Accounting Concepts. BRIEFLY define each of the following:

  (i)   Cost Concept
  (ii) Prudence Convention
  (iii) Realisation Concept
  (iv) Materiality Convention

  (8 marks)

(b)   Explain how the concepts and conventions both apply in the following examples:

  (i)   Fixed Assets (Cost concept and Prudence convention)
  (ii) Stock of Stationery (Realisation concept and Materiality convention)

  (12 marks)
  (Mar 92)

1.5   THE ACCOUNTING EQUATION

The dual aspect concept identified the accounting equation. This is vital to the understanding of how accounting records are kept prior to the drafting of the end of year accounts which show the profit or loss of the firm.

The dual aspect concept basically states that all items in a business can be classed as either items that belong to the business or, alternatively, as items that are owed to the owner or other parties outside the business. The totals of the two groups will always be equal to each other, hence the equation:

Assets = Capital + Liabilities

This equation can easily be proven.

Example: Tom starts a business by investing £10,000 of his own money into a business bank account.

The business entity concept states that the business will only record the transactions of the owner that directly affect the business (ie depositing or withdrawing money). Therefore the equation will show:

Assets (Bank account) £10,000 = Capital £10,000

Example: Tom buys a motor vehicle for £3000 on credit for use in the business.

Although Tom has not yet paid for the motor vehicle he has taken delivery, so according to the accruals concept it should be included in the accounts. The accounting equation will now show:

Assets(bank) £10,000 + (motor) £3,000 = Capital £10,000 + Liability £3,000

£13,000 = £13,000

Example: Tom buys business premises for £4000 using some of the money in the business bank account.

Assets		=	Capital + Liabilities	
Bank	£6,000		Capital	£10,000
Motor vehicle	£3,000		Liability	£3,000
Premises	£4,000			
	£13,000			£13,000

The equation is still true even though no further capital or liabilities were involved in the last transaction. This shows that the dual aspect concept is true in that every single transaction will affect two items in the accounts.

Example: Tom buys stock worth £2500 on credit.

Assets		=	Capital + Liabilities	
Bank	£6,000		Capital	£10,000
Motor vehicle	£3,000		Liabilities	£5,500
Premises	£4,000			
Stock	£2,500			
	£15,500			£15,500

Once again the equation is proved, purely because every transaction affects two items.

The main problem at this stage will be in deciding what assets, capital and liabilities are (see Figure 1.3).

Assets are all items that can be classed as "property" and have a value to the business, for example premises, motor vehicles, office furniture, machinery, stock, cash in hand and at the bank, debtors (people who owe money to the business), etc.

Liabilities are all items that are owed by the business to outsiders and usually consist of trade creditors (people from whom the business has bought goods on credit), bank loans, mortgages, etc.

Capital is the money invested in the business by the owner(s).

Figure 1.3 The accounting equation

Exercises

17 Complete the columns to show the effects of the following transactions:

	Assets	Liabilities	Capital
Bought a car on credit			
Bought stock paying by cheque			
The owner invests money in the firm's bank account			
Pay a creditor in cash			
Buy office equipment on credit			
Receive cash from a debtor			
Sell stock on credit			

18 Enter the missing figures in the following:

Assets £	Liabilities £	Capital £
19,000	12,000	?
?	7,500	23,000
16,200	?	11,800
31,700	?	21,400
?	6,400	11,200
8,500	3,900	?

19 What is the difference between fixed and current assets? Give two examples of each.

20A Complete the columns to show the effects of the following transactions:

	Assets	Liabilities	Capital
Bought premises for £20,000 on credit			
Invested £30,000 capital in a bank account			
Bought £2,000 of stock on credit			
Paid £3,000 for a motor vehicle			
Paid £2,000 for amount owing in respect of stock			

1.6 THE BALANCE SHEET

The information provided by the accounting equation is a very important part of accounting information. However, the problem with the accounting equation is that it does not give sufficient information. For example:

Assets £20,000 = Capital £8000 + Liabilities £12,000

does not provide a great deal of useful information, therefore in practice a more acceptable way of presenting the information is used. This involves the balance sheet. The idea behind this is that more information can be provided in a standard layout, so that anyone with some experience of balance sheets can easily find the information that they are looking for. A typical balance sheet would read as Figure 1.4.

	£		£
Fixed Assets		Capital	
Premises	10,000	Capital	20,000
Motor vehicles	7,000	Add profit	8,000
Fixtures & fittings	3,000		28,000
		Less drawings	5,000
			23,000
Current Assets	£	Liabilities	
Stock	4,500	Creditors	5,150
Debtors	2,000		
Cash at bank	1,500		
Cash in hand	150	8,150	
		28,150	28,150

Tom

Balance Sheet as at 31/12/89

Figure 1.4   Sample balance sheet layout

This layout is an improvement over the accounting equation because it shows all separate items under appropriate headings. Therefore, any person wanting to use the accounts to find some information can see quite easily where that information is.

Notice that the balance sheet splits assets between fixed assets and current assets. The difference between the items is:

Fixed assets will tend to be more costly (although this may not always be true) and will have a longer "life". Items such as premises, motor vehicles and machinery will usually be kept for more than one year. These items are essential for the efficient operation of the business.

Current assets are more likely to be lower in value and the individual items will be constantly changing; few businesses would want to keep the same items of stock for more than a few weeks, nor would they want their debtors to be owing them money for more than a few weeks.

Exercises

21   Draw up the balance sheet to record the following items using the standard layout:

	£
Premises	20,000
Stock	4,500

Cash in hand	50
Cash at bank	500
Creditors	4,250
Office equipment	1,200
Debtors	1,550
Machinery	3,400

Insert the appropriate figure for capital.

22　Draw up the balance sheet to record the following items using the standard layout:

	£
Premises	10,000
Capital	25,400
Stock	3,200
Creditors	6,200
Motor vehicles	5,000
Profit	6,100
Cash in hand	200
Debtors	4,600
Drawings	5,500
Machinery	6,100
Cash at bank	1,500
Office equipment	1,600

23　Why is the owner's capital shown on the same side of the balance sheet as liabilities?

24　Draw up the balance sheet to record the following items using the standard layout:

	£
Premises	120,000
Motor vehicles	50,000
Stock	12,000
Cash	750
Creditors	16,500
Bank	2,100
Fixtures and fittings	10,300
Debtors	12,750
Machinery	5,200
Drawings	4,800
Profit	12,400
Bank loan	25,000

Insert the appropriate figure for capital.

25A　Why is the balance sheet an improvement on the accounting equation when it basically shows exactly the same information?

1.7   CLASSIFYING ITEMS

It should already be apparent that there are different ways of classifying accounting data, the most commonly used classification is to categorise items as Asset, Liabilities or Capital. In the next chapter these items will be broken down into the sub-categories of Fixed and Current Assets and Current or Long-term Liabilities. An additional classification of Expenses will also be introduced. Chapter 4 will consider another alternative way of classifying costs.

These classifications are important for the computer programmer as it will almost certainly be necessary to include some means of defining the categories in the computer program. One major advantage of computerised systems is that, providing there has been some forethought, it should be possible to make any codes used for classifying items flexible enough to cater for later alterations to include new items or simply to redesign the existing classifications. The need for flexibility is especially important if the program is intended for use with a number of different firms who may all have their own different ways of classifying items.

Most computer programs classify items by allocating unique code numbers to each category. These code numbers are usually sub-divided into different sections so that any one item can be examined under different headings. The following example shows one possible way of categorising items:

Code number: 100   used to designate all Assets

Code number: 100 001   used to classify Fixed Assets

Code number: 100 001 10   used to designate Premises

This example shows that it would be possible to examine all Assets (including those that are Fixed and including the Premises) by examining Code 100, examining Code 100 001 would only include the Fixed Assets (and Premises), and examining Code 100 001 10 would exclude all items except Premises.

The amount of analysis undertaken will be determined by the Management Information System and the power of the firm's computing equipment; more powerful computers should allow a more detailed analysis. Most "off the shelf" software packages will allow the user to specify their own coding system and some forethought needs to be given to this area.

The following principles should be considered where designating codes:

CERTAINTY   Each code should be unambiguous, it should not be possible to confuse it with another code.

ELASTICITY   Each "Code group" should be flexible enough to allow for the creation of additional codes in the same area.

BREVITY   All codes should be kept as short as possible, long codes are more difficult to commit to memory and may lead to errors.

UNIQUENESS   Each code should be unique and relate to one specific item only.

1.7.1 Types of codes

Most codes are basically similar but there are some minor differences that exist. These different types of codes can be used in conjunction with one another and may be requested as part of a program.

Sequential codes

These are the most common sorts of codes and are allocated in order when new accounts are being created; they are usually numerical.

eg:	Code	Account
	0001	Tom Lee
	0002	ABC Limited
	0003	F & S Singh
	0004	K & G Engineering Ltd

Block codes

These are used to collate similar items under a specific area and are often used in conjunction with sequential codes. Most software packages refer to the "blocks" as Major and Minor divisions.

eg:	Code range	Account types
	100 - 199	Fixed Assets
	200 - 299	Current Assets
	300 - 399	Current Liabilities

The "Minor divisions" within these blocks could be as follows:

eg:	Code	Account
	200 001	Bank
	200 002	Cash
	200 003	Stock

Mnemonic codes

This type of code is designed so that it is easier to remember. The code will include some aspect that will refer to the item recorded in the account. This type of code is most frequently found in the Sales and Purchase Ledgers (see Section 2) for designating accounts, for customers or suppliers. This is because this type of code can contain some element of the customer/supplier's name.

eg:	Code	Account
	SMITH100	J. Smith
	CHAN20	H. Chan
	ABCLTD10	ABC Limited

Section codes

This type of code can be used to store details of exact specifications by coding the separate items included in the specification. They are very commonly found in stock control programs as the code itself can store the exact details of a particular item of stock.

eg: | *Code* | *Item* |
|---|---|
| IBM640HD40M | IBM, 640K RAM, 40 Mb Hard Disk, Mono Monitor |
| IBM520TDCM | IBM, 520K RAM, Twin Drive, Colour Monitor |
| TDN640HD30CM | Tandon, 640K RAM, 30 Mb Hard Disk, Colour Monitor |

Exercises

26   A company uses the following codes in its Nominal Ledger Program:

001/200/8 - refers to sales of computers in India
002/200/5 - refers to purchases of computers in Malaysia
001/300/7 - refers to sales of printers in Hong Kong
002/400/6 - refers to purchases of diskdrives in Singapore

What would the code be for SALES OF DISKDRIVES in Malaysia and PUR-CHASES OF PRINTERS in India?

Briefly suggest what benefits can be derived from this type of coding in a computer system.   (Sep 89)

27   Suggest a suitable code for the following items:

Epson LX500 9 pin Dot matrix printers 80 characters wide
Epson LQ850 24 pin Dot matrix printers 132 characters wide
Epson Laser printer A4 size
Star LC-10 9 pin Dot matrix printer 80 characters wide
Star NL-10 Colour 9 pin Dot matrix printer 80 characters

28A   A firm has created the following codes for its accounts:

100 - 500	Categories of computer hardware/software
01 - 08	Suppliers of computer equipment
300 - 700	Country supplied to

The following codes have been used recently:

100 01 403	Computers, Epson, Hong Kong
400 04 300	Keyboards, Hewlett Packard, New Delhi
200 06 500	Printers, Honeywell, London
400 05 301	Keyboards, Wyse, Baroda
100 02 401	Computers, IBM, Singapore
100 02 600	Computers, IBM, New York
200 01 601	Printers, Epson, Washington

Suggest which codes may be suitable for the following:

Computers, Honeywell, Paris
Monitors, Wyse, Kuala Lumpur
Computers, Tandon, Chicago
Software, IBM, Rome
Keyboards, Wyse, Los Angeles

29   A company uses the following codes in its Nominal Ledger:

210/001/009   Sales of Computers in Malaysia
210/003/008   Sales of Printers in India
210/005/101   Sales of Disk Drives in USA
100/006/202   Purchase of Monotone Monitors from Italy
100/008/203   Purchase of Keyboards from France

Suggest what codes would be used for the following:

(i)   Purchase of Disk Drives from India
(ii) Sales of Monitors to Singapore
(iii) Sale of Keyboards to Canada
(iv) Purchase of Printer cables from United Kingdom
(v)   Sale of Colour Monitors to Germany

(10 marks)
(Mar 92)

1.8   THE PROCESSING FUNCTION

Without going into too great detail, data processing at its simplest can be said to involve three distinct activities:

Data - Processing - Information

There is often a tendency to assume that this sequence only applies to computer operations. This is not true: accounting had been following this data processing cycle for years before computers were invented. In fact, many very small businesses will still be performing the same activities without the aid of computers. But it is a fact that a great number of firms do now use computers as part of the accounting function, so it is worthwhile considering how computers and accounting are affected by the data processing cycle.

Data

This is obtained from the details of each transaction. In practice it involves a source document such as an invoice, credit note, delivery note, or even a cheque. Computers will affect this part of the cycle because firms may use a computer to produce the source document. Other source documents such as order forms may be "read" by a computer using optical mark or optical character recognition devices. Firms will use computers to prepare such documents because computers are generally quicker and more accurate than humans.

Processing

The most common application of computers will be in the actual processing of accounting data. As we have already seen, the majority of accounting data is numeric and there are clearly defined rules that we have to follow. These two factors make computerisation fairly straightforward. This is because it is easier to make a computer process numbers than text. Also, a computer program has to follow a series of set instructions; the rules of accounting provide these set instructions. The advantages of using a computer to process accounting data are that computers should be faster, more accurate and capable of updating a number of accounts all in one go.

Information

The output (information) from one system is often the input (data) for another. Using computers means that the output can be easily and quickly converted into the required input. Information is generally used by management for decision-making purposes. The most modern computers can now make some of these decisions, but even apparently obsolete computers are still an improvement over manual methods, because they can provide the information more quickly and at much more frequent intervals. Firms have to produce a profit and loss account and balance sheet once a year, the reason being that an annual account is the obvious period to select but also, in manual operations the preparation of these accounts takes so long that it would be too costly to produce them more frequently. With a computerised system the profit and loss account and balance sheet can be, and often are, produced monthly. These monthly accounts are not published but are used by management for decision making.

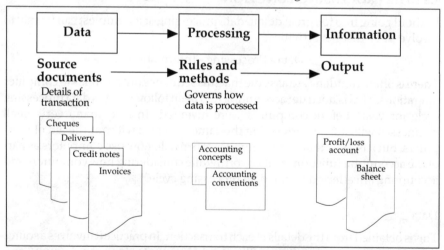

Figure 1.5   The processing function

Exercises

30   The data processing cycle is often expressed as data - processing - information. What are the advantages of using a computer to process accounting data for each of these areas?

2 Book-keeping

INTRODUCTION

This section aims to provide you with an understanding of the systems and procedures used to record and present accounting information. You should appreciate the theory involved in book-keeping and accounts so that you can then relate this theory to the practical task of writing/operating computerised accounting systems. The contents of this section relate to the subject of financial accounting; this is the record keeping part of accounting, and enables businesses to record transactions with a view to calculating profit.

OBJECTIVES

At the end of this section you should be able to:

— demonstrate the techniques of double-entry book-keeping from source documents through to final accounts, using modern styles of layout

— describe the importance of the trial balance, illustrate its deficiencies, and explain how the use of computers can reduce the deficiencies

— prepare trading and profit/loss accounts from given data in a modern style, and provide a basic interpretation of the results

— describe the relevance of, and techniques used to calculate depreciation, bad debts and other adjustments to final accounts

— explain the reasons for, and methods used in, the "division of the ledger", and identify the uses of the various source documents.

BOOK-KEEPING

The first chapter showed how the accounting equation demonstrates that assets always equal capital plus liabilities, and how the balance sheet is used as a more efficient means of presenting information than the accounting equation. However, there are still problems with the balance sheet and additional methods have been developed to overcome these problems. The additional methods involve the use of "book-keeping" and this is the actual processing activity where computers are most frequently used.

Figure 2.1 shows the balance sheet for a business:

J BROWN				
Balance Sheet as at 31/12/89				
		£		£
Fixed Assets			Capital	
Premises		25,000	Capital	34,000
Motor vehicles		10,000	Add profit	7,000
Machinery		5,000		
				41,000
		40,000	Less drawings	6,500
				34,500
Current Assets	£		Liabilities	
Stock	2,500		Creditors	10,500
Cash in hand	100			
Cash at bank	400			
Debtors	2,000	5,000		
		45,000		45,000

Figure 2.1

As explained in the first chapter this is accepted as the best way of presenting information. But, there are difficulties. If Mr Brown sells some stock worth £400 on credit on 1/1/90 then his stock will decrease and his debtors increase. The balance sheet will need to be rewritten as in Figure 2.2:

J BROWN				
Balance Sheet as at 1/1/90				
		£		£
Fixed Assets			Capital	
Premises		25,000	Capital	34,000
Motor vehicles		10,000	Add profit	7,000
Machinery		5,000		
				41,000
		40,000	Less drawings	6,500
				34,500
Current Assets	£		Liabilities	
Stock	2,100		Creditors	10,500
Cash in hand	100			
Cash at bank	400			
Debtors	2,400	5000		
		45,000		45,000

Figure 2.2

However, on the afternoon of the same day he replaces some of the stock by buying £300 worth, paying by cheque, and £500 worth on credit. This will affect stock, cash at bank and creditors. The balance sheet will need to be rewritten once again, as shown in Figure 2.3.

J BROWN					
Balance Sheet as at 1/1/90					
		£			£
Fixed Assets			Capital		
Premises		25,000	Capital		34,000
Motor vehicles		10,000	Add profit		7,000
Machinery		5,000			
					41,000
		40,000	Less drawings		6,500
					34,500
Current Assets	£		Liabilities		
Stock	2,900		Creditors		11,000
Cash in hand	100				
Cash at bank	100				
Debtors	2,400	5,500			
		45,500			45,500

Figure 2.3

It was previously stated above that the balance sheet is a good way of *presenting* information but it should now be apparent that it is not a good way of *recording* information. The reason that the balance sheet heading includes the words "as at" is because the balance sheet alters with every transaction. Therefore, it is important to show which day it relates to as the figures could be very different on the following day. The balance sheet can only show what the figures were at the close of business on the one day.

Whilst the balance sheet is a suitable means of presenting information it is a very arduous means of recording information if the whole thing has to be completely rewritten after each transaction. It would also mean that some organisations would probably never be able to produce a completely accurate balance sheet as they are having transactions every second, for example nationwide supermarket chains. The solution is to maintain daily records using a different system and then transfer the totals for each item to the balance sheet when it is needed at the end of the firm's accounting year. What is required is a simple means of listing all the details of transactions that can then be added up at the end of the year and transferred to the balance sheet. But, the balance sheet is still going to have to "balance" (ie both sides must be equal), and this will only happen if the dual aspect concept is applied. Therefore, the system for listing transaction details must show the effect on both of the items affected by the transaction.

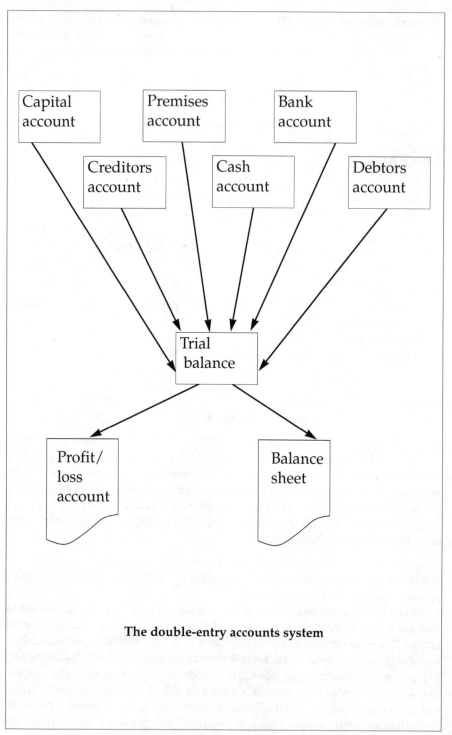

The double-entry accounts system

Figure 2.4 The balance sheet

2.1 THE DOUBLE-ENTRY SYSTEM

The method used to list transaction details for eventual inclusion in the balance sheet is known as the double-entry system because it records each transaction twice, once for each item affected. Each item that appears in the balance sheet will have its own "account" to record each transaction. At the end of the year it is totalled and the final amount is entered in the balance sheet.

The layout of these double-entry accounts has been developed over the years. The obvious way to record items would be as follows in Figure 2.5.

Account for cash in hand	
	£
Received cash from sales	500
Paid for stock	−75
	425
Bought typewriter	−110
Bought stock	−205
Transferred cash to bank	−50
	60
Received cash from sales	120
	180

Figure 2.5

At first sight this system may appear to be suitable, but the disadvantage is that it involves a calculation for every item recorded. This is likely to result in errors and there is no easy way of finding total receipts and total payments. Also, most businesses will have the number of transactions recorded above in a single morning, yet the list has got to be kept for a whole year.

The double-entry system has been developed so that all increases in the item are recorded in one column of the account and all decreases are entered in another column of the account. The columns are given the titles of debit and credit, or dr and cr for short. These terms should not be confused with debtor and creditor.

In order for the balance sheet to balance at the end of the year it is essential that items are recorded in the following way:

Assets and expenses	*Increases in item*	*Debit side*
	Decreases in item	*Credit side*
Liabilities and capital	*Increases in item*	*Credit side*
	Decreases in item	*Debit side*

Section 1.5 explained the definitions of items that are classified as Assets, Liabilities and Capital but the other item shown above, Expenses, has not been mentioned before. An expense item is essentially an asset — assets have already been sub-divided into fixed and current. An expense item is a very short-term asset that is completely used up within one accounting year. They are best defind by the materiality convention — expense items (eg rent, insurance) do have

a value to the firm but they are usually fairly small amounts and there is little, or no value left at the end of the year. Therefore there is no point in including such minor amounts in a balance sheet and the solution is to "write them off" in the year in which they were incurred. The relevance of this will be seen shortly.

Double-entry accounts are usually shown in accounts textbooks as seen in Figure 2.6.

Cash Account

Dr						Cr
1 Jan	Sales	500	2 Jan	Purchases	75	
6 Jan	Sales	120	2 Jan	Typewriter	110	
			4 Jan	Purchases	205	
			5 Jan	Bank	50	
			6 Jan	Balance c/d	180	
		620			620	
9 Jan	Balance b/d	180				

Figure 2.6

This account shows the same information as Figure 2.5 and is the most commonly accepted means of drawing up accounts. The advantages over the other method shown are:

— It only requires adding up at the end of each week or month. The balance b/d, ie brought down, is the balance of cash remaining.

— All increases are shown on one side of the account and all decreases on the other side.

However, although this is the method that is found in most text books, it is not the method that will be used here because it is nowadays rarely used anywhere other than accounts textbooks. Sole traders will use a cash analysis book and large organisations will be likely to use a computer. Therefore it is more relevant to show how computers will record and print the accounts rather than how textbooks will show them. Figure 2.7 shows a computer record of the account detailed above:

Cash Account

Date	Details	Ref	Dr	Cr
1 Jan	Sales	AS123	500	
2 Jan	Purchases	G356		75
2 Jan	Typewriter	QR4562		110
4 Jan	Purchases	G387		205
5 Jan	Bank	23654		50
6 Jan	Sales	AS124	120	
			620	440
	Balance at this date		180	

Figure 2.7

There are a number of variations on this method but most computer programs will produce accounts in virtually the same way so this is the method that will be adopted in this book.

The reasons why computer programs use this method are:

— It is a method commonly used in manual systems.

— It can be printed on a standard 80 column printer (the other method may require more columns).

— It can be displayed on a standard 80 column VDU.

— It looks, and is, simpler than the other methods.

Now that the layout of the accounts has been explained, we need to see some examples of how different transactions would be recorded. Remember that the object of these double-entry accounts is to keep a list of all transactions so that the totals can be entered in the final accounts at the end of the year.

Example: A trader starts a business on 1 January by investing £10,000 of his own money in a bank account for the business.

This transaction will have the effect of increasing his capital and also increasing the bank account for the business. What the records would show can be seen in Figure 2.8.

Capital account			
Date	Details	Dr	Cr
1 Jan	Bank account		10,000
Bank account			
Date	Details	Dr	Cr
1 Jan	Capital account	10,000	

Figure 2.8

The transaction has increased his capital, and increases in capital or liabilities are recorded on the credit side of these accounts, whilst the bank account is an asset, and increases in assets are recorded on the debit side. It is essential that this is done correctly or the balance sheet will not balance. This can be shown better by doing another example:

Example: On 2 January the trader buys a motor vehicle on credit for £4500.

This transaction will increase the assets and also increase his liabilities (see Figure 2.9).

The motor vehicle has increased his assets and therefore has a debit entry, whilst the amount owed is a liability and has therefore increased his liabilities, which means it is a credit entry.

Motor vehicle account				
Date	Details		Dr	Cr
2 Jan	Creditor account		4,500	

Creditor account				
Date	Details		Dr	Cr
2 Jan	Motor vehicle account			4,500

Figure 2.9

If a simple balance sheet is prepared from these accounts it will balance as Figure 2.10 demonstrates.

Bank	£10,000	Capital	£10,000
Motor vehicle	£4,500	Liabilities	£4,500
	£14,500		£14,500

Figure 2.10

This will only be achieved if the dual aspect concept is followed and every transaction is recorded twice. Not every transaction will have the effect of increasing an asset and a liability or capital.

Example: On 3 January the trader buys premises for £8000 paying by cheque.

This transaction will increase one asset, the premises, but will also decrease one of the assets, the bank account. This is shown in Figure 2.11.

Premises account				
Date	Details		Dr	Cr
3 Jan	Bank account		8,000	

Bank account				
Date	Details		Dr	Cr
1 Jan	Capital account		10,000	
3 Jan	Premises account			8,000

Figure 2.11

The premises have been increased and therefore have a debit entry, but the bank account has been decreased and reductions in assets are shown as credit entries. The important thing to do is to make sure that each entry is recorded twice and that each entry is on the opposite side. The balance sheet will still balance as seen in Figure 2.12.

Bank	£2,000	Capital	£10,000
Motor vehicle	£4,500	Liabilities	£4,500
Premises	£8,000		
	£14,500		£14,500

Figure 2.12

A few more examples now follow:

Example: On 4 January the trader buys some office equipment for £500 paying by cheque.

Office equipment account				
Date	Details		Dr	Cr
4 Jan	Bank account		500	

Bank account				
Date	Details		Dr	Cr
1 Jan	Capital account		10,000	
3 Jan	Premises account			8,000
4 Jan	Office equipment account			500

Figure 2.13

Figure 2.13 shows that once again one asset (office equipment) has been increased and one asset (bank) has been decreased.

Example: On 5 January the owner introduces more capital of £300 which he keeps in the cash till.

Cash account				
Date	Details		Dr	Cr
5 Jan	Capital account		300	

Capital account				
Date	Details		Dr	Cr
1 Jan	Bank account			10,000
5 Jan	Cash account			300

Figure 2.14

The "details" recorded for each transaction is the name of the other account where the double-entry can be found — that is the reason for showing "account" after each entry. After some practice it is acceptable to drop the word "account" or use "a/c" as an abbreviation. But it is important to remember that "details" refers to the other account involved in the transaction. Writing the name of the other account is important as it makes it easier to check where errors have arisen if the balance sheet does not balance.

Exercises

All questions ending in A do not have answers supplied.

31A Show how the following would be recorded in a double-entry system:
   May 1   Invested Capital on £10,000 in a Bank account

May 2   Bought premises for £7,500
May 3   Bought a motor vehicle for £2,000 on credit from ABC
        Garages Ltd
May 4   Took £100 from the bank for use in the cash till
May 5   Borrowed £2,000 in the form of a bank loan
May 6   Paid ABC Garages amount owing by cheque
May 7   Bought another motor vehicle for £2,000 by cheque

32A Why is that most Accounting textbooks show double-entry accounts in a "T"
format whereas virtually all computerised packages show the accounts in
the format used in this section?

2.2   DOUBLE-ENTRY OF EXPENSES

Assets, liabilities and capital are not the only items for which accounts are kept.
The materiality convention states that minor assets can be written off in the year
in which they arise. These minor assets are known as expenses. They are treated
in the same way as assets in the double-entry accounts but are not entered in the
balance sheet at the end of the year as they will be used to calculate the profit.

Common expense items are wages, rent, rates, lighting and heating, insurance,
motor expenses, stationery, depreciation and carriage costs. Here are a few
examples of how expense items would be recorded:

Example: On 5 January the owner pays rent of £100 by cheque.

Bank account			
Date	Details	Dr	Cr
1 Jan	Bank account	10,000	
3 Jan	Premises		8,000
4 Jan	Office Equipment		500
5 Jan	Rent		100

Rent account			
Date	Details	Dr	Cr
5 Jan	Bank	100	

Figure 2.15

This is continuing the details of the previous examples. The expense of rent is
treated as an asset and as the "asset" of rent has increased then the rent account
records a debit entry.

Example: The trader pays wages of £150 on 6 January in cash.

Cash account			
Date	Details	Dr	Cr
5 Jan	Capital	300	
6 Jan	Wages		150

Wages account			
Date	Details	Dr	Cr
6 Jan	Cash	150	

Figure 2.16

Once again, as wages are a type of asset, all increases are recorded as debit entries. If in doubt as to which side of the account an entry should be made, remember that all transactions have two entries - one debit and one credit. If you are sure which account has the debit (or credit) entry then the other entry must be on the opposite side. Also, it is worth remembering that all receipts of money are recorded as debit entries in the cash and bank accounts, and all payments are recorded as credit entries in those accounts.

Exercises

33 Show how the following transactions would be entered in a Cash Account (the other entries are not required).

Jan 1 Balance b/d $120.00
Jan 2 Paid wages $75.50
Jan 3 Paid rent $25.00
Jan 4 Cash sales $28.70
Jan 5 Insurance refund $50.00
Jan 6 Carriage Inwards $12.75
Jan 7 Commission received $120.20

Balance off the account on Jan 8.

(8 marks)
(Mar 91)

34 Examine the data shown below and suggest what transactions have taken place between each column. Draw up double-entry accounts to record each transaction. Suggest two possible reasons for the changes in column I.

	A	B	C	D	E	F	G	H	I
Premises	20,000	20,000	20,000	20,000	20,000	30,000	30,000	30,000	30,000
Motor Van	5,000	5,000	5,000	5,000	5,000	5,000	7,000	7,000	7,000
Fixtures	2,000	2,000	2,000	2,000	2,000	2,000	2,000	2,000	2,000
Debtors	3,000	3,000	4,000	2,000	2,000	2,000	2,000	2,000	2,000
Stock	2,500	2,500	1,500	1,500	3,500	3,500	3,500	3,000	3,000
Bank	4,000	4,500	4,500	6,500	6,500	6,500	6,500	6,500	6,500
Cash	1,500	1,000	1,000	1,000	1,000	1,000	1,000	500	1,500
	38,000	38,000	38,000	38,000	40,000	50,000	52,000	51,000	52,000
Capital	30,000	30,000	30,000	30,000	30,000	30,000	30,000	29,000	30,000
Creditors	4,000	4,000	4,000	4,000	6,000	6,000	8,000	8,000	8,000
Loan	4,000	4,000	4,000	4,000	4,000	4,000	4,000	4,000	4,000
Mortgage	—	—	—	—	—	10,000	10,000	10,000	10,000
	38,000	38,000	38,000	38,000	40,000	50,000	52,000	51,000	52,000

(Mar 90)

2.3   THE ASSET OF STOCK

One asset that is shown in the balance sheet but has not yet been mentioned is stock. Stock is the term used to describe the goods that a firm sells. This asset is slightly different from all other assets. In the examples used so far, the bank account is as follows:

Bank account				
Date	Details		Dr	Cr
1 Jan	Capital		10,000	
3 Jan	Premises			8,000
4 Jan	Office equipment			500
5 Jan	Rent			100

Figure 2.17

It should be apparent that there is £1,400 remaining in the bank account and the trader would probably "balance off" the account at the end of the week to calculate the balance:

Bank account				
Date	Details		Dr	Cr
1 Jan	Capital		10,000	
3 Jan	Premises			8,000
4 Jan	Office equipment			500
5 Jan	Rent			100
			10,000	8,600
8 Jan	Balance at this date		1,400	

Figure 2.18

There are a couple of points worth noting at this stage before continuing:

— Underlining a figure twice in accounts means that the figures above the double lines are now finished with. In this example the figures are for the previous week's trading and are now obsolete. Unfortunately, many computer printers do not have the facility to underscore twice so computerised accounts may make do with just one underline.

— Most firms will calculate the "balances" on accounts at weekly or monthly intervals. The reason for this in manual systems is that it makes addition more accurate - the accounts are added regularly instead of once a year so the number of figures to add is much smaller. For example, in the account shown above there are only four figures to add up. Most people can add four numbers together without making a mistake, but if the account is only added up once a year then at the rate of four entries per week there are likely to be 208 figures to add — even with the aid of a calculator there is going to be a high risk of error!

If a computer is being used, then there should not be any addition errors. However, the practice of balancing off accounts is often still continued because the firm will often want to know what amounts are left in various accounts at the end of the month and also, any printout of an account listing over 200 entries is not easy to make any sense of. Accounts that are balanced weekly or monthly are less confusing. Section 2.5 demonstrates an alternative method used by some computer systems.

Consider the bank account shown above and it is possible to see how the balance was arrived at and that the balance remaining in the account is £1,400. An account for stock would show increases (ie stock purchased) on the debit side and decreases (ie stock sold) on the credit side. Such an account might look like Figure 2.19.

Stock account			
Date	Details	Dr	Cr
1 Jan	Cash	400	
2 Jan	T. Brown Ltd		150
3 Jan	Cash		200
4 Jan	Bank	100	

Figure 2.19

If the account were to be balanced off on 8 January the balance would be £150:

Stock account			
Date	Details	Dr	Cr
1 Jan	Cash	400	
2 Jan	T. Brown Ltd		150
3 Jan	Cash		200
4 Jan	Bank	100	
		500	350
8 Jan	Balance at this date	150	

Figure 2.20

This balance clearly implies that the firm has stock left to the value of £150. This is a very false impression as it assumes that stock is being sold at the same price as was paid for it. In fact all firms want to make a profit so goods are sold at a higher price than that paid for them. In the example given it could be that stock of 500 items was bought at £1 each and 175 have been sold at £2 each. If that were the case then the stock remaining is 325 items valued at cost price (using the cost concept) of £1, leaving a balance of £325:

Stock Purchased	500 at £1	
Stock sold	175 at £2	
Balance	325 at £1	= £325

Therefore the stock account is £175 short! This is the only account in which this problem arises and the problem is simply because sales will always be at a higher price than purchases. The difference between the balance shown on the account and the balance worked out above is the profit made by the firm. In order to show the account for stock in a meaningful way it is necessary to divide it into five separate accounts. These are:

The purchases account: This account will record all increases in stock from purchases of goods for resale. As it is dealing with the asset of stock and only records increases, every entry will be debit.

The returns inwards (or sales returns) account: This account will record all increases in stock from goods returned from customers as surplus to requirements or unsuitable. As it is dealing with the asset of stock and only records increases, every entry will be debit.

The sales account: This account will record all decreases in stock from sales of goods. As it is dealing with the asset of stock and only records decreases, every entry will be credit.

The returns outwards (or purchases returns) account: This account will record all decreases in stock from goods returned to suppliers as being surplus to requirements or unsuitable. As it is dealing with the asset of stock and only records decreases, every entry will be credit.

The stock account: This account is only used at the end of the firm's accounting year and will record the unsold stock at the end of the year. It is not part of normal double-entry procedures and the amount shown in this account will be derived from separate stock records. These records can now be very accurate if held on computers but it is also usually necessary to physically count every item of stock (stocktaking) to ensure that the actual stock held agrees with the figure shown in the stock records. It frequently will not agree because some stock will have deteriorated, evaporated, been stolen, etc.

The first four accounts shown are the major ones and they are actually "splitting" the stock account into four separate parts — all of the debit entries for increases in stock are shown in the purchases and returns in accounts and all of the credit entries for decreases in stock are shown in the sales and returns out accounts. Most transactions will be on a credit basis (ie payment is made some time after the goods have been delivered); this should not be confused with the credit side of the accounts. Firms usually buy and sell to a fairly large number of people, therefore it is important to know how much is owed to, or is owed by, each of these people/firms. Consequently, it is necessary to give each debtor and creditor his own personal account.

Example: Goods are purchased from ABC Ltd for £500 credit on 1 January

Purchase account			
Date	Details	Dr	Cr
1 Jan	ABC Ltd	500	

ABC Ltd account			
Date	Details	Dr	Cr
1 Jan	Purchases		500

Figure 2.21

As stated above all purchases will be recorded as debit entries in the purchases account, also ABC Ltd are now owed money by the firm and are therefore creditors; creditors will normally have a credit balance on their account.

Example: On 2 January goods are sold to XYZ & Co for £300

Sales account			
Date	Details	Dr	Cr
2 Jan	XYZ & Co		300

XYZ & Co account			
Date	Details	Dr	Cr
2 Jan	Sales	300	

Figure 2.22

As sales reduce the asset of stock they are always entered as credit entries, whilst debtors will normally have a debit balance.

This is an example of some fully worked transactions covering the first part of this chapter:

1 Jan A trader starts a business by investing £10,000 in a business bank account. On the same day he buys premises for £5,000 and a motor vehicle for £2,000. He pays for both by cheque.

2 Jan He buys stock from A Jones for £700 on credit. He also takes £100 from the bank for the cash till in the business.

3 Jan He buys £200 worth of stock, paying by cheque. He also buys shop fittings for £1,500 on credit from Kwik Fittings Ltd.

4 Jan He sells £650 of goods to D Wilson on credit and £100 of goods for cash.

5 Jan He returns £40 worth of goods to A Jones. Cash of £100 is paid into the bank. D Wilson pays off his account by cheque.

These accounts would be drawn up and balanced off as shown in Figures 2.23(a) to (f).

Capital account

Date	Details	Dr	Cr
1 Jan	Bank		10,000

Bank account

Date	Details	Dr	Cr
1 Jan	Capital	10,000	
1 Jan	Premises		5,000
1 Jan	Motor Vehicle		2,000
2 Jan	Cash		100
3 Jan	Purchases		200
5 Jan	Cash	100	
5 Jan	D Wilson	650	
		10,750	7,300
8 Jan	Balance at this date	3,450	

Figure 2.23(a)

Premises account

Date	Details	Dr	Cr
1 Jan	Bank	5,000	

Motor vehicles account

Date	Details	Dr	Cr
1 Jan	Bank	2,000	

Purchases account

Date	Details	Dr	Cr
2 Jan	A Jones	700	
3 Jan	Bank	200	
		900	NIL
8 Jan	Balance at this date	900	

Figure 2.23(b)

A Jones account

Date	Details	Dr	Cr
2 Jan	Purchases		700
5 Jan	Returns Out	40	
		40	700
8 Jan	Balance at this date		660

Figure 2.23(c)

Cash account

Date	Details	Dr	Cr
2 Jan	Bank	100	
4 Jan	Sales	100	
5 Jan	Bank		100
		200	100
8 Jan	Balance at this date	100	100

Figure 2.23(d)

Shop fittings account

Date	Details	Dr	Cr
3 Jan	Kwik Fittings Ltd	1,500	

Kwik Fittings account

Date	Details	Dr	Cr
3 Jan	Shop Fittings		1,500

Sales account

Date	Details	Dr	Cr
4 Jan	D Wilson		650
4 Jan	Cash		100
		Nil	750
8 Jan	Balance at this date		750

Figure 2.23(e)

D Wilson account

Date	Details	Dr	Cr
4 Jan	Sales	650	
5 Jan	Bank		650
		650	650

Returns out account

Date	Details	Dr	Cr
5 Jan	A Jones		40

Figure 2.23(f)

Notes

1. Accounts that only have one entry in them are not worth balancing off as the balance is obvious (eg capital a/c, premises a/c).

2. Shop fittings and motor vehicles are assets and the purchase of assets is recorded in their own account. These items are not entered in the purchases account as the purchases account only deals with the purchase of goods for resale.

3. The account for D Wilson has been "cleared" as he has paid off the money that he owes.

Exercises

35 Explain why neither manual nor computerised double-entry accounts can be used to record stock, and why even computerised stock recording systems cannot produce the true value of stock.

36 Draw up the double-entry accounts to record the following transactions:

1 June	D Wilkes started his own business using £12,000 in a bank account, his own motor van £8000 and £500 in cash.
2 June	Acquired premises for a rent of £1000 per annum payable quarterly in advance. Paid first installment by cheque.
3 June	Bought stock for £3000 from AC Limited.
4 June	Bought a second-hand lathe for £2500, paying by cheque.
5 June	Advertised the business in the local newspaper, paid £200 cash.
6 June	Sold goods for £750 to H Kelly on credit and another £600 worth of cash.
10 June	Paid £400 cash into bank. Sold goods to D Miles for £300 on credit.
12 June	Sold motor van for £8000 part-exchange for a new vehicle worth £13,000. Paid by cheque.
14 June	Sold goods for £450, paying by cheque.
17 June	Bought more goods from AC Limited worth £1500.
18 June	Paid wages £1300 in cash, after taking cash out of bank.
20 June	Received cheque for £750 from H Kelly.
21 June	Paid AC Limited £2000 on account by cheque.

37 (i)   Show how the following would be recorded in a *Double-entry Bank Account* (NB: the other accounts should be ignored).

   (ii)   Balance off the account at 7th Dec.

Dec 1st   Opening balance was $2,400.
Dec 2nd Owner invested additional Capital of $12,000.
Dec 3rd Bought Office equipment for $7,500.
Dec 4th Bought Stock for $1,1000.
Dec 5th Paid rent $300.
Dec 6th Sold goods $3,000.

(Dec 88)

2.4   CAPITAL AND REVENUE EXPENDITURE

The difference between assets and expenses is very important as it will affect the way that the final accounts are prepared. Basically, all fixed assets are included in the balance sheet and expenses are included in the profit and loss account.

In most cases it is easy to determine which category an item should be classified as, but there are some instances when the difference is not quite so obvious. The definitions of Capital and Revenue expenditure are used to aid classification of items.

2.4.1   Categories

Capital expenditure

Despite the name, capital expenditure refers to any amounts spent on acquiring and installing fixed assets. The term "capital" is used as the source of funds for acquiring fixed assets and is often the owner's capital. As already explained, fixed assets have the characteristics of having long-term use in the business, they usually retain quite a high value and are recorded in the balance sheet.

Revenue expenditure

Revenue expenditure refers to the day-to-day costs of running a business and all of the "expense" items would come under this classification.

The difference is important as these items are included in the profit and loss account and are used to calculate profit. These items will only have a short-term value and in many cases the "benefit" derived from them is used up as soon as they are paid for (eg: wages, rent, motor expenses).

However, it is possible for an item that would normally be classed as revenue expenditure to be classed as capital expenditure under certain circumstances. The cost of a fixed asset is not just the cost of buying that asset but also the cost of installing and setting up the asset ready for use. In normal circumstances the cost of a solicitor's fees or the wages of maintenance staff would be classed as revenue expenditure. But if the solicitor's fees are paid as part of the legal charges incurred in acquiring premises or the maintenance staff wages are associated with installing new machinery, then the costs should be added to the value of the fixed asset and classed as capital expenditure.

This rule will only apply if the expense is incurred in the purchase or improvement of a fixed asset. If the expenditure is merely repairing or renovating a fixed asset then it would still be classed as revenue expenditure. The best way of determining which category is appropriate is to decide whether the expenditure is increasing the value of the asset (capital expenditure) or merely returning the asset to its original value/state (revenue expenditure).

Example: A firm buys some premises for £100,000, they also incur legal charges of £2,000. During the next year an extension is built at a cost of £30,000 and an existing wing is refurbished at a cost of £10,000. The original building is repainted at a cost of £2,000.

Capital expenditure

Purchase price	£100,000
Legal fees	£2,000
Extension	£30,000
	£132,000

All of these items are <u>increasing</u> the value of the building and the Balance Sheet would show the value of Premises as £132,000.

Revenue expenditure

Refurbishment	£10,000
Repainting	£2,000
	£12,000

These items are merely "making good" and are renovations, therefore they will not be increasing the value of the premises but merely returning them to their original value. The cost of £12,000 would be written off in the profit and loss account.

Exercises

38   Classify the following items as capital or revenue expenditure:

 (a) Cost of new machinery
 (b) Petrol and oil for motor vehicle
 (c) Wages of office staff
 (d) Purchase of new typewriters
 (e) Replacement of typewriter ribbons
 (f) Repairs to factory roof
 (g) Extension to factory
 (h) Repainting offices
 (i) Installation of air conditioning system in offices
 (j) Solicitor's fees for purchase of new factory premises
 (k) Stationery
 (l) Repairs to damaged motor vehicle
 (m) Cost of training course for staff using new machinery
 (n) Insurance costs on new factory
 (o) Rates on factory
 (p) Wages of staff installing new machinery
 (q) Wages of staff using new machinery
 (r) Replacement of rotten windows in offices

39A A firm has recently ordered a new computer, the basic cost of which is £1,500, but the company has ordered an extra memory card which costs an additional £150. There is also an additional £140 to pay as the company has requested a colour monitor version.

A printer has also been selected, this will cost £300 and £70 for the optional sheet feeder. The order includes £15 for blank floppy disks, £20 for spare printer ribbons and £30 for printer paper. The company supplying the equipment offer a two day training course for staff which costs £300, the firm has agreed to send its staff on this course.

A discount of 10% is offered on hardware items and 15% on other items. Calculate the cost of the order in terms of:

 (i) Capital expenditure
 (ii) Revenue expenditure

40 John has recently set up his own business as a parcels delivery service. His main investment in the business was the purchase of a Leyland Truck. The list price of this van was £13,500 (excluding number plates and vehicle tax). As John paid in cash he was given a discount of 10% on the list price. John also requested that the suppliers fit some optional extras, namely: a stereo radio/cassette costing £180, tinted windows costing £90 and velour upholstery costing £125.

The suppliers persuaded John to take out a 12 month parts and service warranty for an additional £150. Fitting of number plates cost £48 and one year's road tax cost £100. He had already discovered that the insurance would cost him £380 for a full year.

When John went to pick up the van he bought £22 worth of petrol and also bought an Ordnance Survey road map which cost £13.

(a) REQUIRED: Calculate the cost of the van in terms of "capital expenditure" and give your reasons for incluing items in this list.

During the year John also purchased the following items:

(1)   Replacement windscreen wipers
(2)   Chrome wheel trims
(3)   Purchase and fitting of tow-bar
(4)   Oil for refilling engine
(5)   Purchase of trailer
(6)   Fitted car alarm
(7)   Petrol
(8)   Repainting van to include company name
(9)   Car polish and wax
(10)   Cassette tapes for use on the stereo cassette player

(b) REQUIRED: Consider each item in the above list and categorise them under the headings of either Capital or Revenue Expenditure.

2.5 BALANCING ACCOUNTS ON COMPUTERS

The examples shown so far are typical of most accounting textbooks, and demonstrate the usual procedure for "balancing" accounts at the end of each month. The previous section explained that the system of calculating balances ensures that the quantity of figures to be added is kept to a minimum, and therefore errors should be reduced. Clearly, addition of a large series of numbers should not be a problem in a computerised system and an alternative method has been devised in some computer systems.

The advantage of a "balance b/d" is that it clears the accounts of outdated figures, but if the account is balanced at the end of each week or month then it may be difficult to "match" payments received from customers with the order that it relates to as the value of the order has since been amalgamated as part of the "balance b/d".

Computers excel in storing very large quantities of data and, in addition, it should not be a problem if the account records all transactions that are still outstanding — this is known as the "open item" system. A comparison of the two systems would look something like the following:

BALANCE B/D METHOD Debtors account			
Date	Details	Dr	Cr
1 Jan	Balance at this date	100	
4 Jan	Sales (Invoice No 3429)	110	
5 Jan	Bank (Cheque)		50
17 Jan	Sales (Invoice No 3251)	35	
		245	50
31 Jan	Balance at this date	195	

OPEN ITEM METHOD			
Debtors account			
Date	Details	Dr	Cr
12 Nov	Sales (Invoice No 2876)	50	
8 Dec	Sales (Invoice No 2917)	30	
28 Dec	Sales (Invoice No 3100)	20	
4 Jan	Sales (Invoice No 3429)	110	
5 Jan	Bank (Cheque)		50
17 Jan	Sales (Invoice No 3251)	35	
		245	50
31 Jan	Balance at this date	195	

Figure 2.24

The advantage of this system is that when a payment is received it can be "matched" against the appropriate invoice. In this example the payment obviously relates to the invoice dated 12th November. These entries are no longer "open" and therefore would normally be erased from the records when the account is saved to disk. This system should give a much clearer picture of the situation in any account but is usually only used for "personal accounts" (ie debtors and creditors accounts).

The open item system does make it much easier to identify which transaction a particular payment/receipt relates to but can also use the "sorting" ability of computers to produce a list of "aged debts". Because all items are still recorded and not merged as part of a balance then the computer should be capable of producing a list showing which debtors still owe money from transactions three months ago, two months ago and the previous month. This facility will be considered in more depth in Chapter 5.

As the "Open item" system is only of practical use for personal accounts most systems will allow the user to specify whether each account should be "Open item" or "Balance b/d".

2.6   THE TRIAL BALANCE

At the end of the year, or perhaps more frequently if a computer is being used, a balance sheet must be prepared. The accounting equation and dual aspect concept effectively state that every transaction will affect two items (ie double-entry); unfortunately it is very easy for accounts clerks to forget to make both entries. If an entry is missed out on just one side of the accounts then the balance sheet will not balance. In the example above, if one of the entries had been missed out it would have been necessary to check every transaction to find where the error was. This would be a nuisance but if the error were not discovered until the end of the year, the number of transactions to search through would be fifty times larger!

The trial balance is what its name implies — a test of whether the balance sheet will balance. It is useful because it is quick to draw up and can be done at any time of the year. If the trial balance is done on a monthly basis, when an error does arise it can be pinpointed as arising during a particular month's transactions. In addition, it is always good practice to do a trial balance before starting to draw up a balance sheet, since if the trial balance does not balance, the balance sheet will not either!

The trial balance is a quick and easy check on the accuracy of the double-entry accounts and operates on the principle that if all transactions have been entered twice, the total of all debit entries should be the same as the total of all credit entries. If every single entry has to be added for both sides of the accounts, it would not be a very quick method; however, if all entries have been made correctly, the total of debit balances should equal the total of credit balances. This makes the extraction of a trial balance much quicker and simpler.

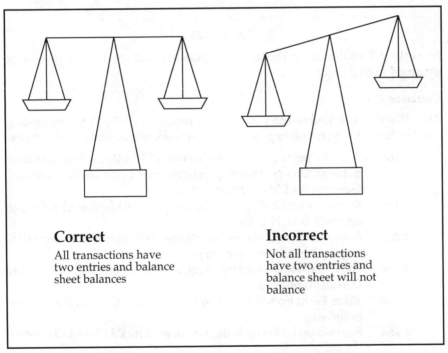

Correct

All transactions have
two entries and balance
sheet balances

Incorrect

Not all transactions
have two entries and
balance sheet will not
balance

Figure 2.25 Balancing the balance sheet

For the double-entry accounts drawn up in the previous example the trial balance would be that shown in Figure 2.26.

A trader		
Trial balance as at 8 Jan		
Account	Dr	Cr
Capital		10,000
Bank	3,450	
Premises	5,000	
Motor Vehicles	2,000	
Purchases	900	
A Jones		600
Cash	100	
Shop fittings	1,500	
Kwik Fittings Ltd		1,500
Sales		750
Returns Out		40
	12,950	12,950

Figure 2.26

Since the debit balances are the same as the credit balances, the accounts can be assumed to be correct.

Exercises

41   Draw up the double-entry accounts to record the following transactions, balance off the accounts at the end of the week and extract a trial balance.

1 Jan   A trader starts a business by investing £10,000 in a business bank account. On the same day he acquires a motor vehicle from ABC Garages for £3500 credit.

2 Jan   Buys stock for £350, paying by cheque, and a further £1000 worth on credit from H Cully.

3 Jan   Pays insurance £100, buys stationery £35, motor expenses £15, paying for all items by cheque.

4 Jan   Pays one month's rent by cheque £300. Sells £455 of goods to D Watkins on credit.

5 Jan   Takes £200 from the bank to use as a cash float on the business premises.

6 Jan   Pays wages £50 in cash. Buys more stock for £350 credit from Worthy Ltd.

42   Show how the following would be recorded in the double-entry accounts and extract a trial balance to check the accuracy of your workings.

1 May   H Wilson starts a business by investing £5500 in a bank account and £300 in cash. He also provides a motor van worth £3000 for use solely in the business.

2 May   He buys premises for £4000 and buy goods for resale on credit

from F Goodby £450, J Oates £1000, W Young £120 and G Mistry £245.

3 May   The bank lend him £2000 with which he buys fixtures and fittings for £750, paying by cheque; he leaves the remainder in his bank account.

4 May   Goods are sold on credit to the following: J Singh £750, H Jones £300, K Sung £1200 and K Patel £450.

5 May   Pays the following by cheque: rates £200, insurance £80, stationery £15, motor expenses £75. He also pays wages in cash £120.

6 May   Goods valued at £120 are returned to J Oates. The amounts owing to F Goodby and W Young are paid by cheque. Cheques are received from J Singh £750, H Jones £200 and K Patel £425. K Patel also returns goods worth £25.

43   The following *Trial Balance* has been drawn up by an inexperienced Accounts clerk, redraft the Trial balance to show the correct entries.

	Dr	Cr
Capital	34,927	
Drawings	10,465	
Bank	4,196	
Cash	500	
Debtors	8,500	
Creditors		4,040
Wages		15,500
General Expenses		25,850
Carriage Inwards	650	
Carriage Outwards		1,540
Purchase Returns		761
Sales Returns		531
Discounts Allowed	1,150	
Discounts Received	2,324	
Sales		107,266
Purchases	50,754	
Motor Vehicles	38,420	
Stock at 1st March 1990		5,830
Accumulated Depreciation	14,568	
	166,454	161,318

(10 marks)
(Mar 91)

44   The following *Trial Balance* has been drawn up by an inexperienced Accounts clerk. Redraft the Trial balance correctly:

	Dr £	Cr £
Wages		20,500
Capital		172,380
Motor vehicles	78,900	
Insurance	2,100	
Debtors		17,500
Light and heat		900
Returns In		1,110
Creditors	13,400	
Sales		65,800
Purchases	45,320	
Returns Out	850	
Premises	98,200	
Discounts received	1,200	
Cash	800	
Bank	3,200	
Accumulated depreciation	12,900	
Rent and rates		4,000
Bank loan		6,000
	256,870	256,870

(Dec 88)

45A   K. Singh started a business on 1st May, paying £7,000 into a business bank account. During the next two months the following transactions occurred.

May 2nd	Purchased goods on credit from J. Sukee Ltd for £170.
May 3rd	Paid rent by cheque (£250).
May 5th	Borrowed £1000 (cheque) from P Lal.
May 8th	Sold goods for £75 cash.
May 9th	Purchased goods on credit from J Sukee Ltd (£850).
May 14th	Paid insurance (£90 cheque).
May 19th	Bought office furniture paying by cheque £2000.
May 23rd	Sold goods £130 cash.
May 27th	Paid telephone bill £76, paying by cheque.
Jun 1st	Bought kitchen equipment for self £90 cash.
Jun 2nd	Sold goods for £200 cash.
Jun 3rd	Paid rent by cheque £450.
Jun 6th	Paid electricity bill by cheque £180.
Jun 9th	Wages for proprietor (cash £100).
Jun 15th	Banked takings for the day £205.
Jun 18th	Sold goods to J. Moon on credit £190.
Jun 21st	Purchased goods from J. Sukee on credit £100.
Jun 23rd	Repaid part of loan to Lal by cheque £300.
Jun 29th	Paid road tax for vehicle by cheque £100.

REQUIRED Write up all accounts, balancing at end of each month.
Extract a Trial Balance as at June 30th.

2.6.1 Trial balances in computerised systems

Any person writing or designing an accounting system for a computer needs to be aware of the double-entry rule. In some ways it is easier to record data using a computer because the program should not allow the operator to continue with any further transactions until the double-entry rule has been complied with. This is a fairly simple piece of programming and merely requires the program to refuse to proceed until both a credit and debit entry have been made for each transaction. If this rule is included in a program, it would appear that the need for a trial balance would not exist in computerised systems because of the inherent accuracy. To a certain extent this is true but there is still a need for staff other than the operator to check the records (Chapter 3) and many accounting packages will still include a form of trial balance (Chapter 5).

The job of the system analyst is to ascertain what the users, ie the accounts department, require from a system, and in some cases a trial balance may be requested by the users because it is essential in a manual system and it has not perhaps been made clear to them that the computer should not be capable of allowing single-entry only. That is not to say that a trial balance would be obsolete in a computerised system as it may still be required, but for a slightly different reason.

2.6.2 Errors not disclosed by a trial balance

However, in both manual and computerised systems the trial balance will not prevent all errors; in fact, the only errors that will be discovered from a trial balance are those where only one entry is made. The errors that will not be discovered are:

Errors of Omission: If a transaction is completely left out of the accounts, the trial balance will not show this as an error as there is neither a debit nor a credit entry.

Figure 2.27 Errors not discovered by the trial balance

This error can be prevented by ensuring that all source documents, eg invoices, credit notes, debit notes, are stamped or marked in some way to show that they have been entered in the accounts.

Errors of commission: Some errors will arise because one of the two entries is made in the wrong account, eg making an entry in the account of A Williams instead of the account for A A Williams. As there will be both a debit and a credit entry the error will not be identified by the trial balance. The error will only be identified when A Williams receives his statement of account! This type of error is best prevented by employing capable staff, although computerised systems can lessen the risk by giving each account a unique number or identifier.

Errors of principle: This is similar to errors of commission but would relate to errors where one of the entries is put in the wrong type of account, eg the purchase of office equipment is recorded in the purchases account instead of the office equipment account. This type of error can only really be avoided by employing capable, well-trained staff and by including verification checks in a computerised system.

Errors of original entry: This refers to errors concerning the amount of the transaction, eg the transaction may be for £1000 but the entry made in both accounts (debit and credit) records only £100. Again, the best means of avoiding this type of error is to ensure that staff are well-trained and capable or through verification checks.

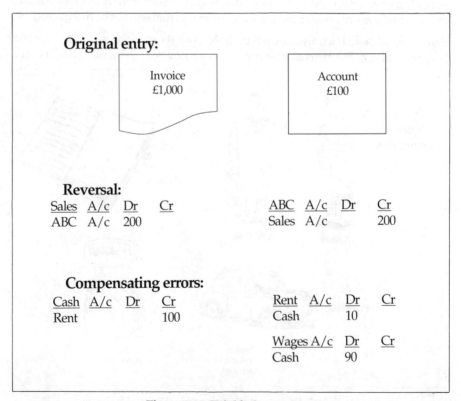

Figure 2.28 Trial balance errors

Errors of reversal: This would apply when a credit and a debit entry are made but both are on the wrong side, eg debiting the sales account for £200 and crediting the account for D Collins by £200. Once again, well-trained and competent staff are essential, but in some cases a computerised system can cut down on errors. In the above example the computer program should identify the fact that debit entries are not possible in the sales account and the entry would not be allowed.

Compensating errors These errors arise when one transaction is entered on one side only but at a later date another transaction for the same amount also has only one entry made but on the opposite side, eg in one week the sales account is credited with £50, no debit entry is made; two weeks later two other accounts have debit entries made, one of £30 and one of £20, no corresponding credit entry is made. In a manual system these errors can be avoided by producing trial balances regularly so that the error is spotted before a compensating entry is made. The problem should be avoided altogether in a computerised system by ensuring that the program refuses to accept single-entries.

Exercises

46 List the names of 5 types of errors that would not be disclosed by a Trial Balance and for each type state how they can be avoided in Computerised systems. (10 marks)
(Mar 91)

47A Fred Jones has recently started trading as a sole trader. He had no prior knowledge of how to keep accounting records and has consequently obtained the services of an accountant. The accountant has agreed to prepare trading, profit and loss accounts and balance sheets, and also to deal with any correspondence from the Inland Revenue and to deal with VAT returns. However, Fred will have to maintain the records of all transactions.

The accountant has demonstrated how records should be kept using the double-entry book-keeping system and shown Fred how he can check the accuracy of his records by drawing up a trial balance. Fred is now satisfied that he can tell the difference between his "debits" and "credits" and is devising a trial balance on a monthly basis to make absolutely sure that he has not made any errors.

REQUIRED

Fred is not necessarily correct in assuming that a trial balance will highlight all of his mistakes. Identify the types of errors that a trial balance will not recognise and give practical examples of the sort of transactions that could be involved.

48 Identify which of the following have been recorded incorrectly and where necessary, specify which type of error has occurred:

(i) Computer printout paper has been recorded under Office Equipment.
(ii) Lawyers fees relating to the purchase of new offices have been recorded under Premises.

(iii) A purchase of raw materials has been recorded as a credit entry in the Purchases account and a Debit entry in the suppliers account.

(iv) A purchase of clothes for the owners has been left out of the accounts altogether.

(v) A sale to A. Ahmed has been entered in the account for A.A. Ahmed.

(vi) A new machine costing $1,000 has been recorded at this value in the Machinery account even though the resale value is now only $750.

(vii) An invoice for $740 has been recorded as $470.

(viii) A pocket calculator costing $9.99 has been recorded as General Office expenses.   (8 marks)   (Mar 92)

49(a) *Errors* have come to light in the *books of account*. You are to explain briefly:

how each is most likely to have occurred,

why they were not detected by a trial balance and

what methods you would adopt to prevent such future errors.

The errors are:

(i)   Black & Co was debited with sales of £350 instead of C. Black.

(ii) Furnishing for the managing director's house were posted to the fixtures and fittings account.

(iii) An invoice from Jones Ltd for £10 was never entered into the books.

(iv) Collins invoiced the firm with goods for £66 but this was recorded as £56. Grahams also sent in an invoice for £544 but this was transcribed as £554.

(v)   Peters paid the firm £89 but was recorded in the books as £98.

                                                                (Dec 89)

50A The following Trial Balance has been drawn up by an inexperienced clerk.

	£	£
Debtors	10,540	
Stock	12,450	
Sales		150,310
Office Fittings	28,300	
Bad debts provision	2,300	
Creditors		12,300
Drawings		22,100
Bank Loan	6,500	
Returns Inwards		3,700
Sundry expenses	6,500	
Discount allowed		12,400
Capital		100,000
Purchases	120,400	
Wages & Salaries	34,520	
Office Fittings: Depreciation for the year	3,100	
Rent & rates	24,560	
Discount received	2,375	
	251,545	300,810

(a) You are required to draw up a corrected trial balance and enter any difference still remaining in a suspense acount.

(b) Upon investigating the difference in the trial balance the following errors are discovered:

(i) An invoice from ABC limited for £1,200 has been posted to their account in the purchase ledger as £2,100.

(ii) The discount allowed column in the cash book has been undercast by £250.

(iii) A purchase invoice from F. Green for £890 has been entered in their account but not in the purchases account.

(iv) Sales of £800 on credit to D. Williams has been entered in their account but not in the sales account.

Show how the errors would be recorded in the suspense account and calculate the amount of the errors still not discovered.

(c) Suggest the names given to five of the errors that would not be discovered by a trial balance.

2.7 THE FINAL ACCOUNTS

At the beginning of the book we discussed the purpose of the balance sheet and this is the reason for keeping double-entry accounts. However, there are some items, eg sales, purchases and expenses items, that do not appear in the balance sheet. If these items are ignored, the balance sheet will not balance. Most firms would choose not to ignore them because these are the items that will determine profit.

At the end of each accounting year, the firm will use the expense accounts to calculate how much profit has been made. The figure for profit will then be entered in the balance sheet, thus showing the financial position of the firm at the end of the year, and revising the figure for capital to include profit made during the year.

There are usually two accounts used to calculate profit, both of which are normal double-entry accounts, although nowadays they are not drawn up like double-entry accounts because a double-entry type layout would not give information clearly enough.

The first account is the trading account, which calculates gross profit. Gross profit is equal to sales less the cost of goods sold. The cost of goods sold is the total of opening stock plus purchases less closing stock (with additional amendments for returned goods and carriage costs). The figures for each item will be transferred from the double-entry accounts with the exception of stock, which will be explained later. A typical layout for the trading account is shown in Figure 2.29.

Note that gross profit is calculated by the formula:

Sales – cost of goods sold

and that the cost of goods sold is calculated:

Opening stock + purchases – closing stock

Although purchases is first adjusted to take into account the goods that incurred carriage costs and to remove those that were returned to the supplier.

A trader

Trading account for the year ending 31 Dec 1989

	£	£	£
Sales			15,000
Less returns inwards			500
			14,500
Opening stock		3,500	
Purchases	8,000		
Carriage inwards	200		
	8,200		
Less returns outwards	700	7,500	
		11,000	
Less closing stock		4,000	
Cost of goods sold		7,000	7,000
Gross profit c/d			7,500

Figure 2.29

All of the double-entry accounts will be adjusted to show that these items have now been transferred to the trading account. Assume the sales account showed the following before the trading account was prepared, as in Figure 2.30.

Sales account

Date	Details	Dr	Cr
1 Dec	Balance at this date		14,000
10 Dec	Cash		100
13 Dec	Bank		350
20 Dec	K Thomas		400
29 Dec	Bank		150
		Nil	15,000
31 Dec	Balance at this date		15,000

Figure 2.30

The account would show the transfer to the trading account as illustrated in Figure 2.31.

Sales account

Date	Details	Dr	Cr
1 Dec	Balance at this date		14,000
10 Dec	Cash		100
13 Dec	Bank		350
20 Dec	K Thomas		400
29 Dec	Bank		150
		Nil	15,000
31 Dec	Balance at this date		15,000
31 Dec	Trading account	15,000	
		15,000	15,000

Figure 2.31

The account is now cleared (ie reduced to nil) and is ready to start recording the transactions for the following year. All of the other accounts except stock will be cleared in the same way. The totals for stock will be obtained by referring to stock records or a computerised stock recording package (in conjunction with a stocktake). Stock differs from the other items as it does not come from a proper double-entry account and it is the only item that will also appear on the balance sheet.

The other account associated with profit is the profit and loss account, which calculates net profit. Net profit is derived from gross profit less expenses. Figure 2.32 shows a typical layout.

Profit and loss account for the year ending 31 Dec 1989		
	£	£
Gross profit b/d		7,500
Commission received		1,500
		9,000
Wages and salaries	1,000	
Rent and rates	500	
Lighting and heating	300	
Stationery	50	
Carriage Outwards	150	
Motor expenses	1,000	
Insurance	500	
Interest paid	500	
	4,000	4,000
Net profit	5,000	

Figure 2.32

The double-entry accounts will be cleared in a similar way to those in the trading account; for example the wages and salaries account may look like Figure 2.33.

Wages and salaries account				
Date	Details		Dr	Cr
1 Dec	Balance at this date		800	
7 Dec	Cash		50	
14 Dec	Cash		50	
21 Dec	Cash		50	
28 Dec	Cash		50	
			1000	Nil
31 Dec	Balance at this date		1000	
31 Dec	Profit and loss account			1,000
			1,000	1,000

Figure 2.33

All of the other expense accounts will be cleared in the same way . This will ensure that the balances on all of these accounts are reduced to nil so that each account starts the new year afresh.

In practice the trading and profit and loss accounts will be shown together instead of as two separate accounts, the normal layout is shown in Figure 2.34.

A Trader

Trading and profit and loss account for the year ending 31 Dec 1989

	£	£	£
Sales			15,000
Less returns inwards			500
			14,500
Opening stock		3,500	
Purchases	8,000		
Carriage inwards	200		
	8,200		
Less returns outwards	700	7,500	
		11,000	
Less closing stock		4,000	
Cost of goods sold		7,000	7,000
Gross profit			7,500
Commission received			1,500
			9,000
Wages and salaries		1,000	
Rent and rates		500	
Lighting and heating		300	
Stationery		50	
Carriage Outwards		150	
Motor Expenses		1,000	
Insurance		500	
Interest paid		500	
		4,000	4,000
Net Profit			5,000

Figure 2.34

The figure for net profit will be transferred onto the balance sheet as it represents the increase in the owner's capital. This is effectively the same as someone who deposits cash in a bank account; at the end of each year the deposit will earn interest which is automatically added to the original deposit. The depositor may then decide to withdraw some or all of the interest earned and this withdrawal will be recorded in the bank's account for the depositor. The balance sheet will record transactions in a similar way - profit is added to capital in the same way that interest is in a bank, and withdrawals are recorded as drawings.

2.7.1 Final accounts in computerised systems

The computer programmer has to include an option in the accounts program for the production of trading and profit and loss accounts. Under normal circumstances these accounts would only be produced once a year for external use, eg for taxation purposes, and if that remains the case, the program should calculate the balances on all accounts, transfer the balances to the trading account or profit and loss account, and then clear the account balances to nil. This should be a simple enough procedure, but what frequently happens is that the accounts department soon realises that the final accounts can be prepared in a few minutes rather than the few weeks that it took under a manual system. As it suddenly becomes so easy to produce profit figures, the majority of firms will soon decide that a monthly profit and loss account is needed. This account will be the same as the final end of year version in all respects except that it will be for a one month period rather than a one year period, and that it will be for internal use only.

One of the major advantages of computers is that they can provide more information and more quickly than manual systems. The production of monthly profit and loss accounts is a perfect demonstration of this. What the computer programmer/systems analyst has to be aware of is that the double-entry accounts should only be cleared to nil at the end of the year. Consequently, if profit and loss accounts are prepared on a monthly basis, only the balances for that month need to be calculated and the files must not be updated.

A further advantage to be gained by producing final accounts on a computerised system is that it should be possible to produce simplified versions relating to just one product, or just one geographical area. The ability to do this will depend upon what sort of classification the firm has used for coding items (see Chapter 1). If sales have been coded by reference to different products then it should be a simple matter to incorporate a program that will extract the relevant sales and purchase figures for individual products only. These can then be used to draft a trading and profit and loss account that relates to one specific product or region only.

2.7.2 Accrual and prepayments

There will often be occasions when some items are not fully paid for at the end of the year. The items most frequently involved will be rent, rates, lighting and heating, and insurance. However, in theory any item can be involved under the above heading.

An accrual arises when an item is not paid in full, for example rent is usually payable quarterly in arrears, for instance on 1 April, 1 July, 1 October and 1 January. If the firm's accounts year ends on 31 December, the final payment will not have been paid when the final accounts are drawn up. Therefore the figure for rent in the double-entry account will only show £300, whereas the firm has clearly "used" rent of £400, £100 of which is still owing.

A prepayment is the opposite to an accrual and refers to instances when payment is made in advance. If a firm takes out an insurance policy which runs from 1 July to 30 June, and the firm's accounts year runs from 1 January to 31 December, then half of the first payment relates to the first six months of the next accounting year. Therefore, if the insurance premium was £100 and was paid on 1 July, only £50 of this should be included in the first year's accounts; the remaining £50 is a payment in advance and should be included in the following year's accounts.

As a general rule the amount to be included in a profit and loss account for any year should be limited to the amount "used" rather than the amount "spent" in the year (ie the Accruals concept). This would be shown in the profit and loss account as follows:

Example Rent paid during the year 1989 was £500, of which £250 relates to 1990. Insurance paid during the year 1989 was £900, but £100 is still owing. The trial balance figure for rent is £500 and for insurance £900 (ie the amounts paid), but there is a prepayment of rent of £250 and an accrual for insurance of £100. These would be shown in the profit and loss account as follows:

Rent	500	
Less prepaid	250	250
Insurance	900	
Plus accrued	100	1000

The amount of the accrual is shown in the balance sheet as a current liability and the prepayment is shown as a current asset.

2.7.3   Balance sheets

Once the trading and profit and loss accounts has been prepared, the balance sheet can be produced. Balance sheets were shown in Chapter 1 but in practice most organisations will not use the layout shown in Chapter 1 but will use the "vertical layout". Using this method the balance sheet to accompany the trading and profit and loss account just drawn up might be as seen in Figure 2.35.

The main difference between this balance sheet and the one shown previously is that the information is now shown running down the page whereas in the original example it was shown as having two distinct "sides". The above method is most commonly used as it shows information more clearly, and it is more suitable for computer use as it can easily be produced on a basic 80 column printer.

There are a few items shown on the balance sheet that have not been mentioned as part of double-entry; these are the items under Acc Dep for fixed assets and provision for bad debts. These items are often only calculated at the end of the financial year and, although recorded in normal double-entry accounts, they do require additional calculations and as such are slightly different from the usual entries. Because of this, it is important that computer programmers are aware of their existence and of the need to include some provision for their use in any accounts program.

A trader

Balance sheet as at 31 Dec 1990

	Cost £	Acc Dep £	NBV* £
Fixed Assets			
Premises	100,000	—	100,000
Motor vehicles	30,000	17,000	13,000
Fixtures and fittings	25,000	10,000	15,000
Plant and machinery	40,000	25,000	15,000
Office equipment	11,000	5,000	6,000
	206,000	57,000	149,000
Current assets			
Stock and work in progress		25,000	
Trade debtors	15,650		
Less provision for bad debts	650	15,000	
Cash at bank		8,000	
Cash in hand		1,200	
Prepayments		500	
		49,700	
Current liabilities			
Loans (overdraft)	5,800		
Trade Creditors	16,200		
Accruals	500	22,500	
Working Capital		27,200	27,200
Net assets employed			176,200
Financed by			
Capitals as at 1/1/90	159,000		
Add profit	9,000		
	168,000		
Less drawings	10,000		158,000
Long-term liabilities			
Mortgage	18,200		18,200
			176,200

Figure 2.35

*Net book value

Exercises

51A The following Balance Sheet has been drawn up by an inexperienced clerk and is clearly incorrect. Use the information given to draft the correct Balance Sheet using the <u>vertical</u> layout.

Balance Sheet

Assets	£	Others	£
Capital	110,000	Mortgage	45,000
Motor Vehicles	35,200	Cash	400
Amount owing for rent	275	Fixtures	16,550
Debtors	17,400	Rent	1,500
Profit	22,300	Drawings	16,300
Creditors	10,150	Insurance	500
Rates paid in advance	500	Depreciation:Vehicles	7,100
Provision for Bad debts	1,700	Premises	99,000
Depreciation: Fixtures	3,100	Stock	12,955
		Bank	1,320
	200,625		200,625

2.8 DEPRECIATION

It should be apparent to everyone that the cost concept has some weaknesses. The cost concept states that assets should be recorded at the value paid for them as this is the only value to which there will be universal agreement. Whilst this is partly true, it is also true that assets decrease in value because of age, wear and tear through use, etc. Consequently firms attempt to show what the estimated current value of assets is by working out how much they have reduced in value, ie depreciated. The reduction in value is shown on the balance sheet as accumulated depreciation (Acc Dep for short).

Fixed Assets can depreciate for a variety of reasons; the more common reasons are as follows:

— *Wear and tear:* the asset simply devalues or wears away through excessive use or prolonged exposure to the elements.

— *Economic factors:* the asset becomes of limited use because of obsolescence or inadequacy as a result of changes in the general economy. Obsolescence means that the asset becomes out of date due to improved assets becoming available. Many firms have discovered that their computers have rapidly become obsolete due to improvements in technology.

— *Time factor:* some assets will have a predetermined life. An example of this would be a lease for the rent of the firm's premises; the premises are only of value during the lifetime of the lease. When the lease expires the asset has no remaining value to the firm. Other similar examples could be patents or copyright agreements to produce goods under a licence from the inventor/designer.

Cost 1975 £5000 - value now £5000?

Depreciation = Wear and tear

True value only found by selling the assets

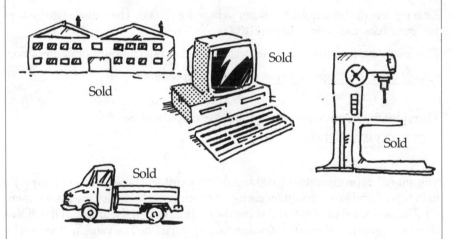

Provision for depreciation = Estimate of wear and tear

Figure 2.36 Cost concept

— *Depletion:* in some cases the asset will become physicially exhausted; an example of this type of depreciation would be a coal mine where all of the coal has been extracted.

The difficulty with depreciation is that the true amount of depreciation can only be found by selling the assets, the difference between what the assets are sold for and what they originally cost being the depreciation. But, this method is not suitable as no firm would want to dispose of all its assets at the end of each year simply to work out what the depreciation was.

To overcome the difficulty, firms estimate depreciation using one of two accepted methods, the "straight line" and the "reducing balance".

Method 1: Straight line

To calculate depreciation using this method, firms must first decide how long they will keep an asset and estimate the scrap/disposal value. This might seem difficult but in practice many firms have an established policy for replacing assets and, if they buy in bulk, also have a fair idea of how much they will receive for part exchange or scrap.

Example A firm has acquired a motor vehicle for £5,000. The vehicle will be kept for four years and then sold for £1,000.

The following formula is used to calculate the annual amount of depreciation:

$$\frac{\text{Cost price less disposal value}}{\text{Years in use}} = \text{Annual depreciation}$$

Therefore the depreciation for the above example will be:

$$\frac{\text{£5,000-£1,000}}{4} = \text{£1,000}$$

The annual depreciation is £1,000 and this amount will be entered as an expense in the profit and loss account for each of the four years for which the asset is owned. The balance sheet must still show the original cost of the asset but it will also show the present value after allowing for depreciation. The value will reduce by £1,000 for each year that the asset is kept. The balance sheet entries for each of the four years would be:

		Cost	Acc Dep	NBV
		£	£	£
Year 1	Motor vehicle	5,000	1,000	4,000
Year 2	Motor vehicle	5,000	2,000	3,000
Year 3	Motor vehicle	5,000	3,000	2,000
Year 4	Motor vehicle	5,000	4,000	1,000

At the end of the fourth year the asset is sold and there will be no entry at all in the balance sheet for year 5 in respect of the motor vehicle. The balance sheet will only balance at the end of each year if the increase in accumulated depreciation has been entered as an expense in the profit and loss account (ie £1,000 for each year).

Straight line method

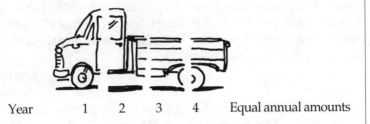

Year   1   2   3   4   Equal annual amounts

$$\frac{\text{Cost less scrap value}}{\text{Number of years in use}}$$

Simple to calculate but unrealistic

Reducing balance method

Year   1   2   3   4

More realistic interpretation of value

Recording depreciation

Profit loss account	Balance sheet
Depreciation for current year	Total depreciation for all years

Figure 2.37 Methods of depreciation

Method 2: Reducing balance

This method can be used where the firm does not know how long it will keep the asset or what the disposal value will be. The method is much simpler in that it merely requires the firm to estimate how much the assets depreciate and then deduct that amount in each year. The "annual amount of depreciation" is a percentage figure and is deducted from the previous year's NBV. If the same asset is used as in the previous example, the firm might decide that 25% is a realistic amount to allow for annual depreciation. In that case the balance sheet and profit and loss account entries would be as follows:

		Cost	Acc Dep	NBV	
		£	£	£	£
Year 1	Motor vehicle	5,000	1,250	3,750	1,250
Year 2	Motor vehicle	5,000	2,188	2,812	938
Year 3	Motor vehicle	5,000	2,891	2,109	703
Year 4	Motor vehicle	5,000	3,419	1,581	528

The main difference with this method is that depreciation is calculated on the previous year's NBV and the effect of this is that the annual amount of depreciation (as shown in the profit and loss account) will reduce each year. This is a better reflection of how assets reduce in value as most assets, and motor vehicles in particular, will depreciate most rapidly in their first few years of use. As the asset gets older its disposal value (NBV) becomes lower but the annual amount of depreciation is also very low.

The double-entry of depreciation is the same regardless of which method is used to calculate the depreciation. The entries for the above transactions are shown in Figure 2.38.

The difficulty of including depreciation in accounts programs is that it is only an estimated amount and does not involve the actual payment of cash to anybody. This means that the figure of net profit will be lower than normal because it has been reduced by the amount for depreciation that has not involved the physical movement of cash. Despite this fact it is still necessary to include an amount for depreciation under the rules of the prudence convention - the firm knows that eventually it will dispose of its assets and that they will be sold for a price less than that paid for them. Consequently the true position of the firm can only be shown if a provision (estimate) is made for depreciation.

Some accounting packages will include accounts specifically created for the firm to enter depreciation; however, the taxation rules of different countries will vary in how depreciation is treated. In the UK, depreciation is excluded from the net profit when calculating tax payable, therefore an accounting package for a very small firm such as a sole trader will probably not include any reference to depreciation. The reason for this is that the only users of the accounts of sole traders will generally be the sole trader and the taxation authorities. Whilst the UK taxation authorities will not accept depreciation as valid expenditure they will allow something very similar called "balancing allowances", which is somewhat more complex than the calculation of depreciation and would be determined by the sole trader's accountant.

Motor vehicle account

Date	Details	Dr	Cr
1 Jan 1981	Bank	5,000	

Provision for Depreciation account

Date	Details	Dr	Cr
31 Dec 1981	Profit/Loss account		1,250
		Nil	1,250
1 Jan 1982	Balance at this date		1,250
31 Dec 1982	Profit/Loss account		938
		Nil	2,188
1 Jan 1983	Balance at this date		2,188
31 Dec 1983	Profit/Loss account		703
		Nil	2,891
1 Jan 1984	Balance at this date		2,891
31 Dec 1984	Profit/Loss account		528
		Nil	3,419
1 Jan 1985	Balance at this date		3,419

Figure 2.38

Larger firms in the UK can still only claim for balancing allowances and not depreciation but the published accounts will be used by a much larger group of users and therefore should include depreciation, even though the taxation authorities will remove the figure when determining tax payable. The upshot of these differences for the programmer is that, in the UK at least, the decision as to whether to include an account for the provision for depreciation will depend upon the size of the firm.

Exercises

52 A firm has acquired three motor vehicles for £6,000 each. They will be kept for four years and then sold for a disposal value of £2,000. Calculate the total annual depreciation for all three vehicles using the straight line method of depreciation.

53 For the vehicles used in question 52 calculate the total depreciation for each of the four years using the reducing balance method (assume depreciation is 25%).

54 A firm has the following balances on its accounts at 1 November: capital £15,500, loan £500; creditors: P Parkes £770, D Parkin £120, G Taylor £350, G Palmer £1,000; sales £9,500, returns in £250; premises £6,500,

motor vehicles £3,500, fixtures and fittings £1,000, bank £2,000, opening stock £5,500, cash £300; debtors: D Wagstaffe £355, P Knowles £710, J McAlliog £200, D Dougan £800, S Kindon £300; purchases £4,500, returns out £115, carriage in £500; wages £500, motor expenses £250, insurance £70, advertising £90, rates £230, lighting and heating £300.

Draw up the double-entry accounts as they would appear at 1 November and extract a trial balance to ensure that your accounts are correct.

The following transactions took place in November and need to be entered in the accounts:

1 Nov	The following payments are made to creditors by cheque: P Parkes £120, G Taylor £200, G Palmer £450.
2 Nov	Advertising of £50 is paid in cash. Cash sales £250.
3 Nov	Cheques are received for the following: D Dougan £350, S Kindon £150, J McAlliog £200. Rates are paid by cheque £60.
5 Nov	Goods are purchased on credit from D Parkin £300, M Bailey £750. Carriage inwards costs of £15 are paid in cash.
8 Nov	S Kindon has been declared bankrupt and a final payment of £50 is received; the balance remaining must be written off as a bad debt.
12 Nov	Additional fixtures are purchased by cheque £300.
14 Nov	Wages are paid in cash £50.
16 Nov	Goods are sold on credit to D Dougan £120, P Knowles £200, H Curran £150.
19 Nov	Stationery is bought for cash £25.
23 Nov	Wages are paid in cash £50.
25 Nov	Drawings of £200 cash and £500 bank are taken by the owner.
27 Nov	P Knowles returns goods worth £30.
29 Nov	Lighting and heating are paid in cash £40. Cash sales £110.
30 Nov	Advertising paid by cheque £20.

Balance the accounts at 30 November and extract a trial balance. Draw up the trading and profit and loss account and balance sheet as at 30 November, using the following information:

(a) Closing stock £5,700
(b) Fixtures and fittings and motor vehicles are to be depreciated at 25% on initial cost.

55   A firm buys some office equipment for £5,000. It is estimated that the equipment will depreciate at a rate of 20% per annum. Use the reducing balance method to calculate the depreciation that will be included in the profit and loss account for each of the first four years that the equipment is owned and also show the entries in the balance sheet for each of the four years.

56(a) A firm has recently bought a motor vehicle costing $8,000, they expect to keep this vehicle for three years and to receive $2,000 as its disposal value at the end of that time.

Calculate the annual depreciation for each of the 3 years using:

(i) the *Straight-Line method*
(ii) the *Reducing Balance method* (at 25%)

(b) Show how these items would be entered in the *double-entry* accounts and the *profit/loss account* and *balance sheet* extracts (for *reducing balance* method only).

57　The following Trial Balance has been extracted at 31st August 1988.

Trial Balance as at 31 August 1988

	Dr $	Cr $
Sales		425,100
Purchases	280,900	
Drawings	15,400	
Wages & Salaries	42,350	
Rent & Rates	18,100	
Light & Heat	17,500	
Loan Interest	2,900	
Debtors	64,340	
Creditors		38,900
Cash	2,100	
Bank	11,760	
Stock at 1st Nov 1987	18,390	
Equipment — at cost	94,000	
accumulated dep.		28,200
Loan		30,000
Capital		45,540
	567,740	567,740

The following information is also available:

(1) Loan interest owing is $150.

(2) Equipment is to be depreciated at 10% per annum using the *STRAIGHT-LINE METHOD*.

(3) Closing Stock was $16,300.

Required

Prepare the *TRADING, PROFIT AND LOSS ACCOUNT* for the year ended 31st August 1988 and a *BALANCE SHEET* at that date — use the vertical layout throughout.

(Sept 89)

58(a) List four factors that will cause fixed assets to depreciate.

(b) Which of these factors will cause depreciation for each of the following:

(i) Coal mine

(ii) Land

(iii) Motor vehicles

(iv) Ferry used for transporting passengers across a river after a bridge has been built

(v) 25 year lease on a building

(vi) Licence to manufacture goods in a specific country

59A The following are the balances on the accounts of G. Wilkes as at 31st January 1990.

Prepare the Trading and Profit/Loss account for the year ended 31st January 1990 and a Balance Sheet as at that date.

	£
Capital	24,927
Drawings	8,465
Cash at Bank	2,197
Cash in Hand	199
Trade Debtors	6,340
Trade Creditors	4,380
General expenses	21,850
Wages and Salaries	15,300
Returns from customers	761
Returns to suppliers	531
Discounts received	1,150
Discounts allowed	1,324
Sales	101,890
Purchases	48,760
Plant and Machinery:	
Cost	36,420
Accumulated Depreciation	14,568
Stock at 1st February 1989	5,830

NOTES:

(i) Stock at 1st January was £6,140.

(ii) £172 has been paid in advance in respect of General expenses.

(iii) General expenses also has accruals of £233.

(iv) Plant and machinery are to be depreciated by 20% on cost.

(v) General expenses include:

	£
Carriage inwards	650
Carriage outwards	1,540

60A Tom Brown is a small retailer whose sales are mainly for cash although he allows credit to a few valued customers. The cash takings are paid into the bank each day and all payments are made by cheque.

A summary of his bank account for the year is as follows:

	£		£
Balance, 1st June 1987	147	Drawings	1,600
Cash takings	28,630	Trade creditors	19,300
		Fixtures	1,500
		Trade expenses	1,750
		Motor expenses	920

Tom estimates that of the Motor Expenses approximately half relates to his private use of the car, and that he has also taken goods for his own use of £1,000.

Additional information available at 31st May 1988 is:

	1987 £	1988 £
Stock	1,210	1,340
Debtors	95	62
Trade creditors	740	930
Trade expenses owing	230	345
Fixtures and fittings (cost £8,400)	4,200	?
Motor Vehicle (cost £6,000)	3,700	?
Premises	30,000	30,000

Tom charges depreciation on fixtures and fittings at 10% per annum on cost and at 20% on the Motor vehicle on reducing balance. A full year's depreciation is charged regardless of the time of acquisition.

Required: Prepare the trading and profit/loss account for the year ended 31st May 1988 and the balance sheet at that date. Show all workings.

2.9 BAD DEBTS AND PROVISION FOR BAD DEBTS

As most organisations operate on a credit basis for trade, it is logical to assume that occasionally the debtor will not pay off his debts. Most firms will take steps to ensure that customers are creditworthy before delivering any goods. However, manual credit control systems are frequently not applied properly or are unable to keep up to date. Computerised accounting systems are much more likely to be updated at more regular intervals and all programs should include some means of checking the creditworthiness of customers when the order details are keyed in to the computer. The most effective checks are those carried out by the computer where the program makes a check on a credit file held on disk, thus cutting out the need for any manual operation. If the customer is not creditworthy, the program should refuse to process any further orders.

Despite the advantages of computer programs in reducing the number of customers who do not pay their debts, there will always be some debts that become "bad". This is because customers may be physically unable to pay their debts (ie they have died); also even the most effective means of gathering information on creditworthiness may not be able to pick up details of all firms about to go bankrupt.

Organisations will have to accept that some debtors' accounts will never be fully paid off and that they will need to clear some accounts by creating a bad debts account. Here the irrecoverable amounts can be entered prior to being written off as expenses in the profit and loss account. This will be a straightforward double-entry transaction between the debtor's account and the bad debts account. For example, T Wilkins owes the firm £75 and has died; there is no prospect of the amount owing being paid. This is shown in Figure 2.39.

T Wilkins Account		Dr	Cr
Date	Details		
12 Mar	Balance at this date	75	
23 Mar	Bad Debts		75
		75	75

Bad Debts account		Dr	Cr
Date	Details		
23 Mar	T Wilkins	75	
31 Dec	Profit and loss account		75
		75	75

Figure 2.39

What will also become evident to firms that have been trading for a few years is that it becomes possible to predict what percentage of debtors will eventually become bad debts; in these cases it is necessary to create a provision for a bad debts account. This account is similar to the depreciation account in that it is an estimate and involves an annual figure which is included in the profit and loss account and a cumulative total which is deducted from trade debtors in the balance sheet.

The difference between the two types of bad debts is that the former is actual and related to a named debtor (eg T Wilkins) whereas the latter is an estimate and is a general figure expressed as a percentage of total debtors and is not "attached" to any named debtor. The difference between the two types of bad debts often causes confusion for students and one way of differentiating is to call the "Provision for Bad Debts" the "Provision for Doubtful Debts" instead.

The double-entry for the Provision for Bad (Doubtful) debts is quite straight-forward as it simply involves transferring the total into the Profit/Loss Account.

Example: A firm has debtors of £10,000 at the end of the year. The owner of the firm feels that it is unlikely that all debtors will make full payment of their debts and therefore has decided to create a provision for doubtful debts set at 2% of debtors, as shown in Figure 2.40.

Provision for Doubtful debts a/c			
Date	Details	Dr	Cr
31 Dec	Profit/Loss A/c		200
		Dr	Cr
Profit/Loss A/c (Extract)			
EXPENSES:			
Provision for Doubtful debts		200	
BALANCE SHEET (Extract)			
CURRENT ASSETS			
Debtors		10,000	
Provision for Doubtful debts		200	9,800

Figure 2.40

The other aspect of bad debts that often causes confusion is the "clearing" of the provision for doubtful debts. The provision for doubtful debts is an "estimate" of *future* bad debts, at the end of the year the owner of a business may have identified that some specific debtors have become "bad debts" but this will not affect the provision for doubtful debts figure as the amount calculated for this item will always be an estimate of future years — therefore it is impossible for the actual bad debts (from the current year) to ever catch up with the provision for doubtful debts, which is always for future years.

The entries in the provision for doubtful debts account in subsequent years are treated in a similar manner to the other provision, depreciation. A provision is

Provision for Doubtful debts a/c			
Date	Details	Dr	Cr
31 Dec 88	Profit/Loss A/c		200
		Nil	200
1 Jan	Balance at this date		200
31 Dec 89	Profit/Loss A/c		40
		Nil	240
1 Jan 90	Balance at this date		240
Profit/Loss A/C (Extract) Year 89			
EXPENSES:			
Increase in Provision for Doubtful debts		40	
BALANCE SHEET (Extract)			
CURRENT ASSETS			
Debtors		12,000	
Provision for Doubtful debts		240	11,760

Figure 2.41

an estimate of future expenditure. This must be shown in the balance sheet to reflect the true state of the business, which means that the business cannot record fixed assets at the cost price or the total debtors if the owner knows that these values are inaccurate. Therefore the provision for both items should be used to show the more accurate, estimated value.

The amount calculated as a provision can be deducted as an expense in the profit/loss account. But if the provision remains the same in future years, then no other entries need to be made in the profit/loss account as the provision will have been written off in an earlier year. Normally, provision for both depreciation and doubtful debts will increase, if this is the case then only the *increase* or *decrease* in the provision needs to be entered in the profit/loss account.

Example: At the end of the second year the owner of the business in the previous example decides to keep the provision for doubtful debts at 2% of debtors, debtors at the end of the year have increased to £12,000.

Exercises

61   A Nelson has the following trial balance at 31 December. Prepare a trading and profit and loss account and balance sheet at that date.

	£	£
Capital		17,750
Premises	15,000	
Furniture and Fittings	4,000	
Motor vehicles	5,000	
Accumulated depreciation: Furniture		1,000
Accumulated depreciation: Vehicles		1,200
Purchases and sales	30,000	52,000
Discounts received		1,000
Insurance	750	
Motor vehicle expenses	600	
Opening stock	4,750	
Returns outwards		400
Sundry expenses	375	
Lighting and Heating	450	
Rent and rates	1,000	
Debtors and creditors	7,600	6,125
Wages and salaries	8,500	
Cash	400	
Bank	1,100	
	79,525	79,525

Notes and adjustments:

(a) Closing stock £5,700.

(b) Debtors are to be reduced by £400 in respect of bad debts.

(c) Motor vehicles, furniture and fittings are to be depreciated at 25% on NBV (reducing balance).

62   Use the list of balances provided in question 43 to prepare a Trading and Profit/Loss Account and Balance Sheet, after taking account of the following adjustments:

(i)   Stock at 28th February 1991 was $6,200.
(ii) Wages still owing amount to $250.
(iii) General Expenses paid in advance $180.
(iv) Motor Expenses are to be depreciated at 20% of cost.
(v)   A provision for Bad Debts is to be created at 2% of Debtors.

(20 marks)
(Mar 91)

63   Explain the difference between the *Bad Debts Account* and the *Provision for Bad Debts Account.*

64   Draw up a Balance Sheet from the following information, use the *VERTICAL* layout:

	$
Capital	103,010
Creditors	12,500
Wages & Salaries	45,000
Debtors	18,400
Fixtures & Fittings	45,200
Bank	11,450
Lighting and Heating	7,210
Bank Loan	4,300
Purchases	87,500
Motor Vehicles	25,000
Provision for Bad Debts	600
Discounts Allowed	990
Drawings	7,500
Accumulated Depreciation:	
Fixtures and Fittings	4,520
Motor Vehicles	2,500
Cash	1,100
Mortgage	30,000
Premises	56,000
Insurance	2,100
Sales	112,600
Stock	13,450

Notes:
(i)   Fixtures and Fittings and Motor Vehicles are to be depreciated by 10% of Cost.
(ii) Net Profit for the year was $13,540.
(iii) Payments made in advance amount to $700.
(iv) Amounts owing for expenses are $900.

(Dec 88)

65   A firm has produced the following Trial Balance at 31st May 1988. Prepare a Trading, Profit and Loss account at that date (NB: a Balance Sheet is not required).

	$	$
Capital		120,000
Creditors and Debtors	20,000	21,500
Sales and Purchases	78,405	138,430
Fixtures and Fittings	35,120	
Motor Vehicles	12,500	
Wages	17,410	
Rent and Rates	3,200	
Premises	101,698	
Lighting and Heating	8,422	
Insurance	1,300	
Motor Vehicle expenses	2,545	
Provision for Depreciation:		
Motor Vehicles		7,000
Fixtures and Fittings		13,500
Provision for Bad Debts		860
Cash in Hand	500	
Cash at Bank	4,500	
Bank Loan		9,000
Discounts allowed and received	950	1,100
Returns In and Returns Out	780	900
Loan Interest	1,450	
Drawings	5,210	
Stock at 1st June 1987	18,300	
	312,290	312,290

Notes:
(i)   Stock at 31st May 1988 was $20,080
(ii)   The provision for Bad debts is to be increased to 5% of debtors.
(iii) Motor Vehicles and Fixtures and Fittings are to be depreciated at 10% on the NBV using the reducing balance method.
(iv)   Amounts still owed at the end of the year were: Insurance $120, wages $450.
(v)   Rent paid in advance £45.   (Jun 88)

66   The following final accounts were prepared by an inexperienced accounts clerk. You are to redraft these *CORRECTLY* in the *VERTICAL FORMAT*.

Profit & Loss Account as at 31st December 1989

Purchases	190,000	Debtors		20,000
Less Opening Stock	10,000			
	180,000			
Add closing Stock	15,000			
Cost of sales	195,000	Gross Profit c/d		175,000
	195,000			195,000

Distribution Expenses:		Gross Profit b/d	175,000
Rent and Rates	4,000		
Drawings	12,000		
Motor Expenses	8,000		
Bad Debt Provision	1,000		
	25,000		

Administrative Costs:			
Loan Repayment	10,000		
Property	192,000		
Heating and Lighting	3,000		
Creditors	17,000		
Discounts Received	5,000	Other Operating Income:	
Provision for Depreciation of:		Discounts Allowed	2,000
Motor Vehicles	6,000	Accruals	7,500
Machinery	8,000	Net Profit for Year	52,000
	236,500		236,500

Balance Sheet for the Year Ending 31st December 1989

	Cost	Dep'n for yr	N.B.V.		Cr	Dr
Machinery	23,000	1,500	21,500	Capital Account:		
Motor vehicles	26,000	4,000	22,000	balance b/fwd	110,00	
				Less Profit	52,000	
			43,500			
Current Assets:						58,000
Sales		300,000		Bad Debts Written off		500
Bank Overdraft		11,000				57,500
Stock		10,000				
				Current Liabilities:		
			321,000			
				5 Year Bank Loan		50,000
				Suspense Account		252,000
				Prepayments		5,000
						307,000
			364,500			364,500

(Dec 89)

67   A firm has produced the following Trial Balance. You are required to draw
up a Trading and Profit/Loss Account for the year ended 27th February
1990. A Balance Sheet is not required and marks will be deducted if the
Trading and Profit/Loss Account is not presented in the Vertical layout.

	Dr	Cr
Capital		22,735
Sales and Purchases	53,100	96,210
Motor vehicles at cost	32,100	
Fixtures and Fittings at cost	10,900	
Discounts Received		550
Insurance	1,100	
Wages and Salaries	12,500	
Debtors and Creditors	18,900	11,870
Rent and Rates	2,450	
Bank	9,650	
Stock at 1st March	8,930	
Returns Outwards	1,205	
Carriage Inwards	2,225	
Carriage Outwards	3,540	
Loan		21,900
Motor vehicle expenses	5,425	
Commission received	8,700	
Drawings	11,290	
Lighting and Heating	1,800	
Provision for Bad Debts		150
Accumulated Depreciation:		
Motor vehicle		9,250
Fixtures and Fittings		3,750
	175,115	175,115

Notes:
1. Stock at 27th February 1990 $9,205
2. Rents paid in advance $210
3. Lighting and heating owing $455
4. Depreciation is to be provided as follows: Motor vehicles at 20% of cost,
   Fixtures and Fittings at 10% Net Book Value.
5. The Provision of Bad Debts are to be increased to 2% Debtors.
6. Wages and Salaries include $2,000 which the owner took as "wages".

(Mar 90)

68A   A Trading and Profit/Loss Account for the year ended 31/5/91 has just been
drawn up for a local business. The Balance Sheet needs to be prepared but a
lot of the records have been destroyed in a fire, one of the figures no longer
available is that for Capital. Draw up the Balance Sheet in a Vertical format
from the following data and insert the appropriate figure for Capital.

Debit balances		Credit balances	
Premises	$120,000	Creditors	$6,300
Prepayments	$210	Bank	$5,410
Vehicles	$40,000	Net Profit	$21,450
Debtors	$11,350	Depreciation:	
Stock at 31/5/91	$14,200	Motor Vehicles	$21,000
Drawings	$15,600	Fittings	$5,000
Fittings	$15,000	Stock at 1/6/90	$15,300
		Provision for	
		Bad debts	800
		Accruals	180
		Mortgage	$80,000

NOTES:

Depreciation on Vehicles is determined on a Straight-line basis at 10% per annum. Depreciation on Fittings is determined using the Reducing Balance method at 30% per annum. The balances shown do not include the current years Depreciation charges.

(20 marks)

(Sep 91)

69 The following Balance Sheet has been drawn up by an inexperienced accountant. Redraft the Balance Sheet correctly using the VERTICAL layout.

CAPITAL	$	CURRENT ASSETS	$
Profit	20,000	Motor Vehicles	35,000
Loan	15,000	Stock	5,000
	35,000	Creditors	24,500
CURRENT LIABILITIES		Premises	90,000
Depreciation:		Bank Overdraft	6,400
Motor Vehicles	12,000	Accruals	600
Office Equipment	4,500	Prepayments	700
Prov. for Bad Debts	1,300		162,200
Office Equipment	18,400	FIXED ASSETS	
	36,200	Capital	
		Cash	1,300
		Debtors	31,600

In addition to the above some other items have not been included:

(i) The Provision for Bad Debts should have been increased to 5% of Debtors.

(ii) The Depreciation should be increased by 10% of existing Net Book Values for both Motor Vehicles and Office Equipment.

(iii) Drawings of 50% of the Net profit have been taken by the owner.

(20 marks)

(Mar 92)

2.10   DIVISION OF THE LEDGER

The double-entry principles covered so far reflect the accounting methods used by the vast majority of organisations that need to keep financial records. These records are traditionally kept in books called ledgers.

In old manual systems the ledger would have a separate page or pages for each account. Frequently used accounts such as cash, bank, sales and purchases accounts would require a large number of pages as there would be hundreds of entries in these accounts during a year. At the beginning of the year the book-keeper would designate which pages would be used for each account. For example, pages 1-5 might be reserved for the bank account, pages 6-10 reserved for the cash account, pages 11-17 for the sales account, and so on. All transactions entered in the ledger accounts would state the name of the double-entry account as normal, but would also state on which page of the ledger the double-entry account could be found.

In larger firms, the system of keeping all accounts in just one ledger creates problems as it means that only one member of staff can use the ledger at any one time. As many large firms will need to process literally thousands of transactions each day, it is obvious that more than one book-keeper is needed. The solution to this problem is to divide the ledger so that each book-keeper can work on his or her own part of the ledger, without preventing the other book-keepers from doing their work.

The problem then is how to divide the ledger into different sections, and to be able to continue dividing it as the firm expands. If the profit and loss account and balance sheet are examined, it can be seen that most firms would only need approximately fifty accounts. Most of the transactions will also, at first glance, appear to involve the cash or bank accounts. The main accounts would be sales, purchases, cash, bank, motor expenses, rent and rates, wages and salaries, lighting and heating, motor vehicles, capital, drawings, stationery, insurance, fixtures and fittings, premises, stock, debtors and creditors. In reality by far the largest number of accounts will be the individual debtors' and creditors' accounts: remember the figures in the balance sheet will only be the totals of debtors and creditors! There could be hundreds of accounts for the debtors and creditors.

Separating the ledger to create further books (ledgers) that contain just the accounts for debtors or just the accounts for creditors makes future division easier, because the first stage in dividing the ledger is to have three ledgers:

— *Nominal/general ledger*   This is arguably the most important ledger and would contain the following accounts: Sales, purchases, cash, bank, motor expenses, rent and rates, wages and salaries, lighting and heating, motor vehicles, capital, drawings, stationery, insurance, fixtures and fittings, premises and stock.

— *Sales ledger*   This ledger contains the accounts of all the debtors of the firm, the logic behind this being that one book-keeper can enter the invoice details into the debtor's account and then pass the invoice to the book-keeper responsible for the nominal ledger for him or her to make the corresponding entry in the sales account.

The title given to the ledger does tend to cause confusion amongst students as they assume that it contains the sales account. The confusion is caused because although it is recording details of sales it is only recording them in the debtors' accounts.

— *Purchases ledger* This ledger is the opposite to the sales ledger and records details from the purchases invoices in the creditors' accounts. Once the details have been entered, the invoice is passed to the book-keeper in charge of the nominal ledger so that details can be entered in the purchases account.

The advantage of dividing the ledgers in this manner is that the majority of transactions will relate to either debtors or creditors - either buying or selling more items or paying off accounts. Other transactions such as paying wages will only occur once a week and transactions relating to the purchase of fixed assets may well arise only once a year.

A further advantage is that such a division makes further subdivision easy because the sales or purchases ledger can be divided into alphabetical or geographical sections. So, for example, there could be four sales ledgers:

Sales ledger 1: Debtors whose surnames begin with A-E
Sales ledger 2: Debtors whose surnames begin with F-L
Sales ledger 3: Debtors whose surnames begin with M-S
Sales ledger 4: Debtors whose surnames begin with T-Z

Clearly, these subdivisions could be continued as the firm expands the need to take on additional book-keepers arises. It is important to remember that although the ledgers have been divided, the accounts themselves are still written up in the same way.

Exercises

70   What is a possible technical reason for continuing to divide the ledgers under a computerised system?

71   Why do firms find it necessary to use more than one ledger, and why do they divide the ledger into sales, purchases and nominal?

2.11 BOOKS OF ORIGINAL ENTRY

One of the problems of dividing the ledger as described previously is that it entails flimsy documents such as invoices being moved about from one section to another. The invoice is the "source document" and is extremely important as evidence in audits (see next chapter). As the documents usually comprise only one sheet of paper they are easily lost or damaged. Another disadvantage of the system described above is that it will eventually become "bogged down" by the number of people entering data in the sales and purchases ledgers. Also, there will be an enormous number of entries in the sales and purchases accounts: whilst these are necessary to ensure accurate double-entry it is not strictly essential that they are made in the sales and purchases accounts.

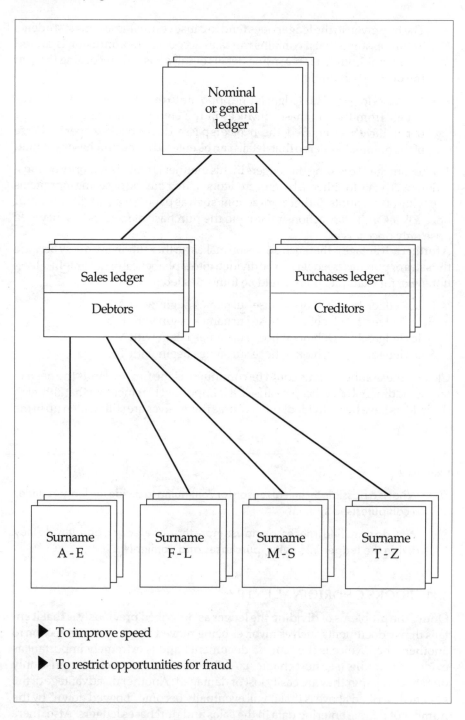

Figure 2.42 Reasons for dividing the Ledger

Many firms find that transactions can be processed more quickly by having "sub-sidiary books" where the details from each invoice are listed. The advantages of using these subsidiary books are that once the invoice details are entered the in-voices can be filed away in a secure place and secondly, the sales and purchases accounts need only record the total sales and purchases for the week or month. If there is any query over the accuracy of these totals, the subsidiary books can be referred to in order to check the double-entry.

As these books are the first record of any transaction other than the source documents, they are known as the "books of original entry". They are simply lists that are retained until the book-keepers in charge of the ledgers are free to enter up the transactions in the proper double-entry accounts. Because they will need to be sent on to another section for final entry in the accounts it is quite common to write the details on loose sheets that can be removed from the books to facilitate transfer.

Most of the books would use a layout similar to Figure 2.43.

Sales daybook				
Date	Details	Invoice	Folio	Amount
3 Jun	L Bodkin	A12767	SL 32	236.80
4 Jun	F Collins	A13276	SL 14	42.20
4 Jun	G Thomas	A12245	SL 44	100.50
5 Jun	H Evans	A12234	SL 23	55.00
5 Jun	L Bodkin	A12353	SL 32	417.95
6 Jun	S Roberts	A12922	SL 16	72.30
6 Jun	K Wilmott	A12102	SL 39	125.10
	Credit sales for the week		NL 6	1049.85

Figure 2.43

The folio number refers to the ledger and the page number in the ledger where the double-entry is written up, for example SL 32 means that the account for L Bodkin is on page 32 of the sales ledger. The sales account is on page 6 of the nominal ledger and will only record the total credit sales for the week. If there is any query concerning the figure for sales, the daybook can be referred to in order to check how the total was calculated. The invoice number is also shown so that each separate transaction can be checked back to the source document if necessary. In other books the invoice number would be replaced by the credit or debit note number.

The daybook used for recording purchases serves a totally opposite function to that of the sales daybook but the layout is usually virtually identical.

Purchases daybook

Date	Details	Invoice	Folio	Amount
1 Sept	J Caan	K20390	PL 32	36.80
2 Sept	J Collins	D39026	PL 24	82.20
2 Sept	L Thomas	SD23	PL 44	104.00
3 Sept	J Collins	LKM234	PL 24	75.00
3 Sept	S Moss	DE345	PL 12	217.95
3 Sept	G Hill	AS2922	PL 26	45.00
5 Sept	J Collins	MA12	PL 24	105.20
	Credit Purchases for the week		NL 6	666.15

Figure 2.44

These entries will be transferred to the purchase ledger at a convenient time and the daybook retained in case there is any need to refer back to check the transaction details. The entries in J Collins account and the purchases account would be as shown in Figure 2.45.

Purchase Ledger				Page 24
J Collins				
Date			Dr	Cr
2 Sept	Purchases Daybook			82.20
3 Sept	Purchases Daybook			75.00
5 Sept	Purchases Daybook			105.20
			Nil	262.40
8 Sept	Balance at this date			262.40
Nominal Ledger				Page 6
Purchase Account				
Date			Dr	Cr
5 Sept	Credit Purchases for the week		666.15	

Figure 2.45

This system has the added advantage of simplifying the data entered in the ledger accounts; it is no longer necessary to clutter up the sales, purchases, returns in and returns out accounts with details of every single transaction as this information can be obtained from the daybooks if required.

The books of original entry are usually called daybooks or journals and there are five in total: the sales daybook, purchases daybook, returns in daybook, returns out daybook and the journal proper. Figure 2.46 shows the source documents and which daybooks and ledgers are involved.

Source documents	Sales invoice	Purchases invoice	Credit note	Debit note	Invoices, receipts (for assets and expense items)
Books of original entry	Sales Daybook	Purchases daybook	Returns in daybook	Returns out daybook	Journal
Account to be debited	Debtors a/c in sales ledger	Purchases a/c in nominal ledger	Returns in a/c in nominal ledger	Creditor's a/c in purchases ledger	Various a/c in nominal ledger
Account to be credited	Sales a/c in nominal ledger	Creditor's a/c in purchase ledger	Debtor's a/c in sales ledger	Returns out a/c in nominal ledger	Various a/c in nominal ledger

Figure 2.46　Source documents and books of original entry

The four daybooks relate to transactions affecting stock and all follow the same layout as the example given previously. Entering items in these daybooks should be quite straightforward as no knowledge of double-entry is required at this stage.

Some organisations prefer to use a more sophisticated version of the daybook layout with the intention of incorporating more data. This alternative style of layout is most commonly used for the sales or purchase daybooks and breaks down sales or purchases into different products.

	Sales analysis book						
Date	Details	Invoice	Folio	Amount	Books	Pens	Paper
1 Jan	T Brown	ZK123	SL4	75.00	50.00	25.00	
2 Jan	D Patel	YR174	SL15	110.00	110.00		
4 Jan	K Hom	YW190	SL10	20.00		15.00	5.00
5 Jan	L Yung	PR210	SL10	30.00	10.00		20.00
Credit sales for week			NL6	235.00	170.00	40.00	25.00

Figure 2.47　Daybooks and journals

The example shown demonstrates how sales can be split into different "analysis" columns so that the firm can quickly calculate total sales and the sales of any one product range as well. The totals of the analysis columns may be calculated purely for statistical purposes, although the firm could devise separate sales accounts for each category, so instead of having one sales account this firm could have a sales: pens account, a sales: books account and a sales: paper account.

The "Analysis" column system can be used on any of the daybooks but is most frequently used on the sales daybook as most firms are more interested in obtaining a more detailed breakdown of sales than they are for purchases. However, if the firm is simply a wholesaler or a retailer than they can calculate gross profit on each of their products by maintaining both a sales and purchases analysis daybook with identical columns.

Exercises

72(a) Show in diagrammatic form the sequence usually adopted in the Division of the Ledger.

(10 marks)

(b) Explain why "books of original entry" are necessary in:

(i) Manual Accounting systems   (5 marks)
(ii) Computerised Accounting systems   (5 marks)

(Sep 91)

73A Enter the following transactions in a Purchase Daybook and then post the totals to the relevant Ledger accounts.

May 1   Invoice 12908 for £1,000 worth of goods from K. Hin Ltd
May 2   Bought £250 of goods from J. Loi, Invoice No 349023
May 3   Invoice No 32190 from D.E.T. Ltd for £570
May 5   Invoice No 4509 for £210 from High Light Eng Ltd
May 6   Bought £1,200 worth of goods from K. Hin Ltd, invoice no 12934
May 7   Invoice No 4510 for £355 from High Light Eng Ltd

74A (a) Enter the following transactions in a Sales Daybook with analysis columns under the following headings; Shoes, Shirts, Trousers and Suits.

Oct 1   Sold £200 shoes, £75 trousers and £155 suits to H & R Ltd invoice number 34560
Oct 2   Sold £340 shirts and £300 suits to GFD Clothing, invoice number 34561
Oct 3   Sold £35 trousers, £2,000 suits and £65 shirts to P. Yin Ltd, invoice number 34562
Oct 4   Sold £455 trousers to N Singh & Co, invoice number 34563
Oct 5   Sold £120 shoes and £75 shirts to H & R Ltd, invoice number 34564
Oct 6   Sold £650 trousers to P Yin Ltd, invoice number 34565

(b) Calculate the total sales for the week and post the figures to the relevant accounts in the Sales and Nominal Ledger.

(c) Suggest some suitable codes that could be used to categorise the different products in a computerised system.

75 Identify (with the aid of a table, if necessary) the various SOURCE DOCUMENTS and BOOKS OF ORIGINAL ENTRY used in manual accounting systems and the appropriate POSTINGS to double-entry accounts.   (Sept 89)

76   Draw up a Sales Daybook to show how the following sales would be recorded:

July 1st   B. Goodall bought $1,200.50 of goods, a trade discount of 10% is offered and VAT (Purchase tax) is payable at 15%. Invoice number W1234.

July 2nd   ABC Limited bought $550.75 of goods, VAT payable is 15%, Invoice number W1235.

July 3rd   Invoice number W1236 is for K & N Engineering and shows the total amount payable as $276.50.

July 4th   Goods sold to PMP Enterprises for $560.90, trade discount of 20% and Cash discount of 2% are offered, VAT is 15%. Invoice number W1238.

(10 marks)

(Sep 91)

77A   A wholesale supplier of sports goods maintains a Purchase Journal which has three analysis columns; Football, Tennis and Others. Write up the following Purchase invoices into the Purchase Journal with appropriate analysis columns.

1987		£
Oct 1	J.Brown;Tennis rackets £75, Golf balls £20	95
Oct 4	D.Cluff; Football strips £550, Badminton nets £50	600
Oct 6	XYZ Ltd; Tennis shoes £80, Running £200	280
Oct 12	D.Evans; Tennis balls	52
Oct 14	K.Santok; Football boots	110
Oct 16	NRD & Co; Golf clubs	493

78A   (a) Draw up a three- column cash book to show how the following transactions would be recorded.
(b) Transfer the entries to the discount accounts at the end of the week.

1988

Dec 1 Balances bought down: Bank £1,900, Cash £560

Dec 2 Received cash £110 from H. Watt after he has deducted £2 for discount.

Dec 4 Paid T. Stephenson £186 by cheque in full settlement of his account (amount owing £200).

Dec 5 Received cheque from L. Davies for £196, he having deducted 2% for discount.

Dec 6 Cash sales £78. Paid R. Evans £35 cash.

Dec 7 Paid amount owing to G. Cotton £150, by cheque after deducting 10% discount.

2.11.1   The journal

The journal proper is slightly different in layout and although most frequently used for recording transactions relating to the nominal ledger, it can be used to record any item as it is most commonly used as a sort of diary to record unusual events. The layout is shown below; notice how each transaction has a "narrative" which is useful for recording unusual items as it provides additional information to that found in the double-entry accounts:

Date	Details	Folio	Dr	Cr
6 Feb	Office equipment a/c	NL 14	250.00	
	N Ford a/c	SL 19		250.00
	Accepted typewriter as			
	payment of amount owing			
12 Feb	Cash a/c	NL 2	565.00	
	Motor vehicle a/c	NL 17		565.00
	Sold Volvo lorry FGH 675A			
	for cash. Surplus to requirements			
15 Feb	Bank a/c	NL 4	120.50	
	Bad Debts a/c	NL 26	80.00	
	G Howard a/c	SL 12		200.50
	Payment received from			
	liquidator in respect of			
	above. No further			
	payments will be made.			

Figure 2.48

The journal is generally shown in the above style with the debit account shown first and the credit account shown second and slightly indented — this is purely to make identification of the accounts easier. The entries are first made in the journal and then at a suitable time are transferred to the appropriate accounts.

The majority of transactions undertaken by most businesses will involve the buying and selling of goods; all of these transactions will be very similar. The journal is useful because of the narrative — this will enable the firm to make comments relating to transactions. If anybody should query a transaction at a later date, the narrative in the journal should provide an explanation, or at least direct staff to a document that will contain the explanation and reason for the transaction.

The journal can also be used where a firm has not previously maintained proper records. In this sort of instance, the journal can be used to show the initial entries for the various items before they are transferred to proper double-entry accounts. In this sort of situation the owner is often able to calculate or estimate the value of most assets and liabilities but is often unsure of how much capital was invested. The journal can calculate the amount of capital by the simple application of the accounting equation (ie if assets and liabilities are known then capital must equal assets less liabilities).

Exercises

79 Show how the following transactions would appear in a journal:

1 Aug   A debtor who owes £350 is made bankrupt and a final payment of £300 is received. The balance will be a bad debt.

3 Aug   A CNC lathe is bought for £12,000, paid by cheque.

4 Aug   £500 is withdrawn from the bank for use as a cash float in the business.

8 Aug   Rent of £500 paid on 27 July included £300 in respect of the owner's living accommodation.

12 Aug   An obsolete computer is sold for scrap for £150 cash.

17 Aug   Two IBM microcomputers are bought for £4000 on credit from Computers Ltd.

21 Aug   Commission of £100 cash is received from ABC Ltd in respect of goods sold on their behalf.

80 Show how the following transactions would be entered in a Journal, complete with suitable narrative:

Mar 1   Stock valued at $4,500 has been taken for the owner's own use.

Mar 2   Bank interest received amounting to $110 from a Deposit Account has been paid in to the Current Bank Account.

Mar 3   A Motor Van has been sold for $2,100, $1,700 of which was paid by cheque and a Machine valued at $400 has been accepted as part payment.

Mar 3   XYZ Limited have gone bankrupt and they still owe $400, the liquidator has made a final payment of 25%.

(14 marks)
(Mar 92)

81 Show how the following transactions would be recorded in a journal:

June 1   Shop fittings are purchased from XYZ Ltd for $10,000 on credit.

June 3   Stock valued at $180 has been taken for the owner's own use.

June 6   A cheque for Commission of $200 is paid to ABC Limited in respect of sales made on our behalf.

June 9   SDT Engineering has been declared bankrupt and still owes us $1,200. The liquidator has authorised a payment of $300 which will be the final sum received in respect of this debtor.

June 15 $300 is transferred from the cash till to the bank account.

June 22   An obsolete computer is sold for scrap $120, cash.

(Jun 88)

82A On 1st March, R Sutterjee had the following assets/liabilities:

	£
Fixtures/Fittings	15,000
Delivery Vans	15,000

Creditors:	
G Patel	3,000
S Dohai	2,800
W Pierce	1,900
Stock	8,720
Debtors:	
T Wing	120
L Cunie	1,200
D Rafael	1,720
P Poon	2,020
Bank	2,250
Cash	320

During March, the following transactions occurred:-

(a)   A debt owed by T Wing is written off as a bad debt.
(b)   Goods taken by the proprietor value £200 had been debited to an account in the Sales Ledger opened in the proprietor's own name.
(c)   A letter had been received from a supplier, P Sohal, stating definitely that £35 cash discount deducted would not be allowed.
(d)   A Machine is taken as payment for amount owing to G Patel.
(e)   A new computer is purchased on credit from Ace Computers Ltd.

Required

(a)   Show Sutterjee's opening entries in the journal, including his capital and open ledger accounts for each item.
(b)   Show all other transactions in the journal and ledger accounts.

83A Why does the journal include a narrative?

2.12 SOURCE DOCUMENTS

Any student of computing will be familiar with the term "source document" but many are not clear what most "source documents" do or what they look like. Source documents are of particular importance in accounting as they serve as proof of the existence of a transaction.

Despite the wide and varying nature of businesses, the number and varieties of source documents are very few. One reason for the similarity between documents is that as accounting systems have become standardised, it has made sense that the documents should also become standardised and nowadays most documents, although produced by different firms, will contain virtually identical information.

The principal source documents used in accounting are as follows:

Invoices: Invoices are used to record details of goods supplied, a sales invoice is sent by the firm to its customers to confirm details of goods ordered. In the majority of cases the invoices will not actually be sent with the goods but will be issued at a slightly later date. A purchase invoice will contain virtually identical data but is issued by a supplier to the firm to show what goods have been purchased. Both invoices are very important as they show what goods have been ordered in detail. It is rarely necessary to record all details in the accounts or daybooks so the invoices should be retained in case there is a query over the items supplied/delivered.

The sample invoice shown in Figure 2.49 contains a column for VAT. This is a form of "direct" or "purchase" tax charged in the UK. Many countries will have a similar type of tax but may call it by a different name.

Invoices are generally used to provide a document for a credit transaction, therefore it is usual to provide details of any credit period offered and of discounts offered if the customer should pay promptly. A "trade discount" is given to firms that are in a similar trade and are likely to return for future orders. This amount can be calculated when the invoice is being prepared so it is possible to deduct this discount from the amount shown on the invoice. A "cash discount" is in fact a discount given for prompt payment. If the customer pays the amount owing within the credit period an extra discount is provided. As it is impossible to tell whether the customer will pay promptly when the invoice is being produced, the amount of this discount is not included in the calculation but the percentage is shown so that the customer can deduct it from the amount paid if it is within the credit period.

Credit notes: These documents are used to describe any items that are being returned to the firm by its customers. Goods are often returned as being damaged or inferior in some way or perhaps merely in excess of the quantity ordered. The document can be sent by the customer or issued by the firm to the customer; it is known as a credit note as the firm will make a "credit" entry in the debtor's account to show that the value of the goods returned has been deducted from the amount owing.

Debit note: This serves the opposite function to the credit note and is used to record details of goods returned by the firm to the supplier. This document is called a debit note as the entry made in the accounts will be a "debit" entry in the suppliers account to show that the goods returned have been deducted from the amount owing to the supplier.

Receipts: A large number of items will not have an invoice as they will be paid for in cash. In these instances it is still necessary to have a source document to refer back to as proof of the transaction taking place. Firms will normally insist that any employee who is paying in cash for an item should obtain a receipt as proof of the transaction occurring. A receipt could be a simple till receipt from a shop or a formal contract for the purchase of new premises. In a number of cases the original cheque can be used as a source document and a copy of the cheque obtained from the firm's bank for the firm's records.

Order forms: Order forms can also be considered source documents as they contain the initial data concerning the products that the customer requires. The customer may send its own order form or may ask for an order form from the firm if the products are of a very technical nature and have a specific product code. Some organisations will supply an order form along with the catalogue/price list of their products; this ensures that all of the required details are included on the

INVOICE			Invoice No. **K 4172**		

NCC International Ltd
Anyplace
Anytown

Invoice Date **16/12/91**

To: ABC Traders
Ltd
New Street
Oldham

Your Order No. **Q120**	Dated **1/12/91**			Terms **2% Cash - 30**	
Quantity	Description	Unit Price £	Total £	VAT rate %	VAT rate %
	1 litre tins - white paint	1.20	12.00	15	
	Large Paintbrushes	2.00	10.00	15	
	1/2 litre tins - thinners	1.50	3.00	15	
			25.00		
	Trade Discount		2.50		
			22.50		3.37
E.&O.E.					

Figure 2.49   Invoice

```
                                                           No. C100

                           CREDIT NOTE

                           NCC International Ltd
                           Anyplace
      Tel. No.  0907 111111  Anytown

                                                   Date  16/12/91

      To:  ABC Traders Ltd
           New Street
           Oldtown
```

Invoice No. **K4172**	Dated **1/12/91**	
Quantity	Description	
3	**Large Paintbrushes**	**6.00**
	+ **VAT**	**.90**
		6.90

Figure 2.50 Credit note

order form and that the correct codes are quoted. Numerous firms now print their order forms on forms that are machine readable in either Optical Character Recognition (OCR) or Optical Mark Recognition (OMR) format. This has the advantage of speeding up the order processing system and will also update stock records at the same time.

Statements of account: The invoice is used to record details of single transactions and goods delivered. It is also a notice that payment is required and will often state the credit period allowed. A statement of account is sent at the end of each month to inform the customer of the balance still owing on their account and to include details of goods recently delivered and payments received. Nowadays, most statements are produced by computers and it is usually possible to include short comments on the statements such as instruction to the customer to pay the outstanding amount immediately or merely to inform of special offers.

ABC TRADERS LIMITED
10 HIGH STREET
NEWTOWN

ORDER FORM

DELIVER TO: .... ACCOUNT NUMBER ....

....

.... DATE: ..../..../....

Please mark your requirements with a — in the appropriate box.

ITEM	PACK SIZE	QUANTITY								
Coffee	Small	(1)	(2)	(3)	(4)	(5)	(6)	(7)	(8)	(9)
	Medium	(1)	(2)	(3)	(4)	(5)	(6)	(7)	(8)	(9)
	Large	(1)	(2)	(3)	(4)	(5)	(6)	(7)	(8)	(9)
Tea	Small	(1)	(2)	(3)	(4)	(5)	(6)	(7)	(8)	(9)
	Medium	(1)	(2)	(3)	(4)	(5)	(6)	(7)	(8)	(9)
	Large	(1)	(2)	(3)	(4)	(5)	(6)	(7)	(8)	(9)
Sugar	1 kg	(1)	(2)	(3)	(4)	(5)	(6)	(7)	(8)	(9)
	2 kg	(1)	(2)	(3)	(4)	(5)	(6)	(7)	(8)	(9)
Biscuits	Medium	(1)	(2)	(3)	(4)	(5)	(6)	(7)	(8)	(9)
	Family	(1)	(2)	(3)	(4)	(5)	(6)	(7)	(8)	(9)
	Extra Large	(1)	(2)	(3)	(4)	(5)	(6)	(7)	(8)	(9)

Figure 2.51   OMR form

Exercises

84A What is the difference between trade discount, cash discount, discount allowed and discount received?

85 What is the main source document for the following daybooks: sales, purchases, returns in and returns out?

86A Design and complete a sales invoice to record the following transaction details:

Goods sold by ABC & Co, New Works, High Green, Midmarsh, Kent to P & S Enterprises, 12 Dallas Road, Newton, Staffs. Invoice dated 31st May 1990, invoice number 20989. Their order number W7646, dated 20th May 1990.

12 Units of Sprockets at £2.50 per unit
6 crates of Cranks at £1.00 each (10 cranks per case)
2 dozen Blocks at £3.00 each
40 Brackets at £250 per hundred
2 pallets of endcovers at £5 per half a pallet

Trade discount of 20% is to be given on the total value of the order and a cash discount of 2.5% is offered for payment within 31 days.

87A Record the following transactions in the Day Books, Cash Book, and Journal, as appropriate.

1989

Dec 1st   Cash in Hand £300; Cash at Bank £30,000; Capital £30,300.
Dec 3rd   Bought Stock from ABC Ltd on credit, at cost of £15,000 less Trade Discount of 20%.
Dec 5th   Paid Rent by cheque £3000
Dec 10th   Cash Sales £4000
Dec 15th   Cash Purchases £2500
Dec 18th   Bought new machine for factory from Ace Products Ltd, credit costing £3000.
Dec 21st   Sold goods on credit to G S Mundy & Co Ltd, for £12,000 less 25% Trade Discount.
Dec 28th   Sold goods on credit to A Mahmood Ltd at cost of £3000 less 30% Trade Discount.
Dec 30th   Paid Ace Products Ltd, by cheque the amount owing to them less 5% cash discount.

88A F Bungar ordered the following goods from Aztec Supplies Ltd., 13 Delhi Road, Bombay, on 1st August 1989, and they were delivered on 31st August to his warehouse at 3 New Road, Calcutta, together with an invoice:

Ref. No. TV210   10 AGC TVs at £200 each, less Trade Discount of 25%.
Ref. No. VCR11   30 AGC Video Recorders at £210 each, less Trade Discount of 10%.
Ref. No. HIFI21   20 AGC Hi-Fi systems at £170 each, less Trade Discount of 10%.

VAT is to be charged at 10%.
(i) Produce the invoice Bungar will receive.
(ii) Before the accounts department pays this invoice state what documents and records they would check.

STATEMENT

NCC International Ltd
Anyplace
Anytown

To: **ABC Traders Ltd**
New Street
Oldtown

Date **31/12/91**

Account No. **ABC123**

Date	Particulars	Debit	Credit	Balance
1/12/91	Balance b/f		120.25	120.25
16/12/91	Invoice K4172		25.87	146.12
20/12/91	Credit note C100	6.90		139.22
27/12/91	Cheque No. 0912131	120.25		18.97

Figure 2.52   Statement of account

89A On 1st September, 1989, John Rafter's debtors were as follows:

D. Noon	£720
P. Lang	£325
M. Dain	£97

His creditors were:

F. Halter	£290
C. Brent	£333
A. Malden	£140
S. Chane	£45

His Daybooks for the month ending September, 1989 were as follows:

Sales Day Book

		Inv No	Folio	Total	VAT	Net
Sep 6	M Dain	1676	SL2	120	12	108
Sep 8	P Lang	1677	SL5	166	13	153
Sep 10	D Noon	1678	SL8	99	9	90
Sep 16	M Dain	1679	SL2	210	21	189
Sep 20	P Lang	1680	SL5	61	6	55

Purchases Day Book

		Inv No	Folio	Total	VAT	Net
Sep 9	F Halter	5651	PL10	170	17	153
Sep 11	C Brent	6367	PL6	110	10	100
Sep 13	S Chane	9191	PL8	66	6	60
Sep 21	A Malden	3838	PL13	220	20	200

Sales Returns Day Book

		Cr Note	Folio	Total	VAT	Net
Sep 20	M Dain	CN346	SL2	55	5	50
Sep 27	P Lang	CN347	SL5	17	2	15

Purchases Returns Day Book

		Dr Note	Folio	Total	VAT	Net
Sep 16	F Halter	CN12	PL10	33	3	30
Sep 28	A Malden	CN19	PL13	20	2	18

In addition to the above transactions, on 30th September, D. Noon paid the balance owing on his account, less 5% cash discount; F. Halter was paid £100 by cheque; and C. Brent £300 by cheque.

REQUIRED;

Write up and balance all necessary accounts to record the above transactions.

2.13 ACCOUNTING SYSTEMS

One of the advantages in using books of original entry is that the daybooks can actually be completed in departments other than the accounts department. The purchasing department will have issued an order for goods and would receive at least one copy of the invoice when the goods are delivered, so that it can up-date its records. Therefore it may be more efficient to have a purchasing department clerk enter details in the purchases daybook and simply send the day's "sheet" on to the accounts department at the end of the day. The same will apply in respect of the sales department and goods inwards (for returns). A further benefit is that each of the departments will be retaining records of their own, which will be in addition to the accounting requirements, and the daybook could be modified to allow additional information to be recorded.

The way that the books of original entry and the different ledgers merge together is often misunderstood and to simplify matters a pictorial representation is given in Figure 2.53. However, this pictorial representation is rather a simplification because in practice there is almost certainly more than one book for both the sales and purchases ledgers. Despite the fact that data can be processed more rapidly by using the system shown, it should be apparent that computerisation of the accounting system would improve the system even further. In the majority of firms the first area to be automated would be the accounting function (see Chapter 1).

Larger firms would not only have the resources to install computers but would also have data in sufficient quantities to warrant computerisation. As one of the reasons for dividing the ledger and using books of original entry was so that more clerks could be employed in entering transactions, it is often suggested that such a division becomes obsolete in a computerised system.

This does not in itself mean that the old divisions of the ledger should not still apply; one reason why the old divisions do still apply is that the technology of most machines is not yet truly multi-user. The firm could have ten terminals all linked directly to one huge accounts file, but what will invariably happen is that the terminal operators will have continuous delays in entering data because the account they require is currently being updated from another operator's terminal. By retaining the divisions of the ledger, delays may still arise as "account currently in use" but the delays will be far less common.

The above explanation is only the technical reason for retaining the manual system methods; there are a number of other equally valid reasons which are more directly related to accounting system requirements and the use of accounting information. Some of these reasons will be explained in the next chapter and the others in Chapter 5.

2.14   INTERPRETATION OF ACCOUNTS

Part 1 described how a range of different groups will want to examine the accounts of a firm for various reasons. Section 1.2 described the particular aspects of the accounts that each group would be interested in. In most cases the users of accounts will primarily be interested in the firm's profit.

However, many of the users will be examining the accounts of the firm in order to compare the profit with the profit of other firms, for instance, prospective shareholders will compare how much profit the firm is making with other

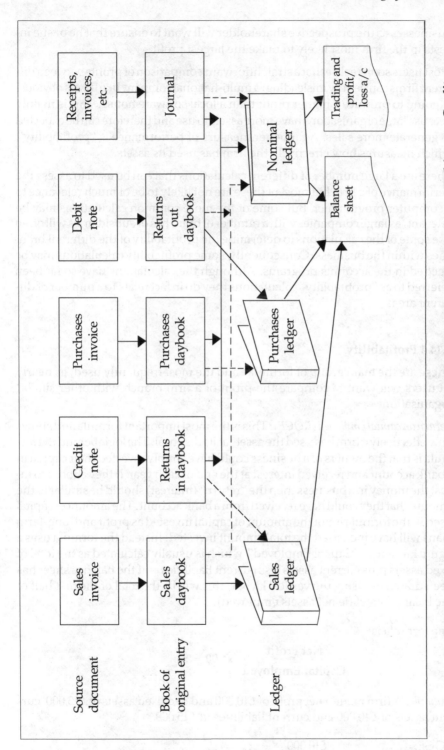

Figure 2.53 Relationship between the books of original entry and the ledgers; — Debit, - - - Credit

businesses as the prospective shareholder will want to ensure that he or she invests in the firm most likely to make the largest profit.

Most users soon realise that a straightforward comparison of profits between different firms can be very misleading; a multi-national company like IBM is obviously going to produce a higher profit than a local software house. This is mainly because large organisations have more assets to use and therefore can be expected to generate more sales. A far better measure of performance is "profitability", which measures how effectively the firm has used its assets.

There are a large number of different calculations that can be used to assess the performance of a firm but most of these are not likely to be of much relevance to a computer programmer. But some of the more common calculations may be relevant, as large companies with a number of branches or subsidiaries will often use some of the calculations to determine the profitability of the different branches within the business. Consequently, some profitability calculations may be needed in the accounts programs. Although the calculations have so far been referred to as "profitability" calculations they do in fact relate to a number of different areas.

2.14.1 Profitability

These are the main group of formulae and the most frequently used, as nearly all users will want to compare the profit of a firm/branch with other similar organisations.

Return on capital employed (ROCE): This is the most important formula and shows how effectively a firm has used the assets at its disposal. The logic behind the formula is that the owners of a business could have simply invested their capital in a bank account and received interest at the end of each year. If they choose to invest the money in a business then the "return" (interest) should be similar to the amount that they could have received from a bank account. The amount of capital used in the formula is not the amount of capital invested as profit and long-term loans will have increased the total amount invested. Instead the formula uses a figure known as "Capital Employed", which is usually calculated as the total of fixed assets plus current assets less current liabilities — if the balance sheet has been drawn up using the vertical layout, this will be the total of the first half of the balance sheet (ie net assets employed).

The formula is:

$$\frac{\text{Net Profit}}{\text{Capital Employed}} \times 100 = \%$$

Example: A firm made a net profit of £10,000 and had fixed assets of £75,000, current assets of £40,000 and current liabilities of £15,000.

ROCE: $\dfrac{£10,000}{£100,000} \times 100 = 10\%$

Many large organisations use this formula to assess the effectiveness of their subsidiaries and many will have company policies to the effect that all subsidiaries will be expected to achieve a ROCE of a set figure.

Net profit/sales: This formula calculates Net Profit as a percentage of total sales; it is useful for showing how effectively the firm has operated and managed to keep expenses down.

The formula is:

$$\frac{\text{Net Profit}}{\text{Sales}} \times 100 = \%$$

Example: The previous firm had made sales of £80,000.

Net Profit/Sales: $\dfrac{£10,000}{£80,000} \times 100 = 12.5\%$

Gross profit/sales: This formula is basically the same as net profit/sales but uses gross profit instead of net profit. This formula is particularly useful for comparing the results of different branches as most large groups will insist that all branches should have the same profit margin.

The formula is:

$$\frac{\text{Gross Profit}}{\text{Sales}} \times 100 = \%$$

Example: The previous firm had a gross profit of £20,000.

Gross Profit/Sales: $\dfrac{£20,000}{£80,000} \times 100 = 25\%$

This formula is especially important for control purposes as it can be used to check that subsidiaries or branches are following company policy and that there is no fraud. This is possible where the firm has a standard pricing policy, such as all goods sold should have a 25% profit margin.

Margin and markup: Prices are normally set as the cost of goods plus a percentage for profit. The **Gross Profit Margin** is where profit is a set percentage of selling price; eg selling price £10, profit margin 25% means that the profit is £2.50 (ie £10 x 25%) and the cost of goods must have been £7.50 (ie £10 – £2.50).

If the firm has a policy of charging a standard **Profit margin** then it should be possible to calculate the selling price for any product. The selling price should equal 100%; if the profit margin required is 20% then that means that the cost of goods must equal the remaining 80%. Therefore if goods cost £20 then the required selling price will be £25 (£20 x 100/80). This gives a profit of £5 which is 20% of the selling price.

Profit markup is very similar but is calculated as a percentage of the cost of goods sold rather than the selling price. This is much easier to work out. If a firm requires that all products have a markup of 25% of cost price then a product which costs £12 will be sold for £15 (£12 x 125/100). Note that the profit margin in this example would be 20% (Profit £3 divided by selling price £15 x 100).

The examples shown are based on just one product and both **Margin** and **Markup** are used extensively for setting prices, but, if all products have the same **markup** or **margin** then the gross profit/sales calculation should be a standard figure. This enables firms to check that all goods have been sold at the correct price.

Margin and **Markup** often cause some confusion to students; the essential difference is that:

Margin is based on the selling price;

Markup is based on the cost price.

2.14.2 Liquidity

Some of the users of account will be equally concerned about a firm's ability to meet its debts. This ability is known as "liquidity"; a firm that has plenty of cash to meet its liabilities is a very liquid firm.

Liquidity is usually measured by comparing current assets with current liabilities because the current assets include those items that can easily be converted to "cash" for use in paying off the current liabilities (long term liabilities are ignored as they do not need paying off in the short term). The two most common measures of liquidity involve simple ratios.

Current ratio: This ratio is also sometimes referred to as the liquidity ratio; it makes a direct comparison between current assets and current liabilities.

The formula is:

Current Assets : Current Liabilities

Example: A firm has current assets of £40,000 and current liabilities of £20,000.

$$£40,000 : £20,000$$
$$2 : 1$$

This shows a ratio of 2:1 which means that the firm has £2 of current assets for every £1 of current liabilities and can therefore easily meet its debts.

NB: This ratio is always expressed as x:1 so that it shows how many current assets there are for each £1 of current liabilities.

Acid test or quick ratio: This ratio is similar to the current ratio but takes a more pessimistic view. It attempts to assess the liquidity of the firm under the worst possible conditions. This means that the only assets included in the calculation are those that can be quickly converted into "cash". Cash and bank balances are already in the form of "cash" so they can be included, debtors may take a long time to pay but it is possible to "sell" debts to a factoring agent. This agent will pay the firm somewhere between 80% and 95% of the amounts owed by debtors and will then undertake to collect the debts. This means that most of the money owing by debtors can be received within 24 hours. Stock is the asset that is most difficult to convert to "cash", especially if the firm is a manufacturing business and the stock is in the form of raw materials or partly finished goods.

Therefore this ratio uses the same formula as the current ratio but excludes stock.

The formula is:

Current Assets — Stock : Current Liabilities

Example: A firm has current assets of £40,000 (including Stock of £10,000) and current liabilities of £20,000.

$$£40,000 - £10,000 : £20,000$$
$$£30,000 : £20,000$$
$$1.5 : 1$$

This shows that the firm has £1.50 of "liquid" current assets for every £1 of current liabilities.
Any ratio in excess of 1:1 is normally satisfactory as it means that a firm has more current assets than current liabilities.

2.14.3 Performance

This last group of formula are used to assess the effectiveness of management, once again there are a large number of different formulae that can be used but it should only be necessary to consider three.

Stockturnover: This formula calculates how often stock is replaced throughout the year. If large quantities of stock are retained then the firm may be able to take advantage of bulk discounts offered by suppliers. But on the other hand they will almost certainly be losing out as they will have large quantities of stock on hand for many months. A full explanation of the problems of overstocking is given in Part 4 under the heading of Inventory Control.

The formula is:

$$\frac{\textbf{Cost of goods sold}}{\textbf{Average Stock}} = \textbf{days}$$

In most cases the "average stock" held throughout the year will not be known (this is usually only possible in computerised systems). An alternative for most businesses is to use a simple average taken from opening and closing stock.

Example: Cost of goods sold during the year was £200,000. Opening stock was £20,000 and closing stock was £30,000.

$$\text{Average Stock} = \frac{£20,000 + £30,000}{2} = £25,000$$

$$\frac{£200,000}{£25,000} = 8 \text{ days}$$

This means that all stock is replaced every eight days on average. This formula should be used with care when comparing different firms as a greengrocer's firm should have a very high Stockturnover - at least 200 days as all stock will need replacing every day or so else it will go rotten, whereas a shipbuilding firm will be quite happy with a Stockturnover of two per year.

Debtors' payment period: This formula calculates how long it takes to receive payment from debtors, on average. This enables a firm to see how effective its credit control procedures are. The formula is:

$$\frac{\text{Debtors}}{\text{Sales}} \times 365 \text{ day} = \text{days}$$

Example: Debtors at the end of the year are £20,000 and sales for the year were £200,000.

$$\frac{£20,000}{£200,000} \times 365 = 36.5 \text{ (37) days}$$

This shows that it takes debtors an average of 37 days to pay their debts. A firm could attempt to improve this time by increasing the amount of cash discount it offers, thereby tempting debtors to pay up sooner.

Creditors payment period: This formula is essentially the opposite of the debtors payment period and calculates the average time taken to pay off creditors. The formula is:

$$\frac{\textbf{Creditors}}{\textbf{Purchases}} \times 365 = \text{days}$$

This formula is not so important except to check that the firm is making sure it takes longer to pay its suppliers than it does to receive money from its customers.

Exercises

90   ABC Limited have recently set up a new branch in NewTown. A manager has been appointed but trade has not yet commenced. ABC Limited is a very large organisation with branches throughout the country. Its managers have full power and authority to run each branch as a separate entity but the Head Office do insist that each branch should achieve certain targets in its accounts. These targets are as follows:

Mark-up	30%
Net Profit as a % of Sales	10%
Return on Capital Employed	5%
Stockturn	8 times
Current Ratio	2.8:1
Quick Ratio	1.55:1
Debtors Payment period	71 days
Creditors Payment period	58.4 days

At the start of the year the manager of the Newtown branch is provided with funds amounting to £130,000 as the capital invested by Head Office. Some of this has already been used to acquire fixed assets worth £112,000. As this is a new branch there is no opening stock.

The Head Office have asked the manager to submit a budgeted profit/loss account and balance sheet to show his expected trading figures.

REQUIRED:

Calculate the figures that will be needed to achieve the targets and devise a Profit/Loss account and Balance Sheet.
NB: Figures for Debtors/Creditors should be rounded up.

91A(i) A firm has produced the following Trading and Profit/Loss Account and Balance sheet for the year ended 30/9/89.

Trading and Profit/Loss Account

	£	£
Sales		210,500
Opening Stock	15,400	
Purchases	93,000	
	108,400	
Closing Stock	17,200	
Cost of Goods sold	91,200	91,200
Gross Profit		119,300
less Expenses		85,100
Net Profit		34,200

Balance Sheet

Fixed Assets	182,000	Current Liabilities	32,600
Current Assets*	51,300	Capital	200,700
	233,300		233,300

*Debtors £12,100

Calculate the following and state any formulae used:

(a) Gross Profit as a percentage of sales
(b) Net Profit as a percentage of sales
(c) Return on Capital Employed
(d) Current ratio
(e) Quick (Acid-test) ratio
(f) Debtors payment period
(g) Stockturn

(ii) The firm would like to produce a Return on Capital Employed of 20%. Assuming that Capital Employed and Net Profit percentages remain the same, what Net Profit is needed to achieve this level and what volume of sales would be required?

92A A Limited Company has produced the following summary of its accounts:

Trading and Profit/Loss account

Turnover	£100,000
Cost of goods sold	£40,000
Gross Profit	£60,000
Admin costs	£10,000
S & D costs	£11,000
Net Operating profit	£39,000
Taxation	£15,000
Net profit after tax	£24,000
Dividends	£12,000
Retained profit	£12,000

Balance Sheet

Fixed Assets			£100,000
Current Assets:			
Stock	£40,000		
Debtors	£55,000		
Bank	£18,000	£113,000	
Current Liabilities:			
Taxation	£15,000		
Creditors	£32,000		
Dividends	£12,000	£59,000	£54,000
			£154,000
Capital:			
Ordinary share capital			
100,000 shares at £1 each		£100,000	
Share Premium Account		£10,000	
Profit & Loss Account		£44,000	

NOTES:
(i) Stock at the beginning of the year was £38,000.

REQUIRED:
(a) Calculate three accounting "ratios" that might be used by the firm's managers.
(b) Calculate three accounting "ratios" that might be used by the shareholders.
(c) Calculate two accounting "ratios" that might be used by the firm's suppliers.
(d) Suggest reasons why these "ratios" might be inadequate and stipulate what other information would be required in order to draw reasonable conclusions.

93A The following Trial Balance was extracted from the books of D. Patel at 31st May 1990.

	£	£
Capital		90,000
Cash	10,000	
Purchases	210,000	
Sales		255,000
Expenses	32,000	
Stock (31/05/89)	49,000	
Creditors		14,000
Debtors	18,500	
Fixed Assets (written down values)	39,500	
	359,000	359,000

D. Patel valued his stock at 31st May 1990 at £52,000.

Required:

(a) Prepare a Trading and Profit/Loss Account for the year ended 31st May 1990 and a Balance Sheet at that date.

(b) Calculate the following:
  (i)   Gross profit/sales ratio.
  (ii) Stock turnover period.
  (iii) Debtor collection period.
  (iv) Liquidity or acid test ratio.
  (v) Return on capital employed ratio.
  (vi) Creditor payment period.

3 Control and audit

INTRODUCTION

This section provides you with an appreciation of the need for control and audit procedures. This involves ensuring that a firm has incorporated various safeguards into its accounting system as a means of preventing error and fraud. As accounting will be the main department concerned with handling money, it is also the most likely target for fraud. The section explains the principal safeguards or controls that firms should apply to prevent fraud and error through incorrect calculations.

OBJECTIVES

At the end of this section you should be able to:

— identify the reasons for including, and the importance of, control and audit procedures in accounting systems

— demonstrate the use of control accounts and suspense accounts, and assess their relevance in a computerised system

— define the various internal controls used to ensure adequate control of accounting data in both manual and computerised systems

— define the various external controls used by an auditor, with particular reference to audit trails

— explain the special difficulties created by the use of computers and identify means of preventing these difficulties.

3.1 CONTROL AND AUDIT PROCEDURES

Part 1 explained how a number of different user groups are interested in the accounts of an organisation and also explained the concept of stewardship. It is important to remember that, in the majority of organisations, the owner is not actively involved in the recording of accounting data. In all organisations there are checks and controls imposed by owners to ensure that the employees are doing their jobs properly and in the best interests of the organisation. These checks apply in all aspects of the business, not just those relating to the accounting function. For example, sales representatives are generally given sales targets which they must meet; if they do not reach these targets then they have to explain why they did not perform to expectations. Similarly, computing staff are given

To check that jobs
are done properly

To prevent theft
and fraud

To provide
reassurance to
users

Managers/
civil
servants

Shareholders/voters

Separation of ownership and control

Figure 3.1   The need for checks and controls

deadlines by which projects should be completed and, if necessary, expected to explain why they exceeded the deadline.

Such checks are clearly much more important for the accounting function for two reasons. First, the employees are handling the owner's money and there need to be checks against fraud. Secondly, the other user groups need to be reassured that the accounts produced are an accurate reflection of the state of the business — in other words the accounts need to be confirmed as being true.

This chapter is concerned with the methods of checking the accuracy of accounting information, and explaining the reasons for imposing those checks. As many firms will now have computerised their accounting functions, it will also be necessary to examine how the checks have had to be altered to take into account the effects of computerisation.

Before continuing it is worthwhile looking at how organisations are structured by comparing the structure of private profit-making organisations with public sector organisations:

	Private sector	Public sector
Owners	Shareholders	Electorate
Policy-makers	Directors	Politicians
Implementation	Managers	Civil Servants

As explained in Part 1, this structure is necessary because the owners are so numerous that they could not all be involved in running the organisation. Therefore they elect directors/politicians to run the organisation on their behalf. The directors/politicians make policy decisions which are carried out by managers/civil servants.

Part of the policy-makers' role is to ensure that the managers/civil servants have actually carried out the policies required. This will involve some of the checks suggested at the beginning of the chapter. These will be internal checks carried out by managers and directors. However, the owners will also want to ensure that the policies are in the interests of the organisation and that the directors/managers are not combining to defraud the owners. This will require external checks carried out by someone unconnected with the organisation.

The first part of this chapter examines some of the internal checks on accounting records and the latter part examines external checks and the role of the auditor.

3.2 INTERNAL CONTROLS

One of the obvious areas to check is the numerical accuracy of the double-entry records. This is not so much a check for possible fraud as a means of saving effort in rectifying errors when they are discovered. The most useful check of this sort is the trial balance which was mentioned in the last chapter. The purpose of the trial balance is to perform periodic checks for errors in double-entry. The errors that the trial balance cannot identify, with suggested remedies, are described in full in Part 2.

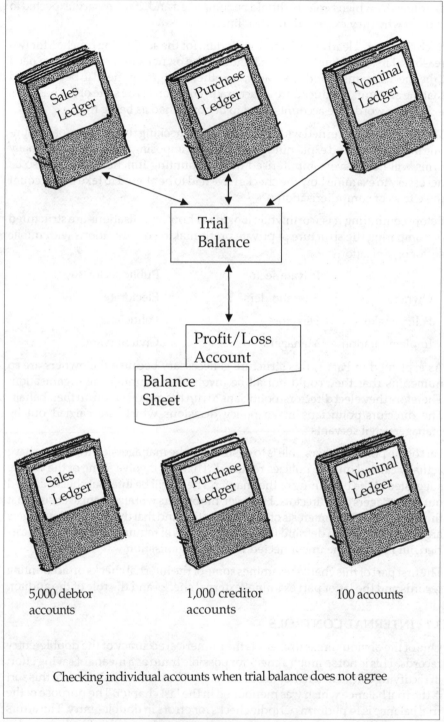

Checking individual accounts when trial balance does not agree

Figure 3.2 Trial balance

Part 2 also describes the "division of the ledger" and such divisions do have repercussions on the use of trial balances. The advantage of the trial balance is supposedly that it is very quick to perform. This is certainly true in small organisations with only a few accounts to include in the trial balance, but in large organisations with a number of ledgers and hundreds of accounts the practice of extracting a trial balance becomes much more cumbersome and prone to error in the extraction of balances. Also, if an error is discovered, it can be a time-consuming task to examine hundreds of accounts to find it. The method can be improved by performing a trial balance on each separate ledger.

Unfortunately, the largest group of ledgers (the sales and purchases ledgers) only contain one of the transactions concerned with the double-entry and therefore a true trial balance is not possible. What is possible, however, is to maintain a master account of all the transactions that should have been entered into the sales or purchases ledger accounts, then the balances of all the debtors or creditors accounts can simply be added and checked against the master account.

The master account is known as a "control account" and is in essence a double-entry account for all debtors or creditors, showing the totals of all entries in the individual accounts. An example of a control account for debtors is shown in Figure 3.3.

Sales ledger control account			
Date	Details	Dr	Cr
1 Jan	Balance at this date	10,000	
	Sales	55,000	
	Bank/Cash received		35,000
	Returns in		1,000
	Discounts allowed		4,000
	Bad debts		5,000
		65,000	45,000
1 Feb	Balance at this date	20,000	

Figure 3.3

What this control account shows is a record of all transactions that should have been entered in each debtor's account in the sales ledger. The entry for "balance at 1 Jan" is the total of balances outstanding on all debtors' accounts, ie the amount owing by debtors. All of the other entries show the alterations that have been made during the month and what the new balances on debtors' accounts should be at the end of January. If the balances on each debtor's account in the sales ledger are added together the total should be £20,000. If the total figure is any different then there is probably an error in the sales ledger and any trial balance drawn up would not balance.

One of the advantages of control accounts is that they are easy to prepare; all of the items included can easily be obtained from the books of original entry such

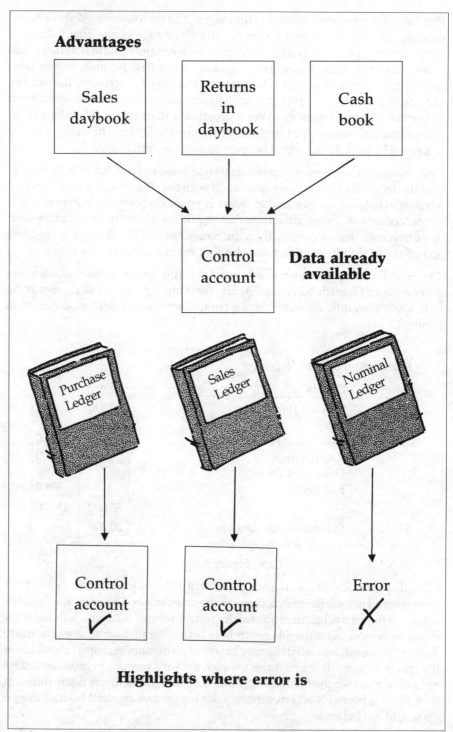

Figure 3.4 Control accounts (1)

as the sales daybook, returns in daybook, cash book and various documents. The appropriate books for purchases would be used to draw up a purchases ledger control account.

A purchase ledger control account may look like Figure 3.5.

Purchase ledger control account			
Date	Details	Dr	Cr
1 Jan	Balance at this date		7,500
	Purchases Daybook		12,100
	Bank/Cash paid	9,010	
	Returns Out	190	
	Discounts Received	1,200	
		10,400	19,600
1 Feb	Balance at this date		9,200

Figure 3.5

Also, if the trial balance does not balance and both the sales and purchases ledger control accounts have been drawn up, the error is clearly in the nominal ledger — thus saving time and effort tracing the error.

If the firm is large enough to subdivide the ledgers in alphabetical or geographical order (eg Wales, England, Scotland) then a separate control account could be used for each ledger.

One of the major advantages of using control accounts is that it is usual to have different people drawing up the control account to those entering data into the ledgers. This means that errors are more likely to be spotted because the chances of two people making the same mistake are unlikely.

The fact that someone else will be checking the accounts will also act as a deterrent against fraud. People are less likely to commit fraud if they know that someone else is going to check their work. This is an important principle and will be discussed more fully later in the chapter.

3.2.1 Control accounts in computerised systems

As the control account serves mainly as a check on the accuracy of ledgers in a manual system, it is quite natural to wonder whether it is still necessary in a computerised system, which should, by its very nature, be inherently more accurate than a manual system. The control account in a manual system does have only one function, but this is not strictly the same function as a control account in a computer package.

The example of a control account given previously shows the type of entries needed in such an account. All of these entries have been taken from various daybooks but all of them could have been taken from the nominal ledger. In computer packages, there is still a division of the ledger, the control account serving as a link between the nominal and sales and purchases ledgers.

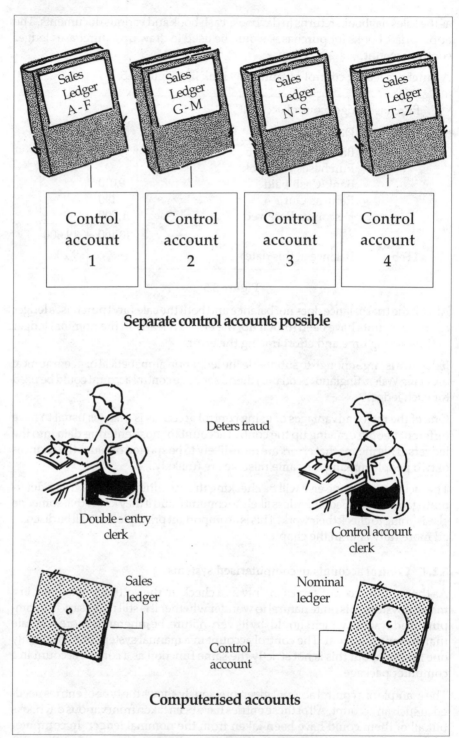

Separate control accounts possible

Deters fraud

Double - entry
clerk

Control account
clerk

Sales
ledger

Nominal
ledger

Control
account

Computerised accounts

Figure 3.6 Control accounts (2)

In microcomputer packages, especially, the different ledgers will be stored on different disks (or at least different tracks on a disk). But the figures from the sales and purchases ledger disks will need to be transferred to the nominal ledger disk whenever a trading and profit and loss account or balance sheet is to be drawn up (this will frequently be more often than once a year as in manual systems). In order to do so the totals from the sales and purchases ledgers need to have an account to be transferred to — this is the control account.

This procedure is not essential and very small firms only use a nominal ledger package because they have such a small number of debtors/creditors. In this case, there should be room for all accounts in just one package: the firm would create the accounts for sales, purchases and all of the individual debtors and creditors in just the nominal ledger package. But larger firms may not have sufficient room to create all of their debtor/creditor accounts on one package and will choose to use separate packages for recording details of debtors/creditors. In this case there must be a control account facility to enable the details of debtors and creditors to be transferred to the nominal ledger program when required, either manually or automatically. Therefore, in computerised systems the control account is not simply an arithmetical check, but a means by which all details can be transferred to one package so that the final accounts can be prepared.

Exercises

Questions followed by A do not have answers supplied.

94 The balances on a firm's control accounts at 31/12/88 were as follows: sales ledger control account £4,500, purchases ledger control account £3,120. During the year 1989 the following transactions took place:

	£
Purchases	120,500
Sales (including £550 cash sales)	278,450
Payments to suppliers	94,300
Discounts received	2,480
Receipts from Customers	226,200
Bad debts written off	4,550
Discounts received	5,710
Goods returned to suppliers	8,340
Refund of customers' overpayment	210
Goods returned from customers	11,140

Prepare the sales and purchases ledgers control accounts for the year ending 31/12/89.

95 A firm has a debit balance of £10,500 on its sales ledger control account on 1 January. During the month, the following transactions took place:

	£
Sales (including £3,000 for cash)	94,500
Discounts allowed	7,200

Goods returned by customers	2,750
Dishonoured cheques	150
Receipts from customers	82,250
Bad debts written off	650

At the end of the month the balances in the debtors' personal accounts come to £9,500. Check the accuracy of this figure by preparing a control account.

96   What function do control accounts serve?

97   The following data was extracted from the books of Lightfoot and Co. at their year end, 30th September 1989. Prepare suitable control accounts to ascertain their accuracy.

	$
Credit sales for the year	75,500
Cash received from debtors	75,600
Creditors at start of year	28,000
Debtors at 30th September 1989	10,900
Bank overdraft at end of year	120
Payments to creditors	78,000
Purchases on credit	70,400
Cash at bank to start	2,600
Purchases/Sales contra entries	100
Returned cheques	300
Returns inward	460
Credit notes received	400
Debtors as at 1st October 1988	12,100
Discounts received	700
Bad Debts written-off	200
Discounts Allowed	640
Creditors as at 30th September 1989	19,200

(Dec 89)

98(a) A firm has obtained the following data from its records, draw up the Sales Ledger and Purchase Ledger Control Accounts.

	$
Opening balance: Debtors	10,450
Opening balance: Creditors	7,346
Cash Sales	804
Cheques received	34,892
Cheques paid	29,428
Discounts received	1,440
Discounts allowed	2,862
Bad Debts written off	925
Increase in Provision for Bad Debts	704

Credit notes issued	1,105
Debit notes issued	1,207
Sales Invoices	36,858
Purchase Invoices	32,324
Purchase incorrectly recorded as a Sale	1,549

(15 marks)

(b) Explain why Control Accounts are used in:

    (i) Manual Accounting systems   (3 marks)

    (ii) Computerised Accounting systems   (2 marks)

(Sep 91)

3.3 SUSPENSE ACCOUNTS

There are occasions in manual systems when the trial balance fails to balance. This is invariably the result of a transaction being entered in one account only. In principle the error should be found; this will mean checking the double-entry of every transaction until the error is discovered. The previous section demonstrated how this job can be simplified by using control accounts to check the sales and purchase ledgers in order to see if the error is in one of those ledgers.

However, sometimes the error will be in the nominal ledger only; or the control account shows that the error is at least partly in either the sales or purchases ledger (NB: the control account does not actually find the error). In these cases it is necessary to go right through the ledgers in order to find the mistake. For firms with a lot of accounts this can be a major job.

The main purpose of the suspense account is to record the previously unentered part of the double-entry transaction and hold it in "suspension" until the error is actually discovered. This system can only be used for minor errors and the concept of materiality would have to be applied to decide whether the mistake would materially affect the accounts or not. For example, if a firm has a net profit of £10,000, a mistake of £500 would probably be considered as being "material", if so, then the error must be discovered immediately. But, if the mistake were only for £50, this would not be considered "material" and the error could be recorded in a suspense account where it would remain until the error was discovered.

Suspense accounts work as follows:

Example: A firm has extracted a trial balance which has the following totals:

  Debit £65,780   Credit £65,850

The difference is £70 and it would be assumed that a transaction for this amount had only been recorded on the credit side of the accounts, therefore the debit total is £70 less than it should be. As this amount is not material it would be simpler to prepare a suspense account rather than spend hours searching the accounts in order to find the error.

Suspense account

Date		Dr	Cr
31 Nov	Re-trial balance	70	

Eventually the error is uncovered and it is found that the error has been caused because:

(a) ABC's account was debited for £220 when the correct amount was £250; the correct amount was entered correctly in the sales account.

(b) The account for S Williams was credited with £80 when it should have been debited.

(c) Cash of £120 paid had not been entered in the cash account.

This shows that the error of £70 was actually the combination of three errors not just one! As some record of the correction of these errors should be kept, an explanation is usually given in the journal.

Journal

Date	Account	Dr	Cr
12 Dec	ABC	30	
	Suspense account		30
	Correction of error:		
	account undercast		
19 Dec	S Williams	160	
	Suspense account		160
	Correction of error: account		
	credited with £80 in error.		
23 Dec	Suspense account	120	
	Cash account		120
	Correction of error: entry not		
	made in cash account		

Note that with the error relating to S Williams it is necessary to debit the account with double the actual amount. This is because it is necessary to remove the existing credit balance of £80 and replace it with a debit balance of £80 (ie £80 + £80 = £160). The accounts would be amended to show:

Suspense account

Date		Dr	Cr
31 Nov	Re-Trial Balance	70	
12 Dec	ABC		30
19 Dec	S Williams		160
23 Dec	Cash account	120	
		190	190

ABC account

Date		Dr	Cr
1 Dec	Balance at this date	220	
12 Dec	Suspense account	30	

S Williams account

Date		Dr	Cr
1 Dec	Balance at this date		80
19 Dec	Suspense account	160	

Cash account

Date		Dr	Cr
1 Dec	Balance at this date*	450	
23 Dec	Suspense account		120

*The opening balance in the cash account has been invented. It is worthwhile considering the effect that these errors would have had on the profit of the firm if they had not been discovered. Obviously, ABC and S Williams are either debtors or creditors and therefore the mistakes in their accounts would mean that the incorrect figures would have been recorded in the balance sheet for debtors or creditors, but the entries in the sales and purchases accounts were correct. If the error had been in either the sales or purchases account, it would have affected the profit reported. Likewise, the error in the cash account would affect the balance sheet but would not have affected the profit reported.

Step 1

Suspense Account

	Dr	Cr
Re trial balance	10	

Step 2

Trial balance

	Dr	Cr
Premises	400	
Vehicles	200	
Suspense	10	
	1,500	1,500

Step 3

Balance sheet (extract)

Current assets	
suspense	£10

Figure 3.7 Trial balance fails to agree

Whilst suspense accounts are a useful tool in manual systems they should not strictly be necessary in a computerised system. The reason for this is that a suspense account is only really used when an entry has been made in one account only. This can easily occur in manual systems if the clerk's attention is distracted whilst halfway through recording a transaction. In a computerised system it requires only a very simple piece of programming to ensure that no transaction is processed until both the debit and credit entries have been made. A good program will refuse to continue any activity until the double-entry for a transaction has been completed.

Exercises

99   A firm has extracted a trial balance which does not agree. The credit side is £45,200 and the debit side £44,989. Create a suspense account for the difference at 1 May.

During the next few weeks the following errors were discovered:

(a) the total of the returns in book £350 had not been posted to the nominal ledger;

(b) a cheque for £75 paid to A Lu had not been recorded in the cash account;

(c) casual wages paid had been recorded as £10 in the cash account when the actual amount was £40;

(d) the balance for T Jones, a debtor, had been recorded as £13 instead of £31.

Enter the above in the suspense account and balance it off at the end of May to show the errors still undiscovered.

100   Is there still any need for control accounts and suspense accounts in a computerised system? If so, why are they necessary?

101   A firm has extracted a Trial Balance which does not agree, the Debit total is $97,540 and the Credit total is $98,320.

(a) Create a Suspense account for the difference at 1st March 1991.

During the next few weeks the following errors were discovered:

(i) A cheque for Motor expenses of $410 has not been entered in the Motor Expenses account.

(ii) The total of the Returns Out Daybook $120 had not been posted to the Nominal Ledger.

(iii) A cheque received from T. Woo for $85 had not been recorded in the Cash Book.

(iv) The Discounts Allowed to Creditors of $305 has not been recorded in the Creditors accounts.

(v) A payment made to R. Naik & Co for $210 has been recorded in their account as $120.

(vi) The Petty Cash float has been restored by transferring $10 but this has not been recorded in the Petty Cash account.

(a) Enter the above in the Suspense account and balance it off at the end of the month. (14 marks)

(b) One of the advantages of Computerised systems is that none of the above errors would have occurred. List 3 other advantages to be gained by computerising the Accounting system. (6 marks) (Mar 91)

102 (a) A firm has extracted a Trial Balance which does not agree. The credit side is $102,346 and the debit side is $101,760. Create a suspense account for the difference at 1st June.

During the next few weeks the following errors were discovered:

(i) The total of the Returns In daybook, $425, for the week ending 25th May had not been posted to the Nominal Ledger.

(ii) A cheque for $68 paid to K. Wong had not been recorded in the bank account.

(iii) Insurance paid of $30 had been recorded in the Cash account as £300.

(iv) The balance for T. Loo, a debtor, had been recorded as £120 instead of £210.

Enter the above in the suspense account and balance it off to show the amount still unaccounted for at the end of June.

(b) Suggest two reasons why controls and checks are arguably more important in the accounting function than in any other function.

103 (a) A firm has extracted a Trial balance which does not agree. The credit side is $20,100 and the debit side $21,150. Create a Suspense Account for the difference at 1st March 1990.

During the next few weeks the following errors were discovered:

(i) The total of the Returns Out book, $755, had not been posted to the Nominal Ledger.

(ii) Cash receipts of $35 had not been entered in the Sales Accounts.

(iii) A creditor was sent a cheque for $126 which has subsequently been returned by the bank as there were insufficient funds in the firm's account to clear the cheque. The bank account has been amended but not the creditor's account.

(iv) The balance for the Motor Vehicles account has been calculated as $2454 instead of $2545.

(v) A sale of goods of £200 was entered in the Sales Account as £300.

(vi) A sum of $25 was taken from Cash and used for Petty Cash, this had not been recorded in the Petty Cash account.

Enter the above in the Suspense Account and balance off at the end of March to show the amount relating to errors still undiscovered.

(b) The Suspense Account should not be needed in a Computerised Accounting system. Explain why. (Mar 90)

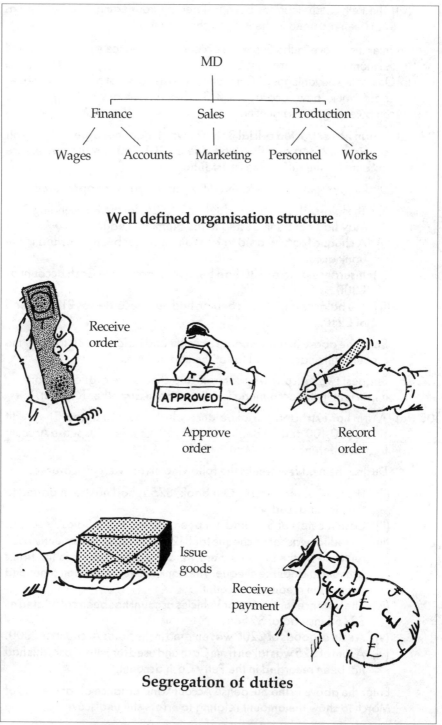

Figure 3.8 Internal controls - what to include (1)

3.4 OTHER INTERNAL CONTROLS

In order to reduce the incidence of mistakes and fraud, management often institutes other controls which should ensure that the accounts are more accurate. Examples of such controls are as follows:

Well-defined organisation structure: This will show how responsibility and authority are delegated and will enable employees to see what they are responsible for. A clearly defined structure ensures that each member of staff is aware of their exact responsibilities. For example, a firm had both a Purchasing Manager and a Production Manager but was continually running short of essential raw materials. Neither manager had a clear idea of their duties and consequently each manager assumed that the other was responsible for ordering raw materials.

Segregation of duties: No one person should fully record and process a transaction. This is very important as, if it is not applied, fraud can be quite simple to carry out. For example, a small firm employed one clerk who had full responsibility for maintaining accounting records, this clerk was systematically defrauding the company by creating accounts for fictitious suppliers, devising invoices for these non-existent suppliers and finally writing cheques to "settle" the accounts which were paid into the clerk's own bank account.

Physical controls: Access to assets and records should be restricted to authorised personnel only. This is also essential to prevent fraud. For example, company vehicles were left in a compound overnight and the car keys were left in the main office; junior staff could quite easily pocket a set of keys on leaving the office and frequently borrowed cars overnight without senior management's knowledge and without any form of insurance.

Authorisation and approval: All transactions over a certain set limit should be authorised by a responsible person. For instance all purchase orders over £500 should be checked by the manager. For example, a firm had segregated duties as much as was possible but did not limit the amount of any order which staff could send out. One clerk sent out an order for unwanted goods to the value of £200,000 from a firm which was run by his cousin. As there was no limit to the amount the clerk could approve the order was sent.

Personnel: Only well-motivated, competent personnel who possess integrity should be employed. For example, a trainee programmer taken on immediately after leaving college managed to deliberately delete all of the firm's files within one week. After he was sacked it was discovered that no attempt had been made to call for references or check his certificates. Subsequent research ascertained that he had never completed his course as he had been expelled from the college.

Supervision: The provision of supervisory procedures will help to reduce errors and fraud. For example, clerks in one office were required to perform fairly complex calculations but there was a long record of errors. A senior clerk was appointed as supervisor whose role was to check the calculations and errors were reduced dramatically.

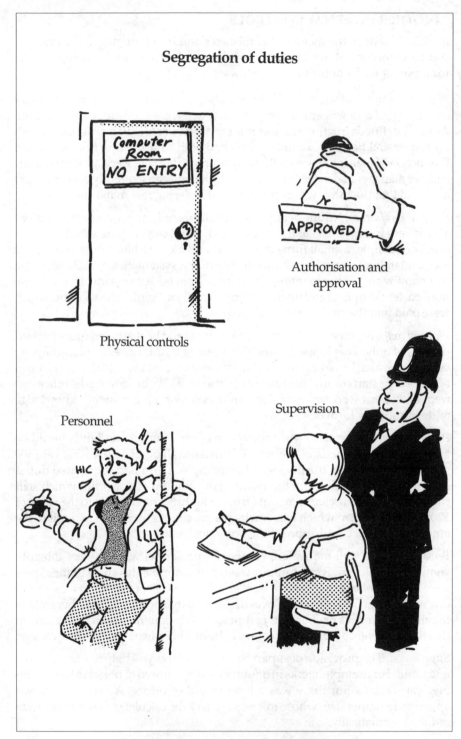

Figure 3.9 Internal controls - what to include (2)

Exercises

104 Suggest examples of suitable internal controls to cover the input and processing of data in a computerised accounting system.

105 Suggest some internal controls that would have prevented the problems in the following:

A disgruntled employee corrupted a firm's entire accounting records by inserting a car key into one of the disk drives. The firm subsequently went into liquidation as it had no records to work from. The employee said that he had done it because he was bored and wanted to see what would happen.

106 Which commonly used term describes each of the following INTERNAL CONTROLS:

(i) Verification checks on data to be processed.
(ii) Restricting access to computer rooms.
(iii) Labeling and indexing systems for data and program disks.
(iv) The use of "benchmarks" on new programs.
(v) No single person should both write and operate programs.
(vi) Preparing feasibility studies on proposed new systems.
(vii) Ensuring that the printouts contain the correct information.
(viii) Running both new and old systems concurrently.
(ix) Ensuring that programs cannot be altered without proper authority.
(x) Making sure that staff know how to use the new system.

(10 marks)
(Mar 91)

107 State which type of Internal Control is being applied in each of the following situations:

(i) One member of staff enters data onto the computer and another member of staff writes the program.
(ii) One member of staff is appointed as head of the computer room.
(iii) Printouts on computer usage and costs are provided for management.
(iv) All staff are thoroughly interviewed before appointment.
(v) All cheques have to be signed by two senior members of staff.
(vi) All invoices figures are double-checked before being entered in the records.
(vii) All staff know what their responsibilities are and who they report to.
(viii) All company vehicles are locked in a compound overnight.

(16 marks)
(Sep 91)

108 (a) Good library facilities are essential to prevent errors and omissions. Identify the features necessary for good file control. (14 marks)
   (b) The complete loss of all records is generally more likely in a computerised system than in a manual system, identify the problems that can be caused through the loss of Accounting records. (6 marks)
(Mar 92)

3.5   EXTERNAL CONTROLS AND AUDITING

As was explained at the beginning of this chapter, one very important reason for checking the accuracy of accounts is to provide reassurance to the owners, ie shareholders, that the accounts they have been shown are, in fact, a true record of the activities of the business. Obviously, the shareholders will not want to rely only on the word of their employees as this could be seen as an incentive to employees to commit fraud. Most nations now have laws which insist that the financial statements, ie accounts, of limited companies are checked by an independent person with a detailed knowledge of accounting; these people are known as auditors.

The auditor should be appointed by the shareholders and his job is to examine the accounting and associated records of a company and report on the accuracy of the accounts. This audit report is intended to provide reassurance not just to the firm's shareholders but to all interested parties. The auditor will also be expected to detect errors and fraud, although it is the duty of management to institute controls to prevent fraud and errors.

The duties of an auditor are to report on all the financial statements issued to shareholders, to carry out investigations in whether proper books of account have been kept and whether the final accounts are in agreement with these books. Most nations have given the auditor legal power to ensure that management and employees do not prevent him from uncovering errors and fraud. The auditor's rights include:

— the right of access to all books, accounts and source documents

— the right to require information and explanation from directors and employees

— the right to attend shareholders' meetings

In addition to the above, it is also usually a criminal offence to give false or misleading information to an auditor.

3.5.1   Audit evidence

The main work of the auditor consists of checking "evidence" that the accounting books and financial statements are correct. This mainly involves selecting samples of transactions and following the "audit trail". This is the sequence in which a transaction is recorded: for example a sales invoice may be the start of an audit trail which the auditor should be able to follow from the authorisation of the invoice to its recording in the sales daybook, then to the double-entry record in the sales and debtor's accounts in the nominal and sales ledgers, then to ensure that the transaction has been included in the total for sales and debtors in the trading account and balance sheet. It should also be possible to follow the trail in reverse by starting with the figure for sales in the trading account and working backwards through all of the accounting books right back to the original invoice.

Figure 3.10 Auditing

An audit trail for a sales transaction would be:

Sales Invoice
Sales Daybook
Sales Ledger (Debtors a/c) & Nominal Ledger (Sales a/c)
Trading & Profit/Loss Account (Total Sales figure)
Balance Sheet (Total Debtors figure)

All other source documents can be traced in a similar way. The auditor will check that the transaction has been correctly recorded at each stage and that all calculations are correct.

The audit trail will simply confirm that the accounting records are properly maintained but will not confirm that the records are correct. A major part of the auditor's work is checking that the records are safeguarded against fraud and errors. An audit trail will only demonstrate fraud if there is no source document at the beginning of the trail. Therefore the auditor will also need to use other evidence to confirm that the transactions actually took place and were not invented for fraudulent purposes.

Other sources of evidence that the auditor might use are:

— statements by independent third parties, eg asking the debtors if the balance owed by the firm is the same as that shown in the accounts

— physical inspection of assets to confirm their existence

— use of flowcharts to identify systems of work

— discussions with management and employees

— minutes of meetings

— reports from the mass media (eg reports on TV or in the papers)

In addition to checking the accuracy of the accounting records the auditor will examine the accounting systems and the methods of working to ensure that management have made every attempt to ensure that errors and fraud are eliminated. This will involve the auditor checking that the internal controls mentioned previously have been instituted by management. If these controls are being used within the firm, it means that the auditor will make sure that they are being adhered to, eg by checking whether purchase orders over £500 are being signed by a manager. If they are, then the auditor can place some reliance on them and concentrate on verifying the accuracy of accounting records.

Exercises

109A What evidence might an auditor use to confirm that the following transactions actually took place?

(i)   The purchase of a motor lorry
(ii) A debt of £2,000 owing to GSL & Co
(iii) A pay increase awarded to skilled workers

Figure 3.11 Additional problems (1)

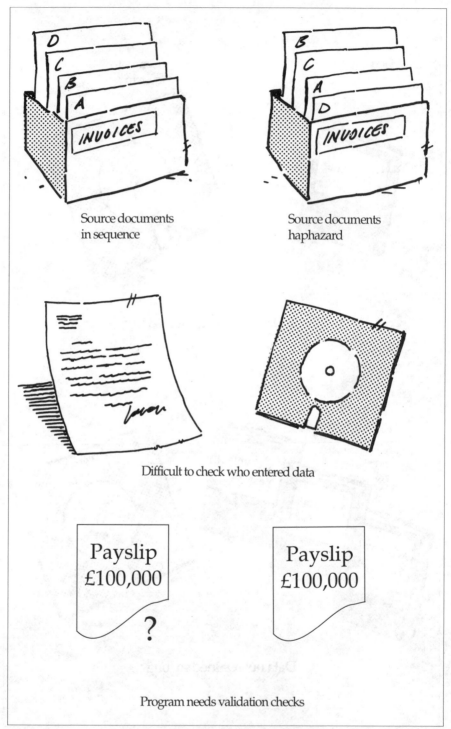

Source documents
in sequence

Source documents
haphazard

Difficult to check who entered data

Payslip
£100,000

?

Payslip
£100,000

Program needs validation checks

Figure 3.12 Additional problems (2)

(iv) A take-over bid for another firm
(v) An explosion at the firm's factory
(vi) The purchase of a spreadsheet package

110 What evidence might an auditor use to confirm the following?

(i) A decision by the Board of Directors to issue more shares.
(ii) A debt of $250 owed by ABC & Co.
(iii) The purchase of new factory premises in a neighbouring town.
(iv) The existence of standard procedures for processing data.
(v) The take-over of a very large competitor.
(vi) The purchase of a random sample of raw materials.

(6 marks)
(Mar 92)

111 Identify FIVE desirable features of an AUDIT TRAIL.

(Dec 89)

112 The Auditor will check the Accounts to ensure that any user can place reliance on their contents. Suggest five items that an Auditor may consider whilst gathering "Audit Evidence".

(Mar 90)

3.6 AUDITING COMPUTERISED SYSTEMS

Most firms of a reasonable size now use computers to process their accounting data. The advantages of computers are that they are more accurate, quicker and can produce more information than manual systems. However, for the auditor they produce additional problems in that:

— The audit trail can be lost as accounts for debtors/creditors held on disk may only contain details of the last three months' transactions. Previous transactions are often deleted to free storage space, but this means that the auditor can have difficulty in checking transactions that are more than three months old.

— The actual task of examining the data is not as straightforward. The auditor cannot simply pick up a disk and read the data as would be possible with documents in a manual system, but instead some knowledge of the firm's computer system will be essential in order for the auditor to display data on the VDU.

— The auditor would normally request the firm to keep all source documents so that he can test the audit trail. In a computerised system, the source document details will usually be sorted by the computer when they are entered, therefore firms will often not bother to sort the original documents into any order. The auditor's search for a particular document can then become a paper chase.

— The task of checking specific accounts has a whole new concept when the data is stored on disk. There may not be any means of finding out which member of staff entered the data.

— Fraud is potentially much easier, particularly if the program is not prepared with care. In a manual system a clerk would query fairly large transactions or large payslips, a computerised system may not!

Many firms would usually involve their auditor in discussions concerning the implementation of new systems to ensure that safeguards are included. Very large firms have taken this practice a step further and now make provision for auditors to run audit test packs and other computer-assisted audit programs on their system. This means that the auditor can use the same technology to perform the audit.

However, in most cases it will suffice for the accounting system to produce daily or weekly printouts that the auditor can use as the audit trail. The other considerations for both the auditor and management will be the effectiveness of internal controls over the computerised system. This is essential in order to minimise the risk of error and fraud.

Internal controls in a computerised system can be placed in three categories:

— *Administrative Controls* over the organisation of the data processing function;

— *Systems Development Controls* over the design and implementation of systems;

— *Procedural Controls* over the day to day running of the system.

Exercises

113   Identify four areas in which computerised accounts create problems for an auditor.

114   What is an audit trail?

3.6.1 Administrative controls

Division of duties

Management should ensure that there is a division of duties as in manual systems, so that no one person will be fully processing any transactions. This is achieved by the use of a clearly defined departmental structure as shown in Figure 3.13. This sort of structure will assist with the division of duties, particularly where there are separate sections for systems development and day to day running. The main reason for this division is to ensure that no one person is responsible for devising and operating systems as this is virtually an open invitation for fraud. However, the division should also ensure that the firm is not totally dependent upon one individual and that staff can be replaced fairly easily. For example, an firm had employed an Analyst/Programmer to set up a Computerised accounts system, when the system was set up the Analyst/Programmer was expected to input all data. Not unnaturally the individual concerned was somewhat frustrated with merely keying in data and left some months later. The firm then discovered that an urgent replacement was needed as no-one else within the firm knew how to operate the system.

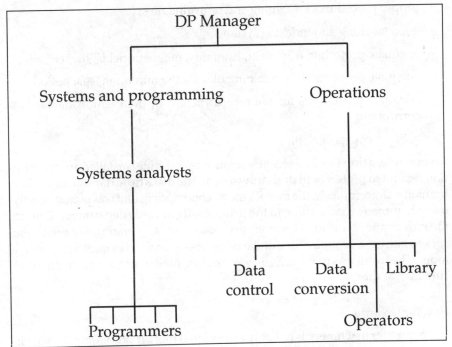

Figure 3.13 Administrative controls

Operation controls

These are essential for ascertaining what the computer and the employees have been doing. They will include such practices as:

— rotation of shift duties;

— duty logs;

— manual of operating instructions;

— controls on attendance times;

— computer log.

For example, a programmer manipulated programs and files in a large organisation through "trapdoors"; these activities merely required a few minutes at the terminal each week and this enabled him to defraud the firm of many thousands of pounds. He remained undetected as there was no procedure for checking on the use of computer time.

File controls

Poor library facilities will lead to errors and omissions. The features necessary for good file control are:

— a skilled technician;

— proper procedures for issuing and returning files;

— good labelling and indexing systems;

— adequate protection from dust, humidity, magnetic fields, fire, etc;

— adequate procedures for retaining files for the minimum legal period;

— adequate procedures for file reconstruction in the event of damage or corruption;

— back-up copies of all files.

For example, a firm that had recently acquired a computer installed an air conditioning unit to protect both the hardware and the disks from damage caused by humidity. Unfortunately, the inlet for the air conditioning unit was placed directly over an unmade road leading to the firm's goods inwards department. During the next summer this road became very dusty and large amounts of dust were sucked into the air conditioning unit which subsequently fed it into the computer room. The result was that many disks were corrupted by a thin layer of dust that spread over them.

Hardware security

The computer machinery is not only an essential tool for processing data but is also a valuable fixed asset in its own right. Managers would not allow workers free use of company vehicles, nor should they allow them free access to computer machinery for similar reasons.

Site security can be achieved by:

— restricting access to sensitive areas, eg CPU room and library;

— fire precautions and a controlled environment;

— adequate insurance for equipment;

— stand-by arrangements for when the computer breaks down.

For example, a large organisation decided that the best place to site its computer hardware would be the basement of the Head Office as this area was easy to make secure and was undesirable as normal office accomodation. Unfortuately, one night the central heating system broke down and the basement was flooded, resulting in irreparable damage to the computer.

3.6.2 Systems development controls

The necessary controls for systems development come under the following headings:

Standardisation

This is the use of standards laid down by management for the design and development of the system. It should include the documentation of the system, including

Figure 3.14 Systems development controls

flowcharts. Apart from other benefits, it should enable the auditor to see how the system is working. For example, a firm had invested a very large sum of money in designing a very powerful on-line order system using the most advanced computer technology, the systems design team convinced senior management that "old-style" controls such as record counts, file controls and audit trails were unneccessary due to the advanced technology being used. However, within a few months of operation it was discovered that numerous problems were arising that could not be solved without normal controls. The cost of putting these controls into the system increased costs by another $400,000

Managerial Involvement

This entails the preparation of feasibility studies, use of budgets for capital and revenue expenditure, and regular evaluation of performance to ensure that each project is viable and cost effective. For example, the computing department of a multi-national organsation decided that it was possible to create one enormous database for storing data from the many hundreds of subsidiaries within the group. A team was established to design a suitable database, and spent nearly two years on the project before coming to the conclusion that the current state of technology prevented such a database from being a viable proposition. At no time were senior management informed of the project and when its existence was discovered a number of senior computing staff were dismissed.

Testing and trials

The thorough testing of programs before they become operational: this should also involve the use of "benchmarks" to determine the optimum time taken for a program. Such benchmarks may be of use to an auditor in checking whether programs have subsequently been tampered with. For example, a new program had just been devised by an organisation and was put on-line immediately with no major trials. Within two months it was apparent that the program contained major flaws and it took 12 months for the program and the problems it caused to be put right.

Training

Training should be provided for staff who will be using the program to ensure that there is a reduction in the risk of errors. For example, a firm bought some "off the shelf" software for use in its accounts department, the supplier also offered one weeks training but the firm decided that it could only afford to pay for three days of training. Accounts staff were sent on the course and on their return set about operating the new package. Within a few days it was evident that there were many problems as staff realised that they had only received training on how to use roughly half of the package.

Conversion

This is the practice of running both old and new systems concurrently so that results can be validated. For example, a firm had devised a new program and given

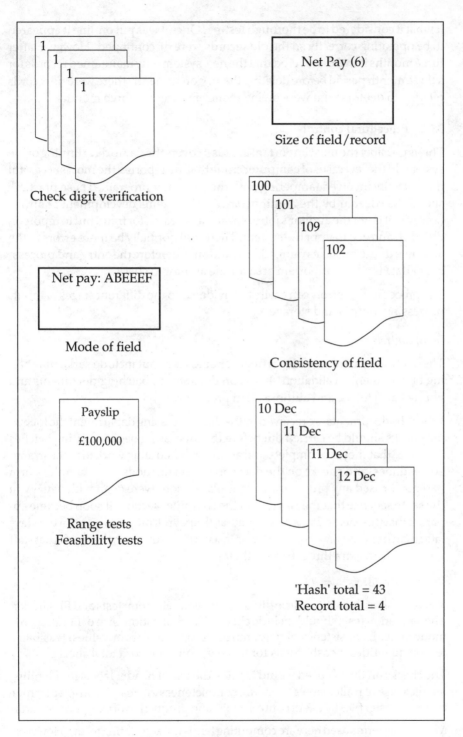

Figure 3.15 Processing controls

it what it considered to be thorough testing. Once it was put on-line it appeared to be operating correctly so the old records were discontinued. However, after three months it was discovered that the new system only maintained records for a three month period before deleting them. Consequently there were no records relating to debtors who were owing money in excess of three months.

3.6.3   Procedural controls

This is possibly the most important area as it covers the day to day running of the system. In the few cases of computer crime that are reported the most successful have usually involved tampering with the computer program. These practices should be covered by the administrative and systems development controls; however, it is not the auditor's job to specifically search for fraud but to report on the truth and accuracy of the system. There will normally be more errors in the accounts due to mistakes rather than fraud and therefore the entry and processing of data is a very important area for the auditor to check.

The procedural controls can easily be divided into the different stages of input, processing, output and storage:

Input controls

The controls that the user department should carry out include serial numbering of documents, validation checks on documents, batching documents and noting batch totals, and authorisation procedures.

When the documents are received by the data processing department the following checks should be carried out before the processing begins: vetting batches to ensure that they are complete and accurate, scheduling work to meet arranged deadlines, and checks on the data conversion methods. For example, a firm had not devised any proper input controls and jobs were dealt with usually in the same seqence that they arrived at the computer section, it soon became apparent that this method was inadequate as the payroll program was run two days later than it should have been on two consecutive weeks with the result that staff had to wait an extra three days for their pay.

Processing controls

The controls at this stage will be divided between validation tests and file checks. The validation tests should include check digit verification, size of field/record, mode of field, consistency of field, range test on numbers or values, feasibility test on quantities, "hash" totals for batches, control/record total checks.

The checks on the file used would include the use of header labels for identifying files, use of trailer labels to ensure completeness of "read", arithmetic proof totals of master files by use of control totals, and production of exception reports.

Many of the terms used here are computing terms not accounting terms. However, it should be obvious that auditors now require a knowledge of computing as well as accounting in order to carry out proper audits.

Output controls

The output from processing will also require some controls, which involve the vetting of output to ensure that input and output are consistent, whether the output needs some action/amendment by the user department, or whether the output is complete. For example, an accountant within a firm had not been invited to participate in the design of the accounting system; his main job each month was to devise a trial balance from the accounting records. At the end of each month the computer section supplied him with 200 pages of printouts showing full details of every transaction. The accountant was continually moaning that what had once been a one day a month job now took him all month.

Storage controls

The controls over storage are very important to ensure that no one can make unauthorised amendments to the program file or accidentally (or deliberately) destroy the master file. Program file security will involve taking steps to ensure that no programs can be altered without authority and that all changes are fully documented. Back-up copies of the program file should be kept in a secure place. All additions, amendments and deletions to standing data in the master file must have the necessary authority and be fully documented. Security copies of the master file are essential to safeguard against damage or corruption.

Most accounting packages that are purchased do include a facility for making back-up copies of master files but it is unfortunately a fairly common practice, particularly in smaller firms, to ignore this facility. Despite the publicity given for cases involving computer fraud, to the author's knowledge no such fraud has resulted in firms going out of business. However, there are numerous examples of firms, particularly in the USA, that have been forced to cease trading because their computer files have been corrupted and they did not have back-up copies. For example, a business had recently acquired its first microcomputers and the typists were all sent on training courses to learn how to use the word processor. Unfortunately the training course concentrated on the word processing package that they were going to use and neglected to provide an introduction to computers. Consequently, all of the typing staff stored all data on the hard disks on their machines without making a back-up copy on floppy disk. This practice was only discovered after an electrical storm caused power surges which corrupted the data held on nearly 50% of the machines. As the typists had not kept hard copies nearly all correspondence with customers/suppliers from the previous three months was lost.

The role of the auditor in computerised accounting systems is still the same as that of an auditor in a manual system: to report on the truth and fairness of the accounts. This will involve checking the accuracy of records and examining the effectiveness of the firm's internal controls. The main difference in a computerised system is that new controls are needed, but some controls can be computerised.

Exercises

115   Suggest five items of audit evidence that the auditor could use to vouch for the accuracy of accounts.

116   What sort of administrative controls would an auditor expect to see in a computerised accounting system?

117   A computer programmer wrote a payroll program and included an unauthorised section whereby 10p or 20p per week was added on to each employee's tax bill. On the last week of the tax year every employee had overpaid tax by £5-£10. The books were balanced by refunding all of this cash to the programmer's salary. Therefore the tax paid by all employees was correct.

The programmer was sacked when the fraud was eventually discovered but whilst working his month's notice he succeeded in:

(a) programming the computer so that every employee received a bonus of £1,000 on the programmer's last day;

(b) entering a subroutine into the accounts program so that exactly two years after he left all financial records were deleted.

What controls could the firm have used to prevent each of these actions from happening?

118   A firm that was involved in work for the nuclear weapons industry had its offices broken into and a double-barrel shotgun was fired at the mainframe computer at very close range. The damage to the computer was irreparable. A pressure group campaigning against nuclear weapons claimed responsibility for the action.

What action could the firm have taken to avoid the above and any disruption to work?

119   (a) *Internal Controls* are essential in both Computerised and Manual Accounting systems to ensure that receipts of Cash and Cheques are properly accounted for. Describe six commonly used Internal controls.
(b) Another type of Control is *"External Control"*. Which person would normally be appointed to oversee this type of control?

(Dec 88)

120   Describe the controls that should be applied in Systems Development as applied to Computerised Accounting systems.

(Dec 88)

121   Define the term "audit trail".

(Jun 88)

122   What problems would be caused by the following and what audit and control procedures are needed to ensure that the business will not suffer:
(i) Machine breakdown
(ii) Loss of file data

(iii) Deliberate sabotage of machinery

(iv) Unauthorised users accessing the system

(v) Resignation of the firm's only programmer

(Jun 88)

123 A firm has recently faced the following problems:

(a) An employee with his own home computer had copied a game program onto the firm's main computer. The firm's main computer has since developed a *computer virus.*

(b) The *computer virus* has corrupted the main accounts program. The firm do have a back-up but are unable to find where they left the disk.

(c) Another firm within the same group uses a similar accounting program which could be amended to work for this firm. They have supplied a copy of this on disk but your programmer is having difficulty in amending it as there is no other documentation available.

(d) The program is eventually amended but is prone to *crashing.* Also, there are occasions when calculations performed have resulted in clearly incorrect answers.

Suggest how each of the above incidents could have been avoided.

(Sept 89)

124 Identify and describe the *procedural controls* that are required for adequate *internal control* of a computerised accounting system.

(Sept 89)

125 A firm is discussing with its bankers the introduction of *electronic funds transfer* (EFT) as a means of improving efficiency. The main proposals are to make payments to suppliers and staff via the purchase ledger and payroll programs respectively.

(a) Suggest *six types of control procedure*, which would be needed to protect the new system against illegal access and fraud and explain *briefly* how each would be applied.

(Dec 89)

3.7 COMPUTER ASSISTED AUDIT TECHNIQUES

Due to the now widespread use of computers by firms as a means of processing accounting data, many auditors realise that the most effective means of testing such systems is to use the accounts program itself.

A fairly wide range of Computer Assisted Audit Technique (CAAT) programs are available for auditors to use with a wide variety of accounting programs. There are two main methods by which accounting data can be assessed by these CAAT packs.

Dead tests

This uses a simple program and the auditor selects a sample of data that has already been processed by the firm's computer program. The same data is fed through the CAAT pack and the solution compared to the solution produced by the firm's program.

Live tests

These use more complicated CAAT programs which can be linked to the firm's program as an extra routine. The auditor can feed in test data with a special code, which is processed as real data would be except that the results are transferred to a test file on the CAAT pack.

The auditor should calculate what the results/postings of this data should have been and compare it with the actual results produced by the system.

A number of large software houses now provide utility programs to accompany their accounting software. These programs will often include programs written for auditors to use. The use of "off-the shelf" accounting packages will simplify the auditors' job to a certain degree, as it should only be necessary to check the transactions and not the program itself, if the package is a well established one.

4   Costing

INTRODUCTION

Now we consider the other main area of accounting — that of cost accounting. This is used, not for record-keeping or calculating profit, but for predicting future costs and profits. The section covers the more commonly used techniques of Cost Accounting and is of relevance as many organisations now "integrate" their financial and cost accounting systems — so computer staff may need to have a knowledge of both areas. Also you may eventually become the head of a computing department and you will then be expected to produce costing information relating to your department, especially in relation to budgets.

OBJECTIVES

At the end of this section you should able to:

- demonstrate the cost accounting techniques for calculating and controlling the cost of materials, labour and overheads
- apply cost accounting techniques to ascertain the cost of specific jobs, and devise operating statements
- apply the techniques used for performing break-even analysis, and interpret the results
- explain the importance of, and prepare, budgets for different departments and the organisation as a whole
- calculate simple variances, and interpret the results
- apply standard costing and marginal costing techniques, and show their importance in decision-making.

4.1   COST ACCOUNTING

All of the accounting subjects we have discussed so far have been developed with one purpose in mind: to record financial transactions correctly so that interested parties can rely on the contents of the accounting statements.

One aspect of a firm's financial situation that all interested parties would like to know is what will the firm's future profits be like. The accounts mentioned so far are called "financial accounting" and they deal with what has already happened. But many firms attempt to predict what their future profits will be and this uses the principles of cost, or management, accounting.

At first sight, it would seem that other interested parties such as banks and shareholders would be interested in seeing the figures that the firm produces using these cost accounting principles. Limited companies are obliged by law to publish their financial accounts and all other firms have to prepare such accounts, if only for the taxation authorities. But the preparation of cost accounting records is entirely voluntary and so not all firms bother to prepare them. Those firms that do use such methods do not have to publish their results: the main reason for preparing them is to enable management to make better decisions (hence the term management accounting).

Clearly, as these accounts deal with the future it would be extremely unwise for anyone to insist that firms should publish their cost accounts; the accuracy of financial accounts can be checked by auditors, but even auditors cannot predict the future!

The preparation of cost accounts should enable management to make more informed decisions such as to the effects of increasing/decreasing prices, how to cut costs, whether to introduce new products, how to calculate the cost of products more accurately, etc. This chapter will examine some of the more common cost accounting practices, but you should be aware of the fact that there are many other facets to this subject that are outside the scope of this book.

4.2   CLASSIFYING COSTS

As cost accounting will attempt to predict what costs will be in the future if production is increased or decreased, so it is first necessary to identify how costs "behave" under increases in production. Many large firms use computers to process their cost accounts, and understanding how costs behave will also benefit the computer programmer.

4.2.1   Classifications

Variable costs

These are costs that will increase in direct proportion to the number of units produced. For example, if the cost of leather in one pair of shoes is £5 then the cost of leather for two pairs is £10, for one hundred pairs £500 and so on. The relationship between variable costs and production is shown on a graph in Figure 4.1.

Variable costs are usually only found in the costs of manufacture and are essentially the same as "direct" and "product" costs. All three refer to the actual cost of producing one unit of production and are normally only found in the costs of raw materials, the labour cost of employees making the product (not stores or foremen), and direct expenses. Direct expenses are quite rare in practice and are restricted to such items as patent and royalty fees which are paid for each item manufactured. The computer industry has some examples of direct expenses in that most microcomputers are sold with an operating system which has been designed by a software house. The manufacturer will often have to pay a royalty to the software house for each computer produced. Other direct expenses can be the cost of hiring special machinery in order to make a batch of products.

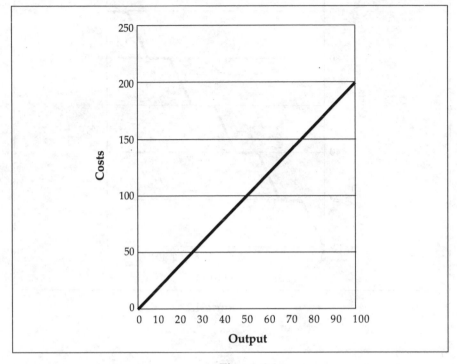

Figure 4.1

Semi-variable costs

These costs are said to have a relationship with the number of units produced, but not in direct proportion to them. These costs will usually increase in stages, for example a firm may only need one foreman every five workers, but as production increases so do the numbers of workers. When another five workers have been taken on then a new foreman is needed, but if only three workers are taken on, then the existing foreman would have to cope with supervising a larger group of workers.

On the other hand, semi-variable costs can increase in proportion to sales or production up to a certain point and then increase at a slightly different rate. Examples of this type of semi-variable cost would be salesmen's commission or the discounts received on the purchase of raw materials. Shown graphically semi-variable costs would look like Figure 4.2.

In reality the majority of costs are semi-variable if only to a small degree; however, they are notoriously difficult to estimate, so most firms prefer to designate them as either variable or fixed costs.

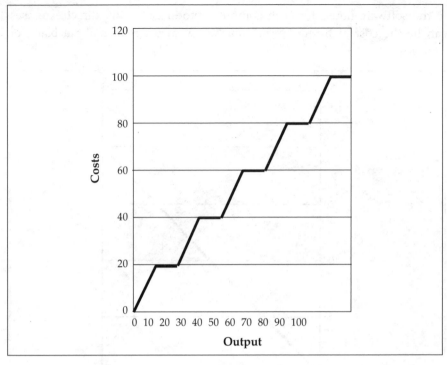

Figure 4.2

Fixed costs

These are costs which have no relationship with production and are generally payable at the same amount whether the firm makes no products or millions of products. Examples are rent, rates, salaries, insurance. Items such as lighting and heating, depreciation, motor expenses and postage, which strictly speaking are semi- variable costs, are normally treated as being fixed as their relationship with production is too complicated to calculate accurately. The graphical representation of fixed costs is seen in Figure 4.3

Fixed costs are the same as "indirect" and "period" costs, in that they have no relationship with production and the charge is frequently calculated over a period (eg rent, rates) rather than the amount of production. Also, any increases or decreases in production will not have a direct effect on these costs.

4.3   THE IMPLICATIONS FOR PROGRAMMING

A knowledge of how costs behave is useful for systems analysts and programmers because there is an increasing use of computers for cost accounting purposes, and an understanding of the behaviour of costs can assist the programmer in devising programs to process costing data. As explained above most firms will classify all costs as either variable (direct) or fixed (indirect). The inclusion

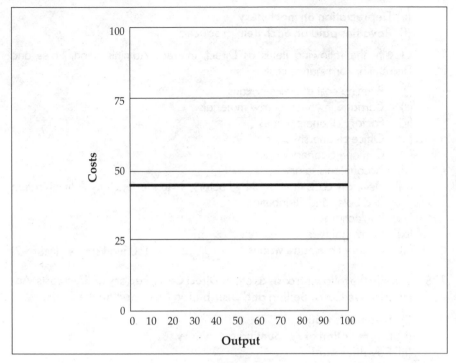

Figure 4.3

of such variables in a computer program should be straightforward in that variable costs could be programmed as V and production in units as P. Therefore a simple instruction such as T = P x V (where T = total variable costs) will ensure that any increases in production create a corresponding increase in variable costs.

Fixed costs will remain constant and again a simple instruction such as F = 2,000 will ensure that fixed costs of £2,000 are included in any future calculations.

Semi-variable costs are often classified as fixed or variable in manual systems as the exact variability is often difficult to define and calculate. In a computerised system this difficulty may not be such a problem. It might be possible to include a matrix or table into the program so that the semi-variable costs can be extracted at any level of production.

Exercises

Questions followed by A do not have answers supplied.

126 State whether the following items are variable, semi-variable or fixed costs:

(a) Foremen's wages
(b) Cost of raw materials
(c) Rent
(d) Cost of wages for machine operators

(e) Depreciation on machinery

(f) Royalties paid on each item produced

127   Classify the following items as Direct, Indirect, Administration, Sales and Distribution, or Finance costs:

(i)   Running cost of Delivery vans

(ii)   Carriage inwards on raw materials

(iii)   Factory cleaners wages

(iv)   Office cleaners wages

(v)   Canteen cleaners wages

(vi)   Accountants salary

(vii) Electricity costs (half used by Factory, 1 quarter each by Administration and Sales and Distribution)

(viii) Bank charges

(ix)   Copyright fees

(x)   Factory Foreman's wages   (10 marks)   (Mar 92)

128   Classify the following costs as either Direct Costs, Factory Indirect costs, Administrative Costs, Selling and Distribution Costs or Finance Costs:

(i) Foremen's wages

(ii) Depreciation of Accounting machinery

(iii) Royalties paid

(iv) Rent of shop

(v) Works manager's salary   (Dec 88)

129A A company has identified the following costs at two levels of output. Complete the table to show the costs for the other levels of output:

	1,000 £	2,000 £	3,000 £	4,000 £
Materials	2,000	4,000		
Machine Operators	4,000	8,000		
Insurance	1,500	1,500		
Rates	700	700		
Depreciation	300	400		
Power	500	550	575	
Carriage In	100	120		
Royalties	100	200		
Storekeepers wages	220	220	440	
Office salaries	600	600		
Advertising	50	60	80	
TOTAL COSTS:	10,070	16,350		
COST PER PRODUCT:	£10.07	£8.17		

4.4   THE OPERATING STATEMENT

Cost accounting is concerned with the future and therefore it cannot produce a proper profit and loss account; however, the figures produced by cost accounting should enable all relevant accounts to be prepared. In order to differentiate the costing profit and loss account from the real profit and loss account, it is known as an operating statement and normally has the following layout, shown in Figure 4.4.

		£
Revenue		100,000
Direct materials		25,000
Direct labour		30,000
Direct expenses		500
Prime cost		55,500
Indirect labour		4,000
Indirect materials		500
Depreciation costs (machinery)		1,000
Lighting and heating		750
Rent and rates		2,250
Manufacturing cost		64,000
Administration costs		
Wages and salaries	15,000	
Rent and rates	1,000	
Lighting and heating	500	
Depreciation (equipment)	750	17,250
Sales and distribution costs		
Commission	3,000	
Advertising	1,250	
Depreciation (delivery vans)	1,000	
Depreciation (shop fittings)	500	5,250
Finance costs		
Audit fees	250	
Bank interest	750	1,000
Total costs		87,500
Profit		12,500

Figure 4.4

The most obvious difference is that a normal profit and loss account would show items by nature of expenditure by function (eg sales and distribution). This style has, in fact, been adopted in the financial accounts of many firms, particularly limited companies.

Prime cost refers to the actual direct costs of making the product and is very important as it only includes variable costs. The significance of the prime cost will become apparent later in the chapter.

As the operating statement is for internal use only, the style of presentation is not so important and some firms would show the above statement simply as:

	£
Revenue	100,000
Direct materials	25,000
Direct labour	30,000
Direct expenses	500
Prime cost	55,500
Manufacturing costs	64,000
Administration costs	17,250
Sales and distribution costs	5,250
Finance costs	1,000
Total costs	87,500
Profit	12,500

Figure 4.5

The most important costs for management will be the cost of materials, labour (especially direct labour) and overheads. Overheads is the name given to the various expenses incurred in the cost of manufacture and other functions. The object of cost accounting is to ensure that the firm knows exactly how much it costs to make its product. This is invariably far more complicated than it sounds!

The operating statement is often expanded to show more information. One of the disadvantages of financial accounting is that it does not show the profit made by each product (not that shareholders would be particularly interested anyway); however, such information would obviously be useful for management. The operating statement shown previously may be broken down by management to show the following information:

Product	Boots	Shoes	Bags	Total
	£	£	£	£
Revenue	10,000	75,000	15,000	100,000
Direct materials	2,000	22,000	1,000	25,000
Direct labour	4,000	24,000	2,000	30,000
Direct expenses		500		500
Prime cost	6,000	46,500	3,000	55,500
Other manufacturing costs				8,500
Administration costs				17,250
Sales and distribution costs				5,250
Finance costs				1,000
Total costs				87,500
Profit				12,500

Figure 4.6

Notice that only the direct (variable) costs are deducted from the revenue of each product. The reason for this is that the other costs are indirect, ie not related directly to the product, and are also fixed, so would be paid at the same amount regardless of how many items of each product were made or sold.

From the table it is possible to calculate that the gross profit earned by the different products is £4,000 for boots, £29,000 for shoes and £12,000 for bags. However, as bags are the most profitable the firm should try to increase the sales of bags rather than shoes.

The above example is just one of the ways in which cost accounting can provide information. What it can also do is provide more accurate costs for products. The costs involved in products fall into three categories:

— the cost of raw materials
— the cost of direct labour
— the cost of overheads (indirect expenses).

All products will incur some of the above costs and the job of the cost accountant is to find out what the cost for each category is. Each category has its own peculiarities, and costing methods have been devised to enable cost accountants to calculate the costs for each category.

Exercises

130 Draw up the operating statement for the following:

	$	$
Revenue		221,350
Raw materials purchased		56,800
Carriage inwards		1,200
Patent fees		2,300
Depreciation		
Plant and machinery	3,500	
Office equipment	1,500	
Delivery vans	2,500	
Shop fittings	1,000	8,500
Audit fees		2,000
Advertising		12,000
Wages and salaries		
Manufacturing wages	45,500	
Foremen's wages	12,200	
Office salaries	27,780	
Salesmen's salaries	12,450	97,930
Lighting and heating		
Factory	5,050	
Offices	3,100	
Shop	2,150	10,300
Rent and rates		
Factory	7,350	

Offices	2,100	
Shop	1,550	11,000

131 Draw up the operating statement from the following figures:

	£	£
Purchases of raw materials		64,500
Wages and salaries		
Direct labour	42,000	
Factory foremen	14,000	
Office staff	24,500	
Salesmen	19,000	99,500
Carriage inwards		350
Returns out		980
Hire of special machinery		2,100
Sales		221,300
Rent and rates		8,000
Lighting and heating		5,000
Depreciation		
Factory machinery	2,000	
Office equipment	1,300	
Delivery vans	4,010	
Shop fittings	890	8,200
Insurance		600
Loan interest		3,120
Royalties		10,562

132 Draw up an OPERATING STATEMENT from the following budgeted figures using appropriate headings:

	$
Revenue	185,900
Materials:	
Direct Materials	13,000
Indirect Materials	12,000
Wages and Salaries:	
Direct Labour	40,000
Factory Foremen	16,000
Office Staff	14,000
Salesmen	13,000
Carriage Inwards on Direct Materials	500
Royalties	1,000
Lighting and Heating	5,000
Rent and Rates	8,000
Advertising	2,500
Depreciation:	
Factory Machinery	3,000
Office Equipment	1,000
Shop Fittings	2,000

NOTES

(i) Rent and Rates are divided 50% to the factory, 25% to offices and 25% to shop.

(ii) Lighting and Heating are divided $2,000 to factory and the balance equally between offices and shop.

(Sep 88)

4.5 THE COST OF RAW MATERIALS

Finding the cost of raw materials included in a product would appear to be quite simple. If the quantity of raw materials included is known, then this quantity is multiplied by the cost of the materials to find the cost for the product. For example, if a pair of trousers requires 2 metres of cotton and cotton costs the firm £2 per metre then the cost of materials for one pair of trousers is £4:

$$2 \text{ metres} \times £2 \text{ per metre} = £4$$

This is the method used to calculate raw material costs but in practice it can become more complicated as the cost of raw materials per metre is not always known.

Most firms will keep stocks of raw materials to ensure that workers never have to stop production and that sales are not lost through having no finished goods ready to sell. This means that firms are continually buying new stocks of raw materials to replace those issued to the factory floor. The problem arises in that the cost of raw materials bought will continually be rising because of inflation and other factors. Therefore the cost of material per metre in January may be £2 but by the following December it may be £3. The stores section will have to notify the factory how much the raw materials they are using actually cost. In some industries it will be possible to work out the cost of each batch of materials issued from stores because they can be separately marked, but this will not be possible with materials such as nuts and bolts or liquids which are usually just emptied into large containers. Different methods have been developed for issuing and recording raw materials to cater for the nature of the materials and variations in price.

4.5.1 Methods used

First in, first out (FIFO)

This method is the most logical approach and states that the first stock to be received, ie the oldest, should be the first to be issued. In many industries this is the only practical method of issuing stock as the raw materials are likely to deteriorate if kept too long, eg greengrocer's.

It should be remembered with all of these methods that the prime concern from the cost accountant's point of view is to put a price on materials used and that these methods are primarily accounting "conventions". That means that a firm might not actually issue the oldest stock first but is only assuming that this is so for accounting purposes. In reality if the raw material is paint which is stored in a vat it is impossible to say whether the oldest or newest stock is used first.

To illustrate how the cost of materials is calculated under the FIFO method the following figures are used:

Date	Receipts	Cost (each)	Date	Issues
January	20	£2.00	February	5
March	5	£2.20	April	15
June	10	£2.50	August	4
September	15	£2.60	October	5
			November	10
			December	3

These entries would be entered on a Stock Record card as shown below in Figure 4.7:

Date	Receipts			Issues			Balance		
	Units	£	£	Units	£	£	Units	£	£
Jan	20	2.00	40.00				20	2.00	40.00
Feb				5	2.00	10.00	15	2.00	30.00
March	5	2.20	11.00				15	2.00	30.00
							5	2.20	11.00
							20		41.00
April				15	2.00	30.00	5	2.20	11.00
June	10	2.50	25.00				5	2.20	11.00
							10	2.50	25.00
							15		36.00
Aug				4	2.20	8.80	1	2.20	2.20
							10	2.50	25.00
							11		27.20
Sept	15	2.60	39.00				1	2.20	2.20
							10	2.50	25.00
							15	2.60	39.00
							26		66.20
Oct				1	2.20	2.20	6	2.50	15.00
				4	2.50	10.00	15	2.60	39.00
							21		54.00
Nov				6	2.50	15.00	11	2.60	28.60
				4	2.60	10.40			
Dec				3	2.60	7.80	8	2.60	20.80

Figure 4.7

With this method the cost accountant is able to say what the cost of materials is for each product made by transferring the cost from this sheet onto a job card which is attached to each item made.

This method can also be used to calculate the gross profit on each item. If the products are sold for £6.00 each then the profit can be calculated thus:

	£
Sales (42 units at £6.00)	252.00
Cost of sales (total of issues)	94.20
Gross profit	157.80

Last in, first out (LIFO)

This method is the opposite to FIFO and involves recording the last goods received, ie the newest, as being the first to be used. This method would be used where materials are stored in bins or vats, but once again there is nothing to stop firms from issuing the oldest stock first and using this method to record issues, as these methods are only accounting conventions.

Using the same figures as above, the method of calculation is as shown in Figure 4.8.

Date	Receipts			Issues			Balance		
	Units	£	£	Units	£	£	Units	£	£
Jan	20	2.00	40.00				20	2.00	40.00
Feb				5	2.00	10.00	15	2.00	30.00
March	5	2.20	11.00				15	2.00	30.00
							5	2.00	11.00
							20		41.00
April				5	2.20	11.00			
				10	2.00	20.00	5	2.00	10.00
June	10	2.50	25.00				5	2.00	10.00
							10	2.50	25.00
							15		35.00
Aug				4	2.50	10.00	5	2.00	10.00
							6	2.50	15.00
							11		25.00
Sept	15	2.60	39.00				5	2.00	10.00
							6	2.50	15.00
							15	2.60	39.00
							26		64.00
Oct				5	2.60	13.00	5	2.00	15.00
							6	2.50	15.00
							10	2.60	26.00
							21		51.00
Nov				10	2.60	26.00	5	2.00	10.00
							6	2.50	15.00
							11		25.00
Dec				3	2.50	7.50	5	2.00	10.00
							3	2.50	7.50
							8		17.50

Figure 4.8

With this method the gross profit calculation would be:

	£
Sales (42 units at £6.00)	252.00
Cost of sales (total of issues)	97.50
Gross profit	154.40

This figure of profit is different from that using FIFO, which is normally the case. Firms have to decide which method to use and then keep to just the one method, as continually changing methods will mean that the profit figures produced will be meaningless. In times of rising prices, the FIFO method will produce the largest profits, LIFO will produce the largest profits when prices are falling.

Average cost (AVCO)

The other commonly used method is to find the average cost of goods received and use this value to price materials issued. This method is only an accounting convention and obviously cannot be used as a practical means of controlling raw materials.

Date	Receipts			Issues			Balance Average Cost		
	Units	£	£	Units	£	£	Units	£	£
Jan	20	2.00	40.00				20	40.00	2.00
Feb				5	2.00	10.00	15	30.00	2.00
March	5	2.20	11.00				20	41.00	2.05
April				15	2.05	30.75	5	10.25	2.05
June	10		2.50 25.00				15	35.25	2.35
Aug				4	2.35	9.40	11	25.85	2.35
Sept	15	2.60	39.00				26	64.85	2.494
Oct				5	2.494	12.47	21	52.38	2.494
Nov				10	2.494	24.94	11	27.44	2.494
Dec				3	2.494	7.48	8	19.96	2.494

Figure 4.9

With this method the gross profit calculation would be:

	£
Sales (42 units at £6.00)	252.00
Cost of sales (issues)	95.04
Gross profit	156.96

Thus it can be seen that each of the three methods of accounting for raw materials will result in different profits being made. This explains why the consistency convention mentioned in Part 1 is so important.

Perpetual or periodic inventory

The normal assumption with stock valuation methods is that items of stock issued and received are recorded at the time of issue or receipt. This is known as the "perpetual inventory" method as stock records are continually (perpetually) being maintained and updated. This method will generally be used if a computer system is in operation, but firms still keeping manual records may consider this method to be too long-winded. As such records form part of cost accounting, they are not a legal requirement and will only be kept if the firm considers that the information gathered is worthwhile. Consequently, some firms will not feel that the effort required in keeping perpetual records of stock can be justified by the benefits derived from such records.

Periodic inventory is a much quicker and simpler way of maintaining details of stock without having to continually update stock records. With the periodic inventory method, the exact date of receipt or issue is irrelevant and only totals issued and received are considered. Therefore the Last In First Out method will assume that the last goods received during the year are the first to be issued, despite the fact that there may clearly have been a substantial number of issues earlier in the year. This apparent discrepancy between what actually happens and the accounting records is not considered to be of major significance as all of the methods for recording materials are merely conventions.

Using the data from the previous examples the cost of stock issued would be:

Last in first out (LIFO)

All stock issued is assumed to be from the last received:

Total issued = 42

Therefore:

15 at £2.60	=	£39.00
10 at £2.50	=	£25.00
5 at £2.20	=	£11.00
12 at £2.00	=	£24.00
42		£99.00

This compares with an equivalent value of £97.50 when using the perpetual inventory method.

Average cost (AVCO)

Using the periodic method it is first necessary to calculate the average cost of all materials received during the year.

20 at £2.00	=	£40.00
5 at £2.20	=	£11.00
10 at £2.50	=	£25.00
15 at £2.60	=	£39.00
50		£115.00

Average Cost of goods received = $\dfrac{£115}{50}$ = £2.30

Therefore, cost of goods issued = 42 units at £2.30 = £96.60.

This compares with an equivalent value of £95.04 using the perpetual method.

First in first out (FIFO)

This method will always produce the same answer whichever method is used.

Total issued = 42

$$
\begin{array}{r l}
20 \text{ at } £2.00 &= £40.00 \\
5 \text{ at } £2.20 &= £11.00 \\
10 \text{ at } £2.50 &= £25.00 \\
\underline{7} \text{ at } £2.60 &= \underline{£18.20} \\
\underline{42} & £94.20
\end{array}
$$

In examination questions, students should always assume that the "perpetual inventory" method is required unless the question specifically asks for the "periodic inventory" method.

4.5.2   Inventory control

Stock control is the term generally used to describe the methods used for recording the issue and receipt of goods and materials into and out of the stores department. The main methods used for this recording process have already been described.

One other aspect relating to the costs of raw materials is the quantities which should be ordered and kept in stock. The techniques used for determining order and stock levels are referred to as inventory control.

Inventory control involves calculating stock levels to ensure that stocks are kept at an economic level. The reason for these techniques is that many firms will order very large quantities of stock in order to obtain higher discounts. Unfortunately, this runs the risk of firms having such large stocks of goods that it may not be necessary to reorder any further goods for some months or years. The problems created by this are that the firm will actually be losing money as:

(1)   The money spent on stocks could have been deposited in a bank and could have been earning money (interest) instead of being tied up in stocks.
(2)   Additional rental costs could be incurred as additional storage space will be required.
(3)   Additional clerical and security costs to record and safeguard stocks.
(4)   Additional costs for Insurance.

In order to find the most economic levels of stock, various inventory control formulae can be used. These formulae use some terms that might need an explanation:

Lead time	— This is the period that elapses between placing the order and receipt of the goods.
Buffer Stock (Minimum stock)	— This is the amount of stock that will be needed to cover demand during the lead time.

Maximum stock	— The maximum economic level of stock for each item.
Reorder level	— The point at which a further order should be placed.
Economic order quantity (EOQ)	— The level of stock that makes the best savings after taking into account a balance between costs of delivery and ordering costs.
Reorder quantity	— The amount of stock to be ordered, usually the EOQ if this has been calculated.

Calculating stock levels

Reorder level
This is calculated by the formula:

Maximum usage x maximum lead time

Example: Maximum usage is 15 units per day, Maximum lead time is 10 days.

15 x 10 = 150 units

This means that an order should be raised whenever stock levels fall as low as 150 units.

Minimum level
This is calculated by the formula:

Reorder level x Average usage in average lead time

Example: Average usage 10 units per day, lead time 6-10 days.

150 x (10 x 8) = 70 units

This means that stock should never be allowed to fall below 70 units.

Economic order quantity
This uses a formula which compares the costs of ordering and carrying (delivery) costs.

$$\sqrt{\frac{2 \times \text{Ordering cost per order} \times \text{Annual demand}}{\text{Carrying cost per item per annum}}}$$

Example: Ordering cost £2 per order, Carrying costs 10%, Unit cost £50 per item, Average usage 10 units per day.

$$\sqrt{\frac{2 \times 2 \times (10 \times 365)}{50 \times 10\%}} = 54 \text{ units}$$

Maximum level
This calculates the maximum amount of stock that should be held:

Reorder level + EOQ − Minimum usage in minimum lead time

Example: Minimum usage 2 units per day, Lead time 6-10 days.

150 + 54 − (2 x 6) = 192 units

Reorder quantity

This is a much more straightforward calculation of order quantities than the EOQ and is probably more frequently used because of its simplicity, however, in order to calculate this quantity the firm must first decide what the maximum stock level should be, this may have to be estimated from previous stock usage figures.

Maximum stock — (Reorder level – Minimum usage in minimum delivery time)

Example: Maximum stock 180 units, Reorder level 150 units, Minimum usage 2 units per day, lead time 6-10 days.

$$180 - (150 - (2 \times 6)) = 42 \text{ units}$$

Average stock

This calculates the average quantity in stock on lead times (not to be confused with Average cost).

Minimum Level + ½ Reorder quantity

Example: Minimum stock level 70 units, Reorder quantity 42 units

$$70 + ½(42) = 91 \text{ units}$$

Exercises

133   Calculate the cost of raw materials issued from the following figures using:

    (a) The FIFO method
    (b) The LIFO method
    (c) The average cost method

	Receipts	Issues
Jan	20 at £1.00	Feb 12
March	10 at £1.05	April 6
May	15 at £1.10	June 11
Sept	25 at £1.20	July 4
		Aug 5
		Oct 10
		Dec 8

134   Using the answers from question 133, if each item were sold for £1.50 calculate the gross profit using:

    (a) The LIFO method
    (b) The FIFO method
    (c) The average cost method

135   Calculate the cost of raw materials issued from the following data using:

    (a) The FIFO method
    (b) The LIFO method
    (c) The average cost method

	Receipts	Issues
Jan	8 at £10.00	March 6
Feb	8 at £10.20	May 12
April	5 at £10.30	Aug 10
June	8 at £10.50	Oct 6
July	4 at £10.60	Dec 12
Sept	10 at £11.00	
Nov	8 at £11.10	

Show what the profit would be for each method if the goods issued were eventually sold for £20 each.

136 A firm has devised the following Stock Record Card:

Date	Receipts			Issues			Balance		
	Qty	$	$	Qty	$	$	Qty	$	$
1 Jun	10	5.00	50.00				10	5.00	50.00
2 Jun	5	5.10	25.50				10	5.00	50.00
							5	5.10	25.50
							15		75.50
3 Jun				4	5.10	20.40	10	5.00	50.00
							1	5.10	5.10
							51		55.10
4 Jun	10	5.20	52.00				10	5.00	50.00
							1	5.10	5.10
							10	5.20	52.00
							21		107.10
5 Jun				10	5.20	52.00	4	5.00	20.00
				1	5.10	5.10			
				6	5.00	30.00			

REQUIRED:

(a) State which method of Stock recording has been used.   (1 mark)
(b) Re-draft the Stock Record Card using an alternative recording method.   (6 marks)
(c) If all Issues are later sold for $10 each, calculate the Gross Profit on both methods.   (5 marks)
          (Sep 91)

137 A Calculate three inventory control levels for a stock control system having the following characteristics:

Average usage	3,000 units per week
Minimum usage	2,200 units per week
Maximum usage	4,200 units per week
Lead Time	10-14 weeks
EOQ	35,000 units

138A Calculate for the following:

    (a) Reorder level
    (b) Reorder quantity
    (c) Minimum level
    (d) Average stock held

Maximum stock level	17,000 units
Expected consumption per month	Max 3,000
	Min 1,600
Estimated delivery time:	Max 4 months
	Min 2 months

139A Annual demand for material 77868 is 100,000 units. One unit costs £4 per annum to store. Ordering costs are £20 per order. What is the Economic Order Quantity?

140A A firm has estimated that its maximum stock required of a particular component should be 5,000. Over the last two years it has used a maximum of 1,100 components per month and a minimum of 900 components. Normal delivery times range between 2 months and 4 months.

141 (a) Calculate the cost of components issued from the following figures using the Average Cost method:

Date	Receipts	Issues
Jan	100 at $12.10	
Feb	60 at $12.50	
March		120
May	210 at $13.00	
July		190
Aug	60 at $13.60	
Sept		40
Nov	80 at $13.90	
Dec		125

(b) Calculate the Gross profit for the above if the components were later sold for £22 each.

(Dec 88)

142A The following information gives details of stock issued and received during the month of July. Calculate the cost of goods issued using the average cost method.

Date	Receipts	Cost (each)	Date	Issues
July 1st	100	1.00	July 14th	75
July 3rd	50	1.18	July 10th	20
July 8th	50	1.21	July 12th	5
July 16th	30	1.25	July 9th	40

(Sept 89)

4.6 THE COST OF DIRECT LABOUR

Direct labour is defined as being the actual cost of making a product. It will therefore include the wages of assembly line workers and bricklayers on construction sites, but it will not include the cost of foremen's wages or those of maintenance staff as they are not actively involved in making the product.

The actual cost of direct labour for each product needs to be calculated and this will involve recording the time spent by workers on each job or product. This is often done by the use of job cards. These are record sheets which are attached to each job and follow its progress through the factory. Every time any work is carried out on the job a record is made on the sheet so that when the job is completed the costing clerk can simply add up the totals to find the total cost of the job. These job cards will also show details of materials used and overheads to be absorbed. An example of such a card is given below.

The calculation of direct labour costs for each job will merely involve multiplying the hours worked by the hourly rate of pay for that section. As many jobs will have work performed in a number of sections the same calculation is performed for each section in order to find the total cost for direct labour.

Example: A firm has three sections: assembly, finishing and packing. The hourly rates of pay for direct labour in these sections are:

	£/hour
Assembly	2.00
Finishing	2.50
Packing	1.50

Two jobs recently completed required the following hours work:

	Job A Hours	Job B Hours
Assembly	4	2
Finishing	3	2
Packing	1	1

The total cost of each job in respect of direct labour is:

	Job A £		Job B £
Assembly (4h at £2.00)	8.00	(2h at £2.00)	4.00
Finishing (3h at £2.50)	7.50	(2h at £2.50)	5.00
Packing (1h at £1.50)	1.50	(1h at £1.50)	1.50
Total direct labour	17.00		10.50

Figure 4.10

Once the cost of direct labour is known it can be added to the cost of raw materials and overheads to ascertain the total cost of each job.

4.7 THE COST OF OVERHEADS

Overheads is the term used to describe the indirect and fixed expenses such as rent and rates, depreciation, foremen's wages, lighting and heating, etc. These differ from materials and direct labour as they cannot be directly attributed to a specific job. By using job cards or other means of recording, it is possible to record and calculate the materials and direct labour used in any one job. However, it is not possible to record how much rent or depreciation has been used in any one job because the overheads are indirect costs and have no relationship with the amount produced.

The overheads are "period" rather than "product" costs because they are charged to the firm over a period of time (usually annually) instead of to an individual job. But if a firm simply includes the direct costs, ie materials and direct labour, in the calculation of its costs then it will eventually get into difficulties since selling prices are usually based on costs, and the firm will be ignoring the cost of overheads. Therefore it is essential that firms develop some means of "absorbing" the cost of overheads between the different items produced. The most common and effective means of doing this is to absorb on an hourly basis.

As the direct labour cost will be calculated on the basis of hours spent making the product it is usual to use a similar method to charge the overheads to a particular job. For example, it is known that total overheads amount to £30,000 and that the total number of hours for which direct labour will be working in the year is 10,000 hours, then an "hourly absorption rate" of £3.00 (£30,000/10,000 hours) can be used to absorb the overheads. Absorbing the overheads means charging the costs of overheads on an equitable basis amongst all jobs undertaken.

Sometimes the idea of using the direct labour hours to absorb overheads is not suitable; in sections where the work is particularly machine intensive, it may be more appropriate to absorb the overheads on the basis of the number of hours that the machinery is used rather than that of direct labour hours.

Also, it is rarely possible to set one absorption rate for the whole factory because different sections will incur more overheads than others, so it is usual to calculate an absorption rate for each specific section. This involves calculating what proportion of overheads relates to each section by apportioning overheads between the different sections on the basis of the number of employees, floor space, cost of machinery or any other suitable measure.

Example: A firm estimates that its overheads for the coming year will be:

Rent and Rates	£10,000
Depreciation	£5,000
Lighting and Heating	£4,000
Foremen's wages	£15,000
Canteen costs	£1,500

It has also obtained the following information relating to its three sections:

	Assembly	Finishing	Packing	Total
Floor area (m²)	3,000	5,000	2,000	10,000
Cost of machinery (£s)	30,000	10,000	10,000	50,000
Use of machines (hours)	6,000	1,000	1,000	8,000
Number of employees	10	3	2	15

By deciding on a suitable basis for apportionment, it is possible to apportion all of the overheads between the different sections.

The firm will be charged rent and rates according to how big its buildings are, therefore the floor size of each department is a suitable basis on which to apportion this cost. Assembly has three-tenths of the total floor space, therefore it will also receive that fraction of the total cost of rent and rates (£10,000 × 3/10 = £3000). Packing will receive one-fifth (£1000).

The costs will be apportioned as follows:

Cost	Basis used	Assembly	Finishing	Packing	Total
		£	£	£	£
Rent and rates	Floor area	3,000	5,000	2,000	10,000
Depreciation	Machine cost	3,000	1,000	1,000	5,000
Lighting and heating	Use of machines	3,000	500	500	4,000
Foremen's wages	Employees	10,000	3,000	2,000	15,000
Canteen costs	Employees	1,000	300	200	1,500
		20,000	9,800	5,700	35,500

Figure 4.11

These figures show how the overheads can be apportioned to the appropriate department to calculate how much each department is costing. But, it will also be necessary to absorb these costs into the cost of each product to ensure that the selling price is determined by adding the required profit margin on to the correct cost. The correct cost for each unit produced will contain three elements: direct labour, direct materials and a proportion of the overheads. The proportion for overheads should ensure that over the whole year each unit sold will be "recovering" part of the cost of the overheads.

However, the overheads need to be absorbed on a fair basis so that each unit only carries a reasonable amount of overheads with it. There are a number of methods for absorbing the overhead costs but the most common is to absorb on the basis of labour hours or machine hours. The choice will depend upon whether the section is labour intensive or machine intensive.

Using the same data as shown above it should be possible to calculate hourly absorption rates for each department. The firm estimates that the following hours will be worked in the coming period:

	Assembly	Finishing	Packing
Direct labour	10,000	2,000	7,000
Machines	1,000	10,000	2,000

It should be clear that the assembly and packing sections are predominantly labour intensive whereas finishing is machine intensive, therefore it would be most appropriate to absorb overheads for the assembly and packing sections on a direct labour-hour basis and to absorb overheads in finishing on a machine-hour basis.

Before any overheads can be absorbed it is first necessary to calculate the hourly absorption rates. This is achieved by dividing the total overhead cost by the labour or machine hours for each section:

	Assembly £	Finishing £	Packing £
Total overheads	20,000	9,800	5,700
Direct labour hours	10,000		7,000
Machine hours		10,000	
Hourly rate (£)	2.00	0.98	0.81

Figure 4.12

This means that every job that goes through these departments will be charged £2.00 per labour hour in Assembly, £0.98 per machine hour in Finishing and £0.81 per labour hour in Packing. Note that these charges will be in addition to normal charges for materials and direct labour and are intended to recover the cost of overheads in these departments. So, if every estimated hour for labour in Assembly is charged at £2.00 for Overheads, at the end of the year a total of 10,000 hours should have been used and £20,000 (10,000 hours x £2.00 per hour) recovered, hence covering the cost of overheads.

This should help illustrate the importance of a later topic, Budgeting. If the estimate of labour hours to be used in the Assembly department should turn out to be inaccurate then the amount recovered for overheads will be wrong. For example, if it turns out that there are only 9,000 hours of labour used in this department then the amount recovered for overheads in this section will only be £18,000 (9,000 hours x £2.00 per hour). Therefore it is very important that all figures used in estimating overheads should be as accurate as possible otherwise the effects can be very severe.

An easy way of remembering how to deal with overheads is to remember to use the three "A's":

Allocate: the obvious costs can be allocated to the appropriate cost centre (eg materials used in Dept A)

Apportion: divide other costs on a suitable and fair basis (eg rent apportioned on the basis of floor area)

Absorb: calculate a suitable hourly or percentage rate to recover the cost of overheads in each department (eg costs recovered on a machine hour basis)

Exercises

143 A firm estimates that it will have the following overheads:

	£
Rent and rates	12,000
Indirect wages	25,400
Depreciation of equipment	10,000
Insurance	1,000
Maintenance	15,000
Lighting and heating	4,000
Canteen costs	6,000
	73,400

There are three sections within the firm and the management would like to calculate an overhead absorption rate for each section.

Section	A	B	C	Total
	£	£	£	£
Floor area (m²)	5,000	10,000	5,000	20,000
Cost of machinery (£'s)	70,000	25,000	5,000	100,000
Use of machines (hours)	33,000	6,000	6,000	45,000
No. of employees (indirect)	3	4	3	10
No. of employees (direct)	10	50	30	90
Direct labour hours	15,000	80,000	45,000	140,000

Use the above information to apportion costs between the different sections and then calculate the hourly absorption rate for each section using either machine hours or direct labour hours.

144 A computer bureau is trying to work out a suitable hourly charge for its services. It is estimated that the costs for the coming year will be:

	£
Labour	345,000
Lighting and heating	10,000
Rates	34,000
Rent	54,900
Insurance of equipment	8,000
Depreciation of equipment	100,000

The bureau expects to be in operation for 60,000 hours during the year. Use this information to calculate an appropriate hourly charge, including a 30% profit mark-up.

145 A firm has three departments: assembly, painting and finishing. The estimated overheads for the year are:

	£
Rent	10,000
Rates	8,000
Fuel for machines	40,000

Depreciation of equipment	30,000
Foremen's wages	120,000
Canteen costs	25,000
Insurance for machinery	3,000
Heating costs	5,000

The following information is also available:

	Assembly	Painting	Finishing	Total
Floor area (sq.ft.)	45,000	31,000	24,000	100,000
Cost of machines (£s)	180,000	50,000	70,000	300,000
Employees	50	16	24	90
Foremen	7	2	3	12
Cubic capacity (cu.ft.)	140,000	92,000	95,000	327,000
Machine hours	40,000	50,000	15,000	105,000
Labour hours	96,000	31,000	46,000	173,000

Allocate and apportion overheads on a suitable basis and then calculate an hourly absorption rate for each department using:

(a) a machine hour basis
(b) a labour hour basis

146A A firm has estimated the following overheads for the coming year:

	£
Rent	20,000
Rates	5,000
Light/Heat	3,000
Depreciation	10,000
Indirect Labour costs	42,000
Canteen Costs	4,000
Foremen's wages	24,000
Insurance (machinery)	1,000
Clerical staff	21,000

The following other information is available:

COST CENTRE:	DEPT A	DEPT B	STORES
Floor area (sq.ft.)	10,000	30,000	10,000
Cubic capacity	30,000	60,000	15,000
Machinery value	70,000	30,000	—
Direct Labour	16	8	—
Indirect Labour	3	2	2

Complete the following table to show how costs would be best apportioned.

	Basis £	Dept A £	Dept B £	Stores £	Total £
Rent					20,000
Rates					5,000
Light/Heat					3,000
Depreciation					10,000
Indirect Labour costs					42,000
Canteen Costs					4,000
Foremen's wages					
Insurance (machinery)					
Clerical staff					
TOTAL:					
Apportionment of Stores					
TOTAL:					

147A A firm has estimated that its overheads for the coming year will be as follows:

		£
Rent		12,000
Rates		30,000
Lighting & Heating		45,000
Canteen costs		18,000
Depreciation on machinery (5%)		20,000
Indirect Material costs:		
Dept A	15,000	
Dept B	10,000	
Dept C	8,000	
Maintenance	12,000	45,000

Direct Materials			230,000
Direct Wages			312,000
Indirect Wages:			
Dept A	7,500		
Dept B	12,000		
Dept C	10,000		
Stores	18,000		
Maintenance	25,000		72,500
Works Managers salary			16,000
			800,500

The following information is also available:

Dept:	Direct Materials used	Dept Area sq.ft.	Direct Labour hours	Wages	Machine hours	Cost of Machines
	£'000	'000	'000	£'000	'000	£'000
A	70	100	100	120	80	90
B	90	150	180	150	100	120
C	70	65	60	42	35	110
Stores		25				
Maintenance		45			95	80
	230	385	340	312	310	400

Required:

(a) Allocate and apportion the costs to the Production depts, using bases that you consider appropriate.
(b) Calculate the overhead absorption rates for each of the three production departments using (i) Direct Labour hours and (ii) Machine hours.

4.8   JOB COSTING

Using the data provided previously it is possible to calculate reasonably accurately what the cost of any job is.

Example: A job has recently been finished and the following data has been collected concerning the job:

Direct materials	£20.00
Direct labour:	Assembly 4 hours
	Finishing 1 hour
	Packing 2 hours
Machine hours:	Finishing 3 hours

The rates of pay for direct labour are:

Assembly — £3.00 per hour
Finishing — £4.00 per hour
Packing — £2.50 per hour

Job cost card

Job number: K101
Completion date: 17/06/XI

Customers name and address:
J Bloggs, New House, Old Town

Start date: 10/06/XI

Special instructions:

Blue fascia required:

	Material	Labour Cost			Overheads			Total
		Hrs	Rate	Total	Hrs	Rate	Total	
One	10	1	2	2.00	1	4.50	4.50	16.50
Two	5	2	3	6.00	2	1.37½	2.75	13.75
Three	-	½	1	0.50	2	1.81¼	3.62½	4.12½
Total	15			8.50			10.87½	34.37½

Selling and distribution costs 5.10
Administration costs 4.10½
43.48
Profit mark-up 10.87
Total 54.35

Figure 4.14 Job Costing

The cost of the job will be determined as follows (using the absorption rates calculated in the previous section):

		£	£
Direct materials			20.00
Direct labour:	Assembly (4h x £3.00)	12.00	
	Finishing (1h x £4.00)	4.00	
	Packing (2h x £2.50)	5.00	21.00
Overheads:	Assembly (4h x £2.00)	8.00	
	Finishing (3h x £0.98)	2.94	
	Packing (2h x £0.81)	1.62	12.56
Total cost			53.56

Figure 4.13

This method of job costing requires management to maintain records of materials used and hours worked for each individual job, as well as determining hourly absorption rates. Firms that use these methods will normally use job cards as a means of recording the necessary data as the job progresses through the different sections. A typical job card would look something like Figure 4.14.

This card is often attached to the product as it passes through the different sections and the different items of data are added at each stage. Factors such as labour rates and overhead rates will already have been determined and staff will only have to enter the hours worked and calculate the total costs for each item.

The amount of selling and distribution expenses, and administration expenses will also normally be calculated as a fixed amount and is often a percentage of total factory cost. However, in some cases the actual amount spent on advertising and delivery could be used for the selling and distribution costs.

The selling price of the product may be determined in line with prices that competitors are charging, but most firms will still want to calculate the cost of making the product in order to ensure that they are covering their costs. In most cases though the firm will determine its selling price by adding an appropriate "mark-up" to the total cost (see Part 2, Section 2.14).

Exercises

148   A software firm has the following costs: Programmers wages $7.50 per hour, Overheads $5.00 per computer hour.

A program has recently been written for a client and involved the following costs/times; Disks $2.20, Photocopying and Stationery $3.50, Programming hours 5, computer hours 3.

Calculate the cost of the job and work out a suitable charge assuming that the firm have a 25% mark-up for profit.   (4 marks)

(Sep 91)

149 A firm has estimated that its Computer Department will have the following overheads:

	$
Rent & Rates	55,000
Depreciation of equipment	80,000
Insurance	20,000
Labour	250,000

The following additional information has been obtained:

	Systems Analysis Section	Programming Section
Floor area (sq metres)	10,000	15,000
Number of staff	20	10
Cost of equipment	$150,000	$650,000
Computer machine hours	40,000	90,000

Apportion the costs between the two sections using an appropriate basis and then calculate an Absorption rate for each section based upon Machine hours.   (14 marks)
(Mar 92)

150 A firm has three different departments used in Production; *Assembly, Refining* and *Finishing*. The *Overhead Absorption* rates have been calculated as: Assembly $3.50 per hour, Refining $4.75 per hour and Finishing $6.10 per hour. *Overheads* in the Assembly and Finishing Departments will be absorbed on a *Labour Hour* basis and on a *Machine hour* basis in the Refining Department.

Hourly Rates of pay for *Direct Labour* are as follows; Assembly $2.30, Refining $1.60 and Finishing $3.10.

Calculate the costs of the following job:

		Job Number 129
Materials used		$15.40
Labour hours:	Assembly	3
	Refining	2
	Finishing	3
Machine hours:	Assembly	1
	Refining	4
	Finishing	2

(Dec 88)

151 A Software house has two departments; Programming and Systems Analysis. The costs for the forthcoming year have been budgeted as follows:

	$
Wages and Salaries	140,000
Rent and Rates	12,000
Light and Heat	9,000

Maintenance on equipment	18,000
Travelling expenses	5,000
Canteen and Catering costs	7,000
General Administrative costs	14,000

The following information has also been obtained:

	Programming	Systems Analysis
Floor area (sq metres)	40,000	20,000
Volume (cubic metres)	50,000	40,000
Cost of equipment ($)	20,250	6,750
Number of employees	8	12
Annual mileage on visits	4,000	16,000

(a)   Use the above information to select appropriate bases for apportioning the costs between the two departments and calculate the cost of each department.

(b)   The staff in each department work a 40 hour week and have 5 weeks annual holiday. Calculate the total labour hours available in each department and then determine a suitable overhead absorption rate for each department.

(c)   One job recently contracted for is expected to require 100 hours of Programming and 175 hours of Systems Analysis. It will also require $25 worth of materials in the form of stationery and printing. The firm expects each contract to have a mark-up on cost of 30%. Labour rates are: Programming $3.50 per hour, Systems Analysis $4.25 per hour.

Calculate the charge to be made for this contract.
(Mar 90)

152A GIANT FUSCHIA STORES LTD

A recently redundant steelworker has to decided to invest his redundancy money in a garden centre specialising in his hobby, rearing fuschias.

He has already built up a collection of varieties for taking cuttings from, and has something of a reputation as a grower in local Fuschia Societies.

Premises have been obtained at a rent of £700 per month and the rates payable will be £4,600 payable in two equal installments. Heating costs are estimated at £80 per week, but heating is only required for 20 weeks between November and March. Power is estimated at £10 per week. His wife will help out as a salesperson and will be paid £100 per week.

An automatic potting machine has been bought for a cost of £20,000, this machine should last for 10 years. The machine is capable of potting up 200 plants per hour and could be run for up to 1,000 hours in the year. The machine operator is paid £100 per week.

The owner of the business takes all cuttings and pays himself £200 per week.

The "raw materials" used will be the plant cutting (free), compost and the plant pots. Compost is bought in 80 litre bags which cost £6.40, each bag is sufficient for potting on 320 plants. Plant pots are bought in batches of 1,000 which cost £38.

Advertising is expected to cost £40 per week and delivery costs will be paid for by the customer.

REQUIRED:

(1) Calculate the most appropriate absorption rate for overheads.
(2) Calculate the cost per cutting.
(3) Calculate the selling price assuming that the owner wants a 20% profit margin.
(4) Calculate what the profit will be for the year.

153A A manufacturing firm produces a variety of products and uses a job costing system to determine the cost of each product produced.
Information available is:

Materials used;	Department	Labour Costs	Overhead rates
Widgets £1.50 per kilogram	Assembly	£2.10	£3.00
Sprockets £4.00 per kilogram	Turning	£1.80	£1.10
Dongles £10.00 per metre	Packing	£3.00	£2.50
Jangles £4 per batch of ten	Finishing	£1.00	£1.00
Wigwams £2.50 per kilogram			

All labour costs and overhead rates are per hour.

All departments except Assembly and Turning absorb overheads on a labour hour basis.

An additional 25% is added onto the manufacturing cost to cover the cost of overheads in Administration and Sales & Distribution, and the Selling price is calculated by adding 30% onto the total cost.

Job number 12485 requires the following:

Assembly Dept:	3 kg of Widgets, 1 kg of Sprockets, 1.5 metres of Dongles. Direct labour 2 hours, Machine hours 3 hours.
Turning Dept:	15 Jangles Direct labour 1 hour, Machine hours 2 hours
Packing Dept:	2 kg of Wigwams Direct labour 1.5 hours, Machine hours 1 hour
Finishing Dept:	Direct labour 0.5 hours, Machine hours nil

Calculate:

(a) the cost of materials used
(b) the cost of direct labour
(c) the overheads absorbed
(d) the total manufacturing cost
(e) the total cost
(f) the selling price

4.9   BREAK-EVEN ANALYSIS

This chapter began with a description of how costs behave and showed how costs can be classified as variable or fixed. These classifications are particularly useful when a firm is considering the introduction of a new product as they can be used to predict the number of units needed to make a profit.

Most organisations will conduct market research before launching a new product to give them some idea of how many items they can expect to sell. Break-even analysis techniques enable management to quickly work out whether it is worthwhile launching the new product.

All manufactured goods will have some variable costs in the form of materials, direct labour and, possibly, direct expenses. They will also have to make some contribution towards the overheads (fixed costs) as fixed costs can only be paid for by adding on a set amount to variable costs.

4.9.1   Contribution

The term "contribution" has great significance in cost accounting but simply means the selling price less the variable costs. Suppose a firm has a product which it sells for £10.00 and the variable costs involved in making this product amount to £6.00, then the contribution is £4.00. If the fixed costs are £10,000 then each product sold is said to be contributing £4 towards the fixed costs. If this firm sells 2500 units it will have covered all of its fixed costs and any additional units sold will be making £4 profit. This is what is involved in a break-even analysis and it is usually calculated from the following formula:

$$\text{Break-even point} = \frac{\text{Fixed Costs}}{\text{Selling price-variable costs}}$$

Example:

$$\frac{\text{Fixed Costs £10,000}}{\text{Selling price £10-variable costs £6}} = 2{,}500 \text{ units}$$

The break-even point is defined as that point where all costs have been covered but no profit has yet been made. If the firm in the above example thought that it could only sell 2000 units then it would not bother to make the product, because it would not be able to cover its fixed costs. This is the basic break-even formula but it can be altered slightly to calculate various factors.

Profit at different levels of sales

By manipulating the formula it is possible to ascertain profit and units sold at various levels. If the firm mentioned above decided that there was a market for 3000 units it might decide to go into production but would first like to know what profit it would be making. This can easily be calculated by:

Assumed level of sales	3,000
Break-even point	2,500
	500 units

Profit = 500 units at £4 each + £2000

Sales required for a specific level of profit

Alternatively, the firm might decide that it is not worth making the product unless it can achieve a profit of £3000. This means that the contribution required will not only have to cover the £10,000 fixed costs but also the £3000 profit. The number of units that need to be sold will be:

$$\frac{\text{Fixed costs } \pounds 10,000 + \text{profit } \pounds 3,000}{\text{Selling price } \pounds 10\text{-variable costs } \pounds 6} = 3,250 \text{ units}$$

It can easily be seen that these techniques are not only very useful but also very simple and quick to calculate.

Profit for desired return on capital employed

A slight variation on the previous example is where the firm has to make a certain Return on Capital Employed (see Part 2, Section 2.14). This is virtually the same as the previous formula except that the firm will have to calculate what the required profit is first.

If the firm have a Capital Employed of £50,000 and the head office insist that all new products must produce a Return On Capital Employed of 10% then the formula would be:

ROCE = £50,000 x 10% = £5,000

$$\frac{\text{Fixed Costs } \pounds 10,000 + \text{ROCE } \pounds 10,000}{\text{Selling price } \pounds 10\text{-variable cost } \pounds 6} = 5,000 \text{ units}$$

Margin of safety

This is a useful figure which compares the break-even point with the expected level of sales. In the example used so far the break-even point was 2,500 units and the expected level of sales was 3,000 units. The Margin of Safety is the difference between the two figures.

Expected sales	3,000
Break-even point	2,500
Margin of safety	500

This gives the firm some idea of how close it is to the break-even point. In this example, the margin of safety is not particularly large and some unforeseen circumstances may mean that sales are lost, in which case they will come dangerously close to making a loss.

4.10 BREAK-EVEN GRAPHS

It is also possible to chart the revenue and costs lines on a graph so that it is possible to calculate profit at any level of sales simply by reading off the appropriate point from the graph.

The revenue line starts at zero because if no products are sold then there is no revenue; the fixed and variable costs line starts at £10,000 because the firm will incur fixed costs of £10,000 whether it makes any products or not. The point at which the lines cross is the break-even point; the shaded area beneath the

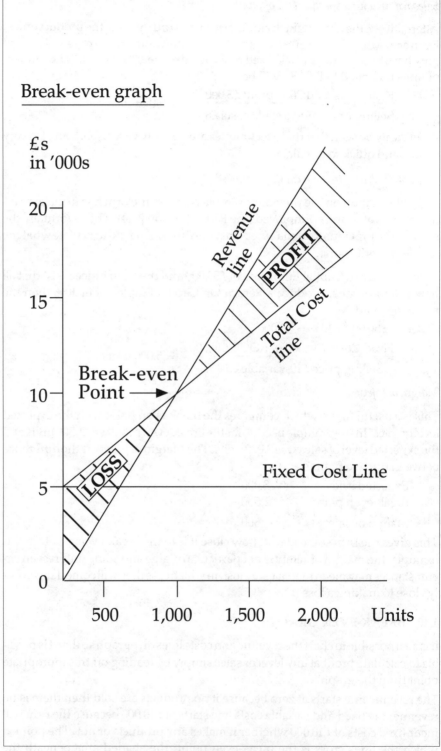

Figure 4.15 Break-even analysis

break-even point shows the loss made by the firm at these points. For example, if the firm makes only 1000 products then the costs line at this point is £16,000 and the revenue £10,000 — the difference is the loss of £6000. The shaded area above the break-even point shows the amount of profit and by using the same method again it should be possible to see from the graph what the profit is at any level of sales.

Exercises

154   A firm is considering whether to introduce a new product. It has estimated that the product will incur costs of £25 for materials, £15 for direct labour and £30,000 of fixed costs. The firm wants to have a 50% mark-up on cost and therefore set the selling price at £60. Market research shows that at this price the firm will only be able to sell 1400 units.

(a) Calculate the break-even point.
(b) Would the firm be wise to sell at this price?
(c) If the price were reduced to £50, what would be the new break-even point?
(d) How many units need to be sold at the new price to make a profit of £10,000?

155   A firm is intending to introduce a new product. It is estimated that the product will incur fixed costs of £100,000 and will also cost £3 per unit for direct materials, £5 for direct labour and £4 for variable overheads. The selling price will be £20 per unit.

Calculate:

(a) The break-even point in units
(b) The break-even point in £s
(c) The number of units needed to make a profit of £30,000
(d) The total income from sales when profit is £30,000
(e) How many units are needed to make a profit of £30,000 if direct labour costs increase to £6.

156A   A firm has fixed costs of £10,000. The variable costs in manufacturing each product are; Direct Materials £4.00, Direct Labour £6.50, Variable Overheads £2.50. The current selling price is £20 per unit. The firm has a policy that all products should produce a Return on Capital Employed of 10%, Capital employed is £150,000.

REQUIRED:
(a) The break-even point (in units)
(b) The break-even point (in £s Sales)
(c) The level of sales required to achieve the required Return on Capital Employed (in units)
(d) The level of sales required to achieve the required Return on Capital Employed (in £s)

157A   A firm has the following costs; Direct Labour £24 per unit, Direct Materials

£15 per unit, Variable overheads £5 per unit, Fixed costs £850,000. Current selling price is £65 per unit. The Budgeted sales for the year are 65,000 units.

The Production manager feels that if the Production system is overhauled then variable costs could be reduced by 5%, however the overhaul would incur an additional fixed cost of £150,000.

The Sales Manager states that a further 10,000 units could be sold to the USA if the selling price (for the additional sales only) were reduced by 10%. This would require an advertising campaign costing £150,000.

The Managing Director wants to reduce Variable costs by making some of the direct labour redundant, he calculates that the cost of Direct Labour per unit could be reduced to £21 per unit. The firm would have to make redundancy payments of £200,000.

REQUIRED:
(a) The break-even point.
(b) The profit made at the budgeted sales level.
(c) The break-even point if the Production manager's proposals are accepted.
(d) The break-even point if the Sales manager's proposals are accepted.
(e) The break-even point if the Managing Director's proposals are accepted.
(f) A recommendation as to which of the proposals (if any) should be accepted.

158A A firm has the following costs:

Direct Materials	£10 per unit
Direct Labour	£15 per unit
Direct Expenses	£2 per unit
Variable overheads	£4 per unit
Fixed Costs	£200,000

The proposed selling price is £45 per unit.

REQUIRED:
(a) The break-even point (in units)
(b) The break-even point (in £s sales)
(c) The number of sales (in units) required to make a profit of £30,000
(d) The break-even point if the selling price is increased to £49 per unit.
(e) The break-even point if the cost of Direct Materials increases to £11.50 per unit.
(f) The break-even point if the Fixed costs are reduced to £180,000.

159A A firm is considering introducing a new product; there are three alternatives available. Alpha will sell for £30 and will have variable costs of £21. Beta will sell for £41 and will have variable costs of £26. Gamma will sell for £56 and will have variable costs of £35.

The firm will incur fixed costs of £700,000 but this figure will increase depending upon which product is selected. If the firm produce product Alpha then Fixed costs will increase by £150,000. If product Beta is produced the Fixed costs will increase by £200,000 and the increase for product Gamma would be £350,000.

Whichever product is selected must also make a Return on Capital Employed (ie Fixed Costs) of 10%.

REQUIRED:

(a) The break-even point for each product
(b) The break-even point for each product to achieve the required return on capital employed.

160 A firm is currently selling its product for $25, the costs involved in manufacturing this product are; *Materials* $6 per unit, *Direct Labour* $4.50 per unit and a *Royalty* of $1.00 per unit payable to the inventor. The firm has estimated that the *cost* of the *Administrative section* will be $120,000 for the coming year and that the *Selling Costs* will be $70,000. Current sales are 17,000 units per year.

Required:

(i) Calculate the *break-even* point in units.
(ii) Calculate the *profit* made.

The firm has been offered a contract for an additional 4,000 units providing that the price for these units is reduced to $20 per unit, if this contract is accepted there will be no increase in Fixed costs.

Required:

(iii) Would you advise that this contract be accepted? Support your answer with calculations.

The Sales manager feels that instead of accepting this special contract the firm should pay sales staff a *commission of $1.00* for every unit sold; he estimates that this would increase total sales to 20,000 units.

Required:

(iv) Calculate the *new break-even* point in units.
(v) Calculate the *profit* made based on the Sales managers figure.

161 A firm is considering whether to introduce a new product. It has estimated that each product will require costs of $4 for materials, $7 for direct labour and $1 for a copyright fee.

An additional cost of $50,000 will be incurred in respect of Fixed Costs if the product is produced. Market research has predicted that 11,000 units could be sold. The firm requires that all products have a mark-up on variable cost of 50% and all products should preferably make a Return on Capital Employed (Fixed Costs) of 25%.

Marks will be awarded for use of formula.

(a) Calculate the selling price.
(b) Calculate the break-even point at this selling price.
(c) Calculate the profit made if 11,000 units are sold.
(d) Calculate how many units need to be sold to make the required Return on Capital Employed.
(e) Calculate the total income from sales if a profit of $10,000 is made.
(f) The firm expect that the price of Materials may increase to $5; what would the break-even point become if this was the case?
(g) Another organisation has advised you that it can make the product for $15, if you bought the product from this manufacturer you could then resell at the same price as in (a) above and the Fixed Costs would only be $20,000. Should you make the product yourself or buy it ready-made from the other supplier?

162A GIANT FUSCHIA STORES

The owner of the business is considering whether to diversify into selling other plants. There appears to be a considerable demand for Geraniums and Carnations.

The owner has done some research into costs and estimates that the following would be likely costs per plant:

	Geraniums £	Carnations £
Materials	0.30	0.20
Labour	0.25	0.20
Variable Overheads	0.10	0.10

A new Greenhouse and heating system would be required for both types of plants, this would cost £40,000 and the owner estimates that there would be an annual Fixed cost of £10,000. Unfortunately the two plants will not grow in the same conditions and therefore the owner needs to select either geraniums or carnations.

The average prices charged by other nurseries in the area are Geraniums £1.50 and Carnations £0.90.

The owner estimates that he could sell 13,000 geraniums or 28,000 carnations a year at the above prices. But ideally he would like to sell sufficient plants to make a Return on Capital Employed of 10% (ie: 10% of the cost of the greenhouse).

If prices are reduced by 10% then the sales could increase to 19,000 for geraniums and 39,000 for carnations.

REQUIRED:

(a) Calculate the break-even point for both plants.
(b) Calculate the profit made for each plant at the expected levels of sales.

(c) Calculate the number of plants that need to be sold in order to produce the required Return on Capital Employed.

(d) Calculate what the selling price would need to be in order to achieve the R.O.C.E. at the expected sales levels.

(e) Calculate the break-even points for the reduced selling prices.

(f) Calculate the number of plants that would need to be sold at the reduced prices in order to achieve the R.O.C.E.

4.11 BUDGETING

4.11.1 Predicting future profit

In order to carry out the technique of break-even analysis as shown above, the firm needs to estimate costs and selling prices. At the beginning of each year, most firms will carry out various exercises connected with predicting what the different costs and selling prices will be for the coming year. This is a very important aspect of cost accounting and is essential as a means of controlling expenditure.

Many organisations will want to know what their profit will be at the end of the coming year. In order to do this it is necessary to make a number of predictions, but the task is not all pure guesswork. The firm should have a reasonable idea of how many sales it will make, based on the corresponding figures from the previous year. If it can estimate sales in this way, then it can also estimate purchases, as the two items are obviously interconnected. It can also estimate various overheads by asking the heads of each of its departments how much they need to spend. The heads of department will be able to estimate this amount by checking how much they needed last year and considering whether they need any additional items this year.

It is essential that managers co-ordinate with one another when devising budgets as it is pointless for the sales manager to budget for 100,000 units of sales in the coming year if the production manager is only budgeting to manufacture 7,000 units and the purchasing manager is only budgeting to buy enough raw materials for 5,000 units. Larger organisations often set up budget committees to ensure that all managers co-ordinate their activities and that each department is fitting in with the requirements of other departments.

The budgets should all inter-relate as shown in Figure 4.16.

Imagine that this exercise has been carried out and the following departments have put in their estimates for the coming year:

		£
Sales department:	Predicted revenue	100,000
	Selling overheads	15,000
Production:	Purchases — 30% of revenue	
	Direct labour — 10% of revenue	
	Overheads	5,000
Administration departments:	Personnel overheads	5,000

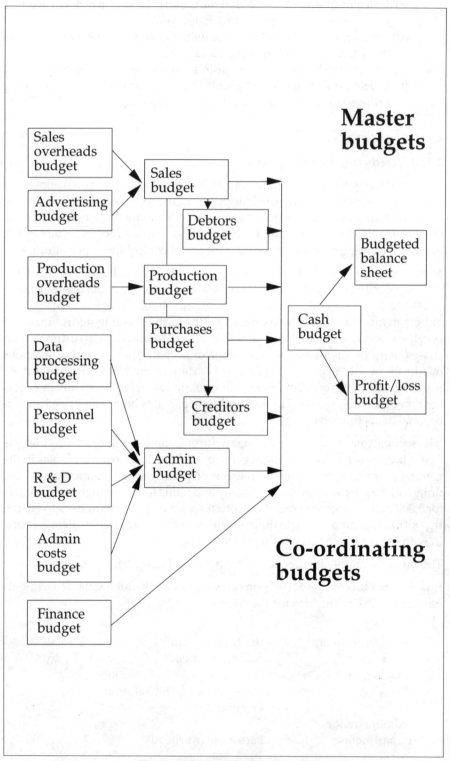

Figure 4.16 Predicting future profit

	General office	10,000
Finance:	Canteen	2,000
	Overheads and salaries	3,000

These items can be merged together to produce the budgeted profit/loss statement:

	£	£
Revenue		100,000
Purchases (materials)	30,000	
Direct labour	10,000	
Production overheads	5,000	45,000
Sales and distribution overheads		15,000
Administration overheads		17,000
Finance overheads		3,000
Net profit		20,000

Such calculations are important for firms as it ensures that some control can be maintained over expenditure: it enables them to plan ahead for replacement of equipment, calculation of dividends, etc, and it ensures that any major falls in profit are predicted so that evasive action can be planned.

Not only will each department have to submit proposals for its budget but an additional budget will be devised by most firms. The disadvantage with profit and loss accounts is that they do not show the flow of cash in to and out of the business. The figure of £20,000 net profit shown in the budgeted profit/loss statement will not mean that the firm has £20,000 in cash. This is because the statement shows the figures for a whole year and any cash received may have been used to pay suppliers, wages, etc, and some of the sales will not yet have been paid for.

Cash budgets or cash flow statements show a firm the "flow" of cash through the business. They enable managers to see when there will be a shortage of cash, so that an overdraft or loan can be arranged, and indicate how much cash is available to purchase new equipment or develop other areas of the business.

The different departments within a firm supply the cost accountant with the following data:

Sales department

This department states that sales are expected to be:

	Dec	Jan	Feb	Mar	Apr	May	Jun	Jul	Aug	Sep	Oct	Nov	Dec
units	100	110	80	70	70	60	80	90	120	140	150	150	110

All units are sold for £20 each. Sales are on credit and debtors pay one month after the month of sale.

A Sales Budget would usually be interpreted as meaning a statement of sales per month, therefore the above list constitutes a Sales Budget already.

It would make life easier if a Debtors budget were prepared, this is based on the

Sales Budget but records when payments for sales are received. The Debtors budget from the above figures would show:

Debtors Budget												
	Jan	Feb	Mar	Apr	May	Jun	Jul	Aug	Sep	Oct	Nov	Dec
Receipts	2000	2200	1600	1400	1400	1200	1200	1800	2400	2800	3000	3000

Figure 4.17

Note that there is a "stagger" in relation to the Sales budget, this is because of the one month delay in receiving payment.

Purchases department

This department states that in order to sell and produce the quantities stated by the Sales Department it will be necessary to purchase the following quantities.

	Nov	Dec	Jan	Feb	Mar	Apr	May	Jun	Jul	Aug	Sep	Oct	Nov	Dec
units	90	60	70	60	50	80	80	100	120	150	160	150	120	90

All units are £10 each. Purchases are on credit and creditors are paid two months after the month of purchase.

This list of figures would normally be called a Purchases Budget, both Sales and Purchases budgets usually show **quantities** of goods to be bought or sold. These are used to draft the Debtors and Creditors budgets which show the **amounts of cash** involved in payments or receipts.

As with the Debtors Budget the Creditors Budget will differ from the Purchases Budget because items bought in one month are not paid for until two months later. The Creditors Budget is shown in Figure 4.18.

	Jan	Feb	Mar	Apr	May	Jun	Jul	Aug	Sep	Oct	Nov	Dec
Purchases	900	600	700	600	500	800	800	1000	1200	1500	1600	1500

Figure 4.18

Other budgets

It is possible, and sometimes much easier, to prepare similar budgets for some of the other items to be included in the Cash Budget. However, in most cases they will be quite straightforward and therefore it is not worth drafting out a separate budget. In reality, very few items would be so straightforward, items such as wages will require very complex budgets as the total wages budget will include wages for staff from a number of different departments with a wide variety of different jobs and an even wider range of salary/wage scales.

Other items to be included in this budget are as follows:

(1) Wages will be £500 per month

(2) Overheads will be £100.

(3) Rates are paid quarterly in March, June, September and December and amount to £200 per quarter.

(4) The firm is buying some new equipment in February costing £600; this will be paid for in three equal installments in March, April and May.

(5) Opening balance of cash in January is £100.

This information can be merged with the Debtors and Creditors budgets to prepare a cash budget for the 12-month period January to December.

	Jan	Feb	Mar	Apr	May	Jun	Jul	Aug	Sep	Oct	Nov	Dec
Sales	2000	2200	1600	1400	1400	1200	1200	1800	2400	2800	3000	3000
Purchases	900	600	700	600	500	800	800	1000	1200	1500	1600	1500
Wages	500	500	500	500	500	500	500	500	500	500	500	500
Overheads	100	100	100	100	100	100	100	100	100	100	100	100
Rates			200			200			200			200
Equipment			200	200	200							
Total cost	1500	1200	1700	1400	1300	1600	1400	1600	2000	2100	2200	2300
Surplus	500	1000	-100	0	100	-400	-200	200	400	700	800	700
Opening balance	100	600	1600	1500	1500	1600	1200	1000	1200	1600	2300	3100
Balance c/f	600	1600	1500	1500	1600	1200	1000	1200	1600	2300	3100	3800

Figure 4.19

This cash flow enables management to see how much cash will be available at any point during the year. For instance, in the above situation, management could afford to buy some more machinery worth £1000 at any point during the year after January as there is always a minimum of £1000 available.

Cash budgets also enable management to decide if it will need to obtain an overdraft from the bank. In the above example there is always a balance of some cash remaining at the end of each month; however, if the overheads increased to £300 per month the situation would look like Figure 4.20

	Jan	Feb	Mar	Apr	May	Jun	Jul	Aug	Sep	Oct	Nov	Dec
Sales	2000	2200	1600	1400	1400	1200	1200	1800	2400	2800	3000	3000
Purchases	900	600	700	600	500	800	800	1000	1200	1500	1600	1500
Wages	500	500	500	500	500	500	500	500	500	500	500	500
Overheads	300	300	300	300	300	300	300	300	300	300	300	300
Rates			200			200			200			200
Equipment			200	200	200							
Total cost	1700	1400	1900	1600	1500	1800	1600	1800	2200	2300	2400	2500
Surplus	300	800	-300	-200	-100	-600	-400	0	200	500	600	500
Opening balance	100	400	1200	900	700	600	nil	-400	-400	-200	300	900
Balance c/f	400	1200	900	700	600	nil	-400	-400	-200	300	900	1400

Figure 4.20

The situation is now very different and the firm would not be able to pay all of its suppliers in the period July to September. If suppliers do not get paid they will be unlikely to supply any more goods and the firm will not have anything to sell. This firm has two choices: it could ask the bank for a loan or overdraft of £600 starting in July; or it could try and explain the situation to its creditors and request two months' extra credit. The advantage in preparing the cash budget is that it gives the firm prior warning of any cash flow problems and a considerable period in which to make arrangements in order to avert any crisis. In the example used the firm has at least five months' notice of the impending cash flow problem and advance notice that the problem is only temporary.

The Master Budget is the term used to describe a budgeted Profit/Loss Account and Balance Sheet; this enables a firm to predict what its Final Accounts will look like at the end of the year. The usual layout for a Budgeted Profit/Loss Account follows that of the Operating statement in section 4.3, although as this is an account solely for internal use it is usually very much abbreviated. The main factors to bear in mind when devising a Budgeted Profit/Loss account is that items not involving cash that are excluded from the Cash Budget (eg depreciation) *will* be included in the Profit/Loss account, but expenditure on Fixed Assets won't be.

Also, the Sales and Purchases figures will usually be different as they will show actual sale/purchases during the year rather than Receipts/Payments during the year.

A Master Budget for the first example given above would appear as in Figure 4.21.

Budgeted Profit/Loss Account		
	£	
Sales	24,600	(12,300 x £20)
Raw Materials	12,300	(12,300 x £10)
Labour	6,000	(£500 x 12 months)
Overheads	2,000	(£100 x 12 months + Rent £800)
Net profit	20,300	

Figure 4.21

It is not possible to prepare a balance sheet as there is not enough information. Note that the figures ignore the cash balances and the amounts paid in respect of installation of the machinery as these items would be included in the balance sheet.

Another common budget is the *Production Budget*; our example does not involve any manufacturing activity so there is no need for a Production department. In those instances where goods are manufactured it is usual to decide whether Production should be at a constant pace (to ensure that employees have always got some work to do) or at a fluctuating amount (to save on storage costs during slack periods).

To calculate Production requirements simply add up the total sales required and then deduct any Opening Stock, and add back any Closing Stock if this is required. For example, suppose a firm has estimated that sales for the year will be 2,000 units and there is already 100 units in Stock. The firm will require a Closing Stock of 200 units at the end of the year.

Sales	2,000 units
less Opening Stock	100 units
	1,900 units
plus Closing Stock	200 units
PRODUCTION REQUIRED	2,050 units

It can be assumed that this would be produced in equal amounts of 175 units per month (2,100/12).

Exercises

163 Draw up a cash budget for the six months from January to June in respect of the following data:

Sales

Sales in units are expected to be:

Nov	Dec	Jan	Feb	Mar	Apr	May	Jun
30	35	25	25	30	35	35	35

All units are sold for £50 each. All sales are on credit and customers are allowed one month's credit, although half of the customers take two months' credit.

Purchases

Purchases are expected to be:

Nov	Dec	Jan	Feb	Mar	Apr	May	Jun
35	30	20	30	30	25	25	25

All units are bought for £25 each on credit; suppliers are paid one month after the items are purchased.

Other items

(a) Wages are £300 per month
(b) Rent is payable on 1 January and 1 April, £400 each installment
(c) Lighting and heating will be payable in March £1000
(d) Other overheads £100 per month
(e) Opening balance of cash is £200

164 A firm has just started trading and has asked the bank for an overdraft to cover the first few months' trading. Use the following information to prepare a cash budget for the first six months of trading and state how much overdraft would be required.

Sales   The firm expects to sell 100 units each month for a price of £24 each. It will offer two months' credit and so will not receive the first payment until March.

Purchases	Purchases will also be at a rate of 100 units per month and will cost £6 per unit. Suppliers offer one month's credit.
Wages	The firm is initially employing two assistants who will be paid £75/week each.
Rent	Premises have been acquired at a rental of £1000 per quarter payable in advance.
Sundry expenses	Other expenses are expected to be £300 for the first two months and £100 thereafter.
Equipment	The firm will require equipment costing £1000 in its first month's trading.

165   Prepare a cash budget from the following information for the six months January to June:
- opening balance £7500;
- sales are 1000 units per month for the months December, January, February and March, and 1500 units for the other months;
- selling price per unit is £5.00, 10% of sales are for cash and the remainder are on credit; debtors pay in one month;
- wages are £300 per month;
- purchases are 2000 units in November and December, 500 in January, February and March, and 1000 in April to June;
- purchases cost £1.50 per unit and are bought on two months' credit;
- rent is payable in January and April and is £200 per quarter;
- rates are payable quarterly starting in February and come to £4000 per year;
- machine is going to be purchased in March for £3000; this will be paid for in three equal installments;
- sundry expenses are £150 per month.

166A A firm is trying to draw up its budgets for the coming year. The following information has been obtained:
(1) Production: Opening Stock will be 600 units, the same number of units should be produced per month to ensure that Labour is used effectively. Production in December was 2,300 units.
(2) Sales: All units are sold for £20.00 each. Estimated sales for the year are: Jan 2,500, Feb 2,500, Mar 2,500, Apr 2,000, May 2,500, Jun 3,000, July 3,500, Aug 5,000, Sep 5,000, Oct 5,500, Nov 4,000, Dec 4,000. Sales in this Dec will be 1,500 units.
(3) Raw Materials cost £5.00 per unit. Materials are bought in the same month as they are used in production. All materials are bought on credit and suppliers allow one months credit.
(4) Direct Labour costs £2.50 per hour, each product takes 2 hours to make. Workers are expected to be given a payrise in August which will increase the hourly rate to £2.75 per hour.
(5) The product is manufactured under licence and a fee of £1.00 is payable for every unit sold. This fee is paid in the month of sale.
(6) Other costs are: Indirect wages £2,000 per month.

(7) Rent & Rates are £16,000 per year, payable in quarterly installments starting in January.

(8) Office expenses are £8,000 per month.

(9) The firm will buy some new machinery in June for £20,000.

REQUIRED:

(A) The Sales Budget (in units).
(B) The Production Budget (in units).
(C) The Direct Labour Budget (in £s).
(D) The Debtors Budget (in £s).
(E) The Creditors Budget (in £s).
(F) The Cash Budget.

167A Draw up the Budget for the six months from January to July using the following information:

(1) Sales: Sales will be as follows: Jan 500 units, Feb 550 units, Mar 600 units, Apr 500 units, May 450 units, Jun 400 units, July 375 units. Sales for December were 450 units.

(2) Purchases: Raw Materials are bought in the month before they are sold. Each unit requires 3 kg of materials. Materials cost £1.20 per kilogram.

(3) Direct Labour is paid at £2.00 per hour. Each unit requires 10 hours of labour.

(4) All units are sold for £45, 25% of sales are for cash and the remainder are on credit. Debtors are allowed one months credit.

(5) Suppliers of raw materials offer a one month credit period.

(6) Other costs are; Factory Overheads £500 per month, Office expenses £250 per month, Purchase of machinery £5,000 in Feb.

REQUIRED

(a) A Debtors budget
(b) A Creditors Budget
(c) A Direct Labour Budget
(d) A Cash Budget
(e) A Budgeted Profit/Loss Account for the six month period

168 DRAW UP A CASH BUDGET for a manufacturer for the six months ended 30th June 1990 from the following information:

i) Opening Cash Balance at 1st January 1990, $640.

ii) Sales; at $12 per unit: cash received three months after sale.

Sales (by units)

1990			1991								
Oct	Nov	Dec	Jan	Feb	Mar	Apr	May	Jun	Jul	Aug	Sep
80	90	70	100	60	120	150	140	130	110	100	160

iii) Production (by units)

Oct	Nov	Dec	Jan	Feb	Mar	Apr	May	Jun	Jul	Aug	Sep
70	80	90	100	110	130	140	150	120	160	170	180

iv) Raw material costs are $4 per unit of production. Materials are paid for two months before being used in production.

v) Direct Labour; $3 per unit paid for in the same month as unit produced.

vi) Other variable expenses; $2 per unit, ¾ of the cost being paid for in the same month as production, the other ¼ being paid in the month after production.

vii) Fixed expenses of $100 per month are paid monthly.

viii) A motor van is to be bought and paid for in April for $6,000.

ix) A sale of some spare land owned by the firm will take place in March and is expected to yield $5,000.

169A GIANT FUSCHIA STORES LTD

The trader has determined his costs and selling prices but feels that he may need an overdraft at some point during the year as most of the sales are condensed in the period January to June.

The predicted sales of cuttings in each month are:

Units in '000's

Jan	Feb	Mar	Apr	May	Jun	Jul	Aug	Sep	Oct	Nov	Dec
10	10	20	40	60	60	5	5	5	3	1	1

Most sales are made to garden centres who pay for plants one month after they have been bought, the remaining 20% of sales are made through the shop or mail order and are paid for at the time of sale.

Compost is bought on credit from ICY Limited and all purchases are paid for one month after delivery. Pots are bought from a local manufacturer who offers a two month credit period.

The potting machine is bought in January and all other expenses also start in that month.

May, June, August and September are "5 week months" for payment of wages and other weekly costs.

The owner starts the business with a bank balance of £15,000 which he obtained from his redundancy money.

REQUIRED:

(1) Calculate the quantities of compost and pots required each month.

(2) Draw up a Sales budget.

(3) Draw up a Purchases budget.

(4) Draw up a Cash budget and ascertain how much, if any overdraft, will be needed.

170A A firm has prepared the Sales budget for the forthcoming six month period; January to June. Units of Sales are expected to be:

Jan	Feb	Mar	Apr	May	June
100	120	120	105	90	130

The Opening stock of units on January 1st is 55 units and a Closing stock of 50 units will be required at the end of June.

All units are sold for £12 each, 10% of sales are for cash and the remainder are sold on one months credit. Sales in December were 95 units.

The cost of raw materials required for each unit is £3. Materials are paid for in cash and are bought in the same month as the unit is manufactured.

Wages are expected to be £500 per month and other expenses £250 per month, increasing to £300 in May and June. The firm intend to buy some new machinery in April for £1,500.

The Opening balance of cash is £200.

REQUIRED:

(a) Calculate the monthly production required (in units) if the firm want to maintain production at an even level.

(b) Prepare the Sales Revenue budget.

(c) Calculate the monthly cost of purchases of raw materials.

(d) Prepare the Cash budget for the six month period.

(e) Prepare the Forecast Trading & Profit/Loss Account.

4.12 STANDARD COSTING

Firms that use budgetary control methods will often also use the methods defined as "standard costing". These methods are most applicable to manufacturing firms but can be applied to any industry.

Standard costing is the technique of defining a "standard cost" for each element involved in the cost of a product; this means that the standard or expected cost is calculated for direct materials, direct labour, variable overheads, fixed overheads and selling price. Without deciding what these costs are expected to be it is quite difficult to actually prepare budgets; put simply, how can budgets for income and expenditure be prepared without knowing what the cost of each item is likely to be?

On the other hand it may appear that it is obvious what the cost of each element is. If management has timed the performance of a job as being two hours and the rate of pay is £3.00 per hour then the cost for direct labour in each product will be £6.00. This is the figure that would be included in the budget as the cost of direct labour. However, it should be apparent that not every job will take two hours for various reasons, such as some workers are quicker than others, some are slower, there may be machine breakdowns, etc.

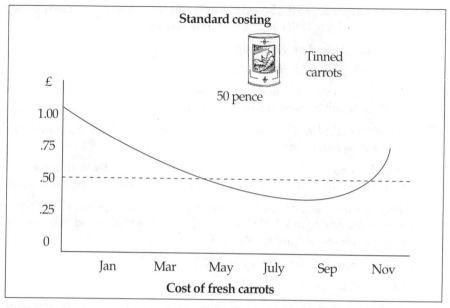

Figure 4.22 Within budget?

The cost of direct materials for a job may be estimated at a set amount per product, but in some industries the cost of raw materials is continually fluctuating. Firms that sell tinned vegetables will be expected to charge roughly the same price throughout the year, yet the price they pay for supplies will fluctuate from very low at harvest time to very high a few weeks before the following year's harvest time because of a scarcity of raw materials.

Standard costing is used by firms that appreciate these problems and that have taken steps to estimate what the average cost of each cost element will be, spread over a whole year. In the previous illustration of direct labour costs, management might decide that although the predicted cost of direct labour is £6.00 per unit, it knows that there will be hold-ups in production during the year and that therefore the average cost will be closer to £6.20 for each unit. This figure is taken as the standard cost and will be used in all budgets and other forecasting methods.

4.13   VARIANCE ANALYSIS

If a firm is using a budgetary control system, it is effectively asking managers of different departments how they expect to perform in the coming year. In order to check whether the managers performed as well as they expected, it is necessary to check the budget figures with the actual figures at the end of the year. This practice involves variance analysis.

At the beginning of each year the standard costs are determined for each cost element; these standard costs are then included in the calculation of budgets. At the end of the year the actual results are compared with the budgeted figures and any difference is known as the variance. Managers can then be asked to explain to senior management why there was a variance from their budgeted figures.

Therefore variance analysis is essentially a technique used to evaluate efficiency. It forms part of the principles of "management by exception" — managers whose budgeted figures are the same as the actual results are not questioned, only those managers whose figures were different from the actual results.

The following budgeted profit and loss account was used in the section relating to budgets and the actual results at the end of the year are shown alongside in Figure 4.23.

The actual profit made is £860 above that budgeted for, but sales are also 100 more than budgeted. So, profit and sales are both more than expected, which is normally accepted as being favourable. Unfortunately, the above figures do not really show whether the increased sales and profit were due to all managers showing greater efficiency. All costs are higher than those budgeted for but as sales increase, most costs will also increase. In order to determine which managers have been most efficient it is first necessary to calculate a "flexible budget". This is a budget which takes the standard costs from the first budget and calculates what the budget figures should have been at the actual level of sales.

	Budgeted units	Actual units
Sales	1,000	1,100
	£	£
Revenue	100,000	108,900
Materials	30,000	35,200
Direct labour	10,000	10,500
Production overheads	5,000	5,665
Sales and distribution overheads	15,000	15,657
Administration overheads	17,000	18,000
Finance overheads	3,000	3,000
Net profit	20,000	20,860

Figure 4.23

Flexible budgets are essential if any comparisons are to be drawn between budgeted and actual figures. As explained, above there will obviously be an increase in some costs if sales are higher than the budget figure, and any comparison of budgets and actual results will be meaningless as they are at different levels. However, the flexible budget shows what the budgeted figures would have been at the actual level of sales: this means that comparisons are possible and meaningful.

The following is an illustration of how the figures can be compared, the last column shows the variance amount. The letter F stands for "favourable" and means that the actual results are better than the budgeted figures; the letter A stands for "adverse" and signifies that the actual results are worse than the budgeted figures.

	Budgeted units	Unit cost	Flexible budget	Actual units	Variance
Sales	1,000		1,100	1,100	
	£	£	£	£	£
Revenue	100,000	100	110,00	108,900	1,100(A)
Materials	30,000	30	33,000	35,200	2,200(A)
Direct labour	10,000	10	11,000	10,500	500(F)
Production	5,000	5	5,000	5,665	665(A)
Sales and distribution	15,000	15	15,000	15,675	675(A)
Administration	17,000	17	17,000	18,000	1,000(A)
Finance	3,000	3	3,000	3,000	
Net Profit	20,000	20	26,000	20,860	5,140(A)

Figure 4.24

This shows that the situation is much worse than the simple comparison of budgeted and actual results predicted. Although net profit is £860 more than the budgeted figure it should really have been £5140 higher than the budgeted figure. Clearly there have been some inefficiencies in the firm.

One point to note from the chart is that in the flexible budget the overheads are not increased from the original budget figure. This is because they are not identified as variable overheads and are therefore presumably fixed overheads. This means that they should not increase in proportion to production or sales but should remain constant, regardless of any changes in output.

It is possible to check that the variances are correct by reconciling budgeted profit with actual profit.

Profit reconciliation	
	£
Flexible budget profit	26,000
— original budget profit	20,000
	6,000
Actual profit	20,860
—original budget profit	20,000
	860
Variance in profit = £6,000 − £860 = £5,140	

Figure 4.25

However, the variance in the profit is only an expression of the results of the inefficiencies and does not explain where the inefficiencies arise. Just because the firm has made less profit than was predicted in the budget does not necessarily mean that all managers and all departments have been inefficient. By calculating the variances for each expense item it is possible to determine more accurately where the inefficiencies lie.

The first variance calculated was the revenue - there is a variance of £1,100 which is adverse. By dividing the revenue by the units sold it is possible to calculate that the selling price per unit was dropped from £100 to £99. The sales manager might be called upon by senior management to explain why he felt it was necessary to do this, rather than sticking to his budgeted selling price. The obvious answer that the sales manager would give is that it was done to increase the volume of sales; unfortunately this excuse would not normally be acceptable to senior management as all of the budgets will be interlocking and it may not be possible for production to maintain increased output to cope with increases in sales. More likely, the selling price might have had to be reduced in order for the firm to retain its market share as competitors had reduced their prices.

The variance on materials is £2200 which means that the cost of raw materials in each product has increased from £30 to £32. The purchasing manager would have to justify this, but it could be due to a general shortage of materials, having to change suppliers to ensure better quality, having to use poorer quality materials due to a shortage and suffering greater wastage through poor quality, etc.

The variance for direct labour is in fact favourable and the cost of direct labour per unit has fallen from £10 to £9.55. This does not mean that the hourly rate of pay for workers has fallen: this is impossible to calculate without knowing the total hours worked. What it does show is that the direct labour force has apparently worked more quickly and produced more goods. This may be because of better training, more highly skilled workers, better supervision, better machinery, fewer industrial disputes, improved bonus schemes, etc.

All of the other variances are adverse and they all relate to supposedly fixed overheads. The reasons for variances in fixed overheads are often outside the control of the firm, for example, rent or lighting bills could have been increased because the supplier decided to increase the charge. Unless substantial prior notice is given then such increases may not be included in budgeted figures. But, particularly in inflationary periods, most organisations will impose annual increases in prices and the managers of different departments would be expected to estimate what these increases would be. Thus the personnel manager would estimate what percentage salary increase would be given to staff and the administration manager would estimate what the increase in lighting, rent, rates etc, would be. It is important that these estimates are fairly accurate as they are included in the master budget and the cash budget. If the increase is more than expected, then there may not be sufficient cash available to pay the extra amount.

What should be remembered is that variance analysis is carried out not as a mathematical exercise but to find the reasons for differences and to identify where improvements can be made.

Reasons for variances

Materials variance:

— cost of materials <u>appears</u> to have increased to £2.10 per unit
— suppliers increased prices
— change of supplier for better quality
— increased scrap and wastage

Labour variance:

— cost of labour <u>appears</u> to have decreased to £1.45 per unit
— reduction in wages (unlikely)
— improved productivity
— original standard set too high
— better trained workers
— improved bonus scheme
— fewer industrial disputes

Overhead variance:

— increase in rent, rates, insurance, etc
— more wastage (eg light and heat)
— climatic conditions (eg long cold spell)

Figure 4.26 Reasons for variances

Many modern, commercially available financial accounting packages for microcomputers allow the user to enter budgeted figures as well as financial accounting details. These packages automatically calculate variances at the end of each period and many can produce variance reports containing details of just the items with a variance.

Exercises

171 A firm that uses budgetary control techniques has devised the following budgeted profit and loss account, and has now obtained the actual profit/loss details in order to make comparisons. Devise a flexible budget, then calculate and comment on any variances.

	Budgeted units	Actual units
Sales	10,000	12,000
	£	£
Revenue	25,000	31,000
Materials	6,000	7,440
Direct labour	4,500	5,760
Production overheads	3,000	2,750
Sales and distribution overheads	3,800	3,800

Administration overheads	4,200	4,400
Finance overheads	750	750
Net Profit	2,750	6,100

172A A firm has estimated that it will be able to sell 10,000 units in the coming year. The selling price per unit has been set at £12.

Materials will cost £3 per unit and Labour £2.50 per unit. The firm has identified Variable Overheads of £1.50 per unit and also predicts Fixed Overheads of £4,000 for the year.

Draw up the Budgeted Profit/Loss account for the year.

At the end of the year the actual results are as follows:

Sales (11,500 units)	£135,500
Materials	£38,500
Labour	£26,500
Variable Overheads	£17,900
Fixed Overheads	£4,200
	£87,100
Profit	£48,400

Draw up a Flexible budget for the actual sales level and identify the variances.

173 A firm has produced the following data:

	Budget Figures	Actual Results
Units	20,000	21,500
	$	$
Sales	80,000	82,775
Materials	10,000	11,825
Labour	25,000	23,650
Variable Overheads	5,000	4,945
Fixed Overheads	12,000	12,900
Profit	28,000	29,445

(i) Calculate all appropriate Variances   (6 marks)
(ii) Suggest reasons why the Materials and Labour Variances have occurred   (4 marks)
       (Mar 92)

174 A firm that uses budgetary control techniques has devised a budgeted Profit/Loss account for the year ended May 1988. The actual figures have now been received and the Profit/Loss account drawn up. The details are as follows:

	Budgeted Units	Actual Units
Sales	100,000	119,000
	$	$
Revenue	850,000	1,029,350
Materials	210,000	255,850
Direct Labour	165,000	184,450
Production Overheads	105,000	113,000
Selling Overheads	45,000	45,000
Administration Overheads	90,000	88,000
Net Profit	235,000	343,050

REQUIRED:

(a) Devise a Flexible budget for 119,000 units.
(b) Calculate any variances.
(c) Comment on the possible reasons for the variances.
(d) Suggest how a spreadsheet could be especially useful in this sort of task.

175   A firm had produced the following budget at the beginning of the year:

Sales	10,000 units
	$
Revenue	200,000
Materials	35,000
Labour	40,000
Variable Overheads	17,500
Fixed Overheads	60,000
Net Profit	47,500

At the end of the year the sales amounted to 11,100 units and the selling price per unit had been $21.50.

The costs of materials were actually $3.65 and Labour was $3.90 per unit. Variable Overheads amounted to $16,800 and Fixed Overheads were $63,000.

REQUIRED

(a) Devise a *flexible budget* for the *actual sales volume*.
(b) Draw up the *profit/loss account* for the actual results
(c) Calculate the *main variances*.
(d) Briefly suggest reasons for the *variances*.

176A GIANT FUSCHIA STORES

In the second year of trading the owner of the business has decided that he could make more money by:

(a) growing the plants "on" and selling larger plants.
(b) selling plants by reference to their growing style.

Consequently the budgeted data for the second year's trading has been drawn up as follows:

TYPE:	Trailing	Bush	Hardy	Standard
	£	£	£	£
Selling price	1.00	1.20	1.40	8.00
Costs:				
Materials:	0.25	0.30	0.30	1.00
Labour:	0.10	0.10	0.10	1.50
Variable Ohds:	0.05	0.05	0.10	0.75
Fixed Ohds:	0.25	0.25	0.25	0.25

These costs have been estimated at a production/sales level of 200,000 plants. Sales of each type of plant are estimated as:

Trailing	70,000 plants
Bush	70,000 plants
Hardy	40,000 plants
Standard	20,000 plants

REQUIRED:

(1) Draw up the Budgeted Profit/Loss Account for the year.

At the end of the year the actual results are obtained and show the following:

TYPE:	Trailing	Bush	Hardy	Standard	Total
Plants sold	75,000	68,000	35,500	18,500	197,000
	£	£	£	£	£
Sales revenue	78,750	85,000	44,375	153,550	361,675
Costs:					
Materials:	18,750	20,400	12,425	20,350	71,925
Labour:	7,500	8,160	3,905	27,750	47,315
Variable Ohds:	4,500	3,400	4,260	16,650	28,810
Fixed Ohds:	20,250	18,360	9,585	4,995	53,190
	51,000	50,320	30,175	69,745	201,240
Profit:	27,750	34,680	14,200	83,805	160,435

REQUIRED:

(2) Draw up a Flexible budget for the actual level of sales and extract any appropriate variances.

177A A company manufactures and sells a microcomputer called the Mango. The following information is available for a reporting period:

	Budget	Actual
Production of Mango	10,000 units	10,000 units
Sales of Mango	10,000 units	8,000 units
Sales revenue	£7,000,000	£7,200,000
Raw materials consumed	8,000 kilos	9,000 kilos
Cost of raw materials	£1,200,000	£1,260,000
Direct Labour hours	500,000 hours	550,000 hours
Direct Labour cost	£2,000,000	£2,475,000
Administration Fixed costs	£3,000,000	£3,260,000

There were no opening or closing stocks of raw materials, and no opening stocks of product Mango.

Stocks are valued at standard production cost.

Required:

(a) Calculate the Budgeted and actual profit for the period.
(b) Calculate appropriate variances for materials and labour.

4.14 MARGINAL COSTING

Earlier in this chapter, under the section on break-even analysis, the term "contribution" was introduced and defined as being selling price less variable costs. The use of contribution is very important in another cost accounting technique called marginal costing, of which break-even analysis is simply one part.

Marginal costing works on the assumption that fixed costs will remain constant regardless of levels of production activity. This is in fact how fixed costs were defined at the beginning of the chapter. The implications of fixed costs remaining constant have already been demonstrated in the use of break-even analysis, but the use of contribution is beneficial in other decision-making situations as well.

If fixed costs remain constant, it means that the difference between selling price and variable costs represents a contribution to fixed costs for every unit sold. For example, if selling price is £10, and variable costs £6 for each unit, the contribution to fixed costs from each unit sold is £4. This simple calculation is adequate for break-even analysis but is not appropriate for many decisions as firms usually sell more than one product, each of which will have a different contribution.

Example: A firm produces three products: alpha, beta and gamma.

	Alpha		Beta		Gamma	
	£	£	£	£	£	£
Selling price		10		15		20
Direct materials	2		3		5	
Direct labour	2		2		3	
Variable overheads	1	5	2	7	3	11
Contribution		5		8		9

Figure 4.27

These contributions would be set against fixed costs. In previous work in this chapter, methods of absorbing the fixed costs have been demonstrated, thus enabling the fixed costs to be divided between the three products on some predetermined basis. However, marginal costing theory is that fixed costs would be incurred regardless of how many units are produced and, more importantly, an additional unit produced will only increase variable costs and not fixed costs. Therefore, it is undesirable to try to apportion fixed costs between the different products; if fixed costs are apportioned, then incorrect decisions can be made.

Consider the following example:

Example: The firm mentioned above has apportioned fixed costs equally between products; the forecast operating statement is as seen in Figure 4.28

	Alpha		Beta		Gamma	
	£	£	£	£	£	£
Sales		20,000		35,000		50,000
Variable costs	10,000		16,000		27,500	
Fixed costs	13,000	23,000	13,000	29,000	13,000	40,500
Profit		(3,000)		6,000		9,500

Figure 4.28

The obvious decision that management have to make is whether to stop production of product alpha. In the above layout it appears to be obvious that alpha should be dropped. However, according to marginal costing theory, this may not be correct as alpha is making a contribution of £5 for each unit sold; the operating statement in marginal costing layout would accordingly be as shown in Figure 4.29.

	Alpha	Beta	Gamma	Total
	£	£	£	£
Sales	20,000	35,000	50,000	105,000
Variable costs	10,000	16,000	27,500	53,500
Contribution	10,000	19,000	22,500	51,500
Fixed costs				39,000
Profit				12,500

Figure 4.29

Using the marginal costing approach only variable costs are attributed to each product and in this method it is apparent that alpha is making a reasonable contribution to fixed costs. Further proof can be obtained by examining what the profit would be if alpha were dropped:

	£
Contribution: beta	19,000
Contribution: gamma	22,500
	41,500
Less fixed costs	39,000
Profit	2,500

Figure 4.30

The difference in profits is solely attributable to the £10,000 lost contribution from alpha. In this example it would be most unwise to drop alpha, unless the spare production capacity could then be taken up by beta or gamma which have a higher contribution.

Marginal costing can also be used to decide whether it is better for a firm to manufacture its own products or buy them in from other suppliers.

For example, an external supplier has offered to supply the firm with product alpha at a cost of £6.50 each. The firm is currently producing and selling 2000 units of alpha.

The price of these units is below the current selling price of alpha but it is not below the marginal cost (ie variable cost) therefore the cost to the firm is £5 to make and £6.50 to buy. If they buy the product in, they may not be able to utilise the production capacity released by not having to make alpha; if this is so they will lose £3000 profit, which is the difference between the buying-in price and the marginal cost of manufacture (£6.50 − £5) x 2000.

Marginal costing can also be used to decide whether to take on a special order. For example, the firm is offered a contract for product gamma in which it would supply 1000 units provided that the price were only £14. This contract would utilise the spare production currently available. The present situation was shown previously and the profit is £12,500. If the firm accepts this order, the figures for the special order will be:

	£
Sales (1000 x £14)	14,000
Less marginal cost (1000 x £11)	11,000
Contribution	3,000

Figure 4.31

As all fixed costs have already been covered by the contribution from existing sales, this £3000 contribution is pure profit. If the firm accepted this order the total profit would be £15,500 (£12,500 + £3,000).

In all of the examples given for marginal costing it is worth remembering that if fixed costs had been absorbed into the cost of each product, the wrong decisions would have been taken and the profit would have been reduced.

Exercises

178 A firm produces three products and has drawn up the following operating statement:

Product	A	B	C
	£	£	£
Sales	130,000	50,000	75,000
Variable costs	70,000	35,000	45,000
Fixed costs	50,000	20,000	25,000
Profit	10,000	(5,000)	5,000

(a) The firm is considering scrapping product B because of its losses. Show an alternative means of calculating the profit and see whether product B should be dropped.

(b) Show the operating statement assuming that product B is dropped.

(c) Show the operating statement in marginal costing format if product B is dropped but sales of product C are increased by £40,000.

179   A firm is making a product which it sells for £4 each. The current output is 85,000 units per year, which is 85% of capacity. Total costs are £280,000 of which £67,500 are fixed costs. A contract could be obtained with a buyer, which would make use of all of the spare capacity but can only be had if the selling price is £3 per unit. Should the firm take the contract and what would be the effect on profit?

180   A firm currently supplies 3 products and has drawn up the following forecast Operating statement:

	Computers	Printers	Software
Sales	$30,000	$37,000	$50,000
Direct Materials	$10,000	$5,000	$1,000
Direct Labour	$10,000	$12,000	$25,000
Fixed Costs	$15,000	$15,000	$15,000
Profit	($5,000)	$5,000	$9,000

The firm is currently considering whether to discontinue selling computers.

(i)   Redraft the Operating statement using an alternative style and state whether in your opinion Computers should be discontinued.   (5 marks)

(ii) Use the same alternative layout to show what the total profit would be if Computers were discontinued.   (5 marks) (Mar 91)

181A A Computer software house produces three software packages and provides a support service for each package. Fixed costs are apportioned equally between the products. The forecast operating statement for the coming year is:

	Word-Processor	Spreadsheet	Database
	£	£	£
Sales	26,000	38,000	17,000
Variable costs	14,000	19,000	9,500
Fixed costs	10,000	10,000	10,000
Profit	2,000	9,000	(2,500)

(a) The firm is considering whether to discontinue the database. Redraft the operating statement using a marginal costing format and state whether the database should be dropped.

(b) Draft the operating statement if the database is dropped and reconcile the figures with those produced in (a).

(c) The spreadsheet currently costs £100 per copy. An overseas distributor has offered to buy 100 copies but only if the price for the order is £68 per copy. Should the firm accept this order?

182   A firm produces four products and has drawn up the following operating statement:

Product:	A	B	C	D
	$	$	$	$
Sales	190,000	250,000	300,000	410,000
Variable costs	125,000	262,000	280,000	320,000
Fixed costs	30,000	30,000	30,000	30,000
Profit	35,000	(42,500)	(10,000)	60,000

(a) The firm is considering whether to scrap products B and C because they are making losses. Redraft the operating statement using a Marginal Costing layout.

(b) Suggest whether the products should be dropped and explain your reasons.

(c) If both products were to be dropped then the spare production capacity could be used by product A and D, sales of both products could be increased by 25% if one product is dropped. Show a summary operating statement to show the effect on profit if Product B only is dropped.

(d) Draw up the summary operating statement to show the effect if product C only is dropped.

(e) If both product B and C are dropped then the sales of A and D will increase by 50%. Show how this would affect profit.   (Jun 88)

183   A computer manufacturer has the following short run costs in relation to the production of 260 of its PCs.

	Fixed Costs	Variable Costs	Notes
Labour	45,626	1,300	$5 bonus for each PC produced
Materials	—	44,946	
Overhead	46,390	260	$1 power cost per PC produced

(a) Briefly explain the terms MARGINAL and ABSORPTION costs.

(b) Calculate the ABSORPTION cost of the PCs.

(c) Calculate the selling price of a PC if the company wishes to make a 20% profit.

(d) Calculate the MARGINAL cost (per unit) of PC production.

(e) If the firm manufactures 260 PCs for the costs above, what would be the cost of producing 280?

(f) If the selling price per unit stood at $700, what would the additional profit be for the firm it if produced the 280 units?

184A GIANT FUSCHIA STORES

The owner of the business has been examining the actual results for the second year's trading *(see sheet on Variance Analysis)*. He is disappointed with the figures for Hardy plants and is considering whether they should be dropped from the "product" range. He is dissatisfied with them as they produce the lowest profit of all four plant types offered.

REQUIRED:

(a) Redraft the actual results in a Marginal Costing format and calculate the Contribution/Sales ratio for each plant type.

(b) Show what the results would have been if Hardy plants had been discontinued.

The owner has also mentioned that sales could have been a lot higher if he had accepted an order from BQ it All (a nationwide DIY/Gardening centre firm). They wanted 5,000 plants of each type but only if he would sell at 50% of normal prices, he had to reject the order as he would only have covered his costs on the Standard type plants.

REQUIRED:

(c) Calculate whether the owner would have covered his costs from this order.

(d) Calculate what effect the order would have had on his overall profit, if it had been accepted.

185A A Computer software house produces three software packages and provides a support service for each package. Fixed costs are apportioned equally between the products. The forecast operating statement for the coming year is:

	Word-Processor	Spreadsheet	Database
	£	£	£
Sales	26,000	38,000	17,000
Variable costs	14,000	19,000	9,500
Fixed costs	10,000	10,000	10,000
Profit	2,000	9,000	(2,500)

(a) The firm is considering whether to discontinue the Database. Re-draft the operating statement using a marginal costing format and state whether the database should be dropped.

(b) Draft the operating statement if the Database is dropped and reconcile the figures with those produced in (a).

(c) The spreadsheet currently costs £100 per copy. An overseas distributor has offered to buy 100 copies but only if the price for the order is £68 per copy. Should the firm accept this order?

186 A firm has budgeted to sell 10,000 computers at a price of $1,000 each. The costs in manufacturing these computers are Direct Materials $350, Direct Labour $240, Variable Overheads $60 and Fixed Costs $200 per unit.

(a) Calculate the break-even point   (2 marks)
(b) Calculate the profit at the budgeted level of sales.   (2 marks)

The sales manager thinks that sales could be increased to 11,000 units if the selling price was reduced to $900.

(c) Calculate the profit at this selling price.   (2 marks)

A well-known retailer has offered to buy 2,000 machines provided that the price on these machines is reduced to $750.

(d) Calculate whether this order should be accepted.   (4 marks)
(e) State what other factors should be considered in this type of situation.   (5 marks)

The same computer could be bought ready assembled for $750 from an overseas supplier.

(f) Calculate whether the computer should be manufactured or bought-in   (2 marks)
(g) State what other factors should be considered in this type of situation.   (3 marks)
                                                                  (Sep 91)

5 Computers and accounts

INTRODUCTION

Lastly, we bring together the topics from the previous sections, and show how the various manual based theories are incorporated into computerised accounting systems. The section shows the different systems and procedures used in computer-based accounting. Note that, whilst the content of this chapter is based on the techniques and styles of most commercially available systems, there is no real substitute for actually using a software package.

OBJECTIVES

At the end of this section you should be able to:

— identify the benefits gained from using computerised accounting systems

— describe the main items required for inclusion/evaluation in a computer-ised accounting package

— define the commonly available printouts of information which a computer-ised accounting should provide

— be aware of the techniques used for data entry and for examination of items in most computerised accounting systems

— identify the similarities and differences between computerised and manual accounting systems

— describe how spreadsheets and other packages can process accounting data.

5.1 COMPUTERISED ACCOUNTS

Organisations intending to use computers invariably make the computerisation of the accounts function their first priority. There are two reasons for this:

— The control of funds coming into and going out of the firm is obviously very important and the use of computers should make such control more effective.

— The vast majority of accounting data is numerical and is always processed with the same method. This makes computerisation relatively easy.

The advantages of having the accounting function computerised are as follows:

— Addition and entries should be more accurate. This is particularly so where there are very large quantities of data to be entered in the accounts. Clerks will tend to get bored or distracted and errors can easily occur in manual systems; computers do not get bored.

— Reports can be supplied more quickly and frequently. This is normally a more important advantage than better addition. Computers can produce profit and loss accounts as frequently as required (once a day if necessary) and all that is needed to produce them is the push of a button and a few minutes wait at most. In a manual system it can often take weeks to produce the profit and loss account for an annual period.

— Many reports can be produced that would not be practical in a manual system because of the time and cost involved. The clearest example of this is the analysis of aged debts. In a manual system clerks will be employed to go through the sales ledger to identify customers who have not paid their debts. Once identified these customers are sent reminders asking for payment. In a computerised system the computer can not only automatically issue reminders but can also examine the accounts to see how long the debt has been outstanding. From this analysis a printout is produced showing the breakdown of debts into the amount owing since last month, the amount owing for two months, for three months, etc.

Computer programs for financial accounting invariably follow the system of dividing the ledger that was described in Part 2 (ie nominal, sales, and purchases ledgers). The reason for continuing the same method of dividing the ledger was partly for continuity - the first firms to use computers were very large organisations whose manual records were already subdivided into the different ledgers. However, the practice has continued because it has distinct advantages for the user firm.

Most commercially available accounting software is available as "integrated packages", which means that it is usually possible to buy any one ledger package, such as sales, nominal or purchases, but if all the packages are bought, they can be integrated so that entries in one ledger will automatically update accounts in another ledger package. This sort of package is ideal for a firm with a large number of customers and suppliers. However, a lot of firms buy from only a handful of suppliers (eg timber merchants) or pay for all purchases in cash (eg scrap metal dealers, antique dealers). For firms which do not purchase "raw materials" (eg a computer bureau) a purchases ledger package would be a waste of time.

Alternatively, a lot of very large businesses have no credit sales (eg supermarkets) or sell to only a few organisations (eg shipbuilders, aeroplane manufacturers). For these firms a sales ledger package would be a waste of time. However, all of the examples given here buy very large quantities of "raw materials" from a very wide range of suppliers so would certainly want a purchases ledger package.

Some organisations have very few purchases or sales on credit and therefore do not need a sales of purchases ledger (eg small shops, football clubs, theatres). For these organisations, a nominal ledger package will often suffice.

The purpose of the above is to illustrate that if the division of the ledger is to be retained in computerised systems, not all organisations will want all of the available ledgers.

The technology available today may mean that there is no longer the need to sub-divide the ledger in order for it to be manageable, but the division is retained because:

- It restricts the opportunity for fraud — if the ledger is divided, one person looks after sales whilst another looks after nominal. Control accounts enable checks to be made on the accuracy of the sales ledger.

- In very large systems, even if they are multi-user, it makes it easier when more than one person is needed to operate the system.

- The reports required from customers' and suppliers' accounts are different from those required from the nominal accounts. For example, at the end of the month a sales ledger package should be capable of printing statements of accounts for customers with outstanding debts. If the sales and nominal ledger were combined this request would mean that unnecessary statements of account for wages, fixtures and fittings, etc, would also be produced.

A fully integrated accounts package will invariably contain more than just the sales, purchases and nominal ledgers. Most software houses also offer packages for payroll, stock control, invoicing and financial planning which can all be integrated into the accounting package so that any entries made will automatically update other packages. This list is by no means definitive and some software houses do offer a variety of other packages such as job costing, production planning, etc. A simple overview of how these packages integrate with each other and the types of reports/printouts obtained is shown in Figure 5.2.

It is perhaps worth mentioning that a number of software houses have in recent years introduced a new type of "integrated package" such as Symphony, Framework, etc. These are packages that generally include a word processor, spreadsheet, database, and a graphics package where data from one element (eg database) can be integrated with data from another element (eg word processor). They are "integrated" but should not be confused with integrated accounts packages.

Improvements in operating systems have enabled more use to be made of "windows" for pull-down menus and for simultaneously viewing other information. These advances should enable programmers to devise packages that are less monotonous to use and therefore should result in less errors in data entry.

Also, developments in database techniques, especially data query tools such as SQLs, have resulted in major advances in the area of data storage and retrieval. Many software houses have already produced accounting packages that can be directly accessible by the more commonly used databases; the objective in doing this is to make accounting data far more flexible and to make the data more widely available in improved report formats or for integration with other packages.

Some software houses have now taken the improved database techniques a stage further and have created "single-ledger systems". These do away with the previous concepts relating to the division of the ledger and store all accounting data in one single database. The advantages of this approach is that a much wider range of reports and analyses can be used and there is far less duplication of data. This "single-ledger system" appears to be gaining in popularity as a means of taking advantages of the improvements in data query tools but any firm developing such a system would have to consider very carefully how it could replace the auditing safeguards that would automatically form part of a multi-ledger system.

Despite the fact that there is a huge range of accounting packages available there are very few major differences between the packages. This is primarily because they all have to follow the basic accounting concepts and conventions and therefore there is little scope for individuality. Most are menu-driven which is accepted as being the easiest method for non-computer staff to follow. A typical main menu for a sales ledger package would be:

1	Enter transactions	4	End period
2	Update account details	5	Set system configuration
3	Report on ledger	6	Exit sales ledger

Figure 5.1

The user simply selects the number required and is then usually presented with a sub-menu allowing a second choice of options. The "system configuration" option should appear in all ledger packages and serves to redesign the package so that it is usable by the firm's own computer system. Remember, a software house will write just one program and expect to sell it to many hundreds of organisations, all using different computers or printers.

Exercises

Questions followed by A do not have answers supplied.

187A Recent developments in database techniques have encouraged some software houses to devise "single-ledger systems" using one large database to store all accounting data as opposed to the normal division of the Ledger system. What internal controls will normally be weakened by such a move?

188A What is meant by an "integrated system"?

189 (a) Explain what is meant by the term "Division of the Ledger" and why such a system is necessary in manual systems.   (8 marks)

    (b) The "Division of the Ledger" is not strictly necessary in a Computerised system, but most firms continue to use it. Give 4 reasons why the procedure is still retained.   (12 marks)

                                                              (Mar 91)

5.2   SYSTEM CONFIGURATION

Commercially available software packages will need to be able to run on a wide variety of different machines and use an even wider range of printers. They will therefore have to be "customised" to match the equipment that a particular firm

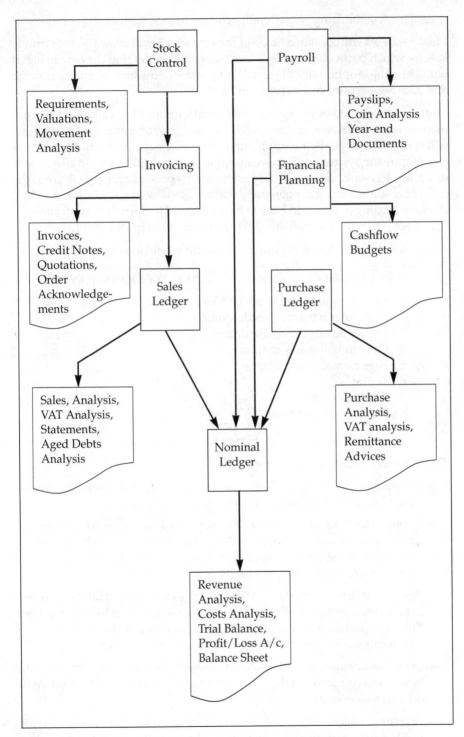

Figure 5.2 Accounting packages

uses. This "customising" is generally referred to as system configuration.

Most packages will contain a range of options which will allow the user firm to specify which particular model of computer and printer that they are using. It will also include options for the equally important items such as company name and address, account codes, passwords, etc.

The options selected by the system configuration should be capable of amendment; it is not unknown for firms to change address, or name, and many firms will certainly change their equipment on a regular basis. If it is not possible to reconfigure the system for the new equipment then the firm would also have to buy a new software package. This in itself may not present a great problem as the cost of accounts software is generally fairly reasonable but it would mean that all of the existing data would have to be transferred to the new system and staff retrained — this would probably be considered as too great a price.

A typical sub-menu for configuring the system would look like this:

SALES LEDGER	SYSTEM CONFIGURATION MENU
1　Company name, address and VAT number	
2　Computer hardware configuration	
3　Printer hardware configuration	
4　Operational configuration	
5　Page format configuration	
6　Tax rates	
7　Alter user table	
8　Return to main menu	

Figure 5.3

These functions have the following purposes:

— *Company name and address*　This is needed to ensure that all documents such as invoices actually contain the firm's name and address.

— *Computer hardware configuration*　The software house is not likely to supply a program which is not compatible with the firm's computer but even so as most computer suppliers sell a range of models it may be necessary for the firm to configure the program for its specific model.

— *Printer hardware configuration*　Many packages will accept a range of printers or allow the user to enter the printer codes appropriate for his or her printer. This is important as many accounts programs require the use of a printer which can switch between 80 and 132 column print mode.

— *Operational configuration*　This allows the user to designate what type of codes to use for account names, how accounts are to be sorted, reference codes for each transaction, etc.

— *Page format configuration*　This is useful if the firm intends to use its own pre-printed stationery; it allows the user to designate the width and length of the paper used. It may also be used to design a "picture" so that reports will be printed in the exact position required for pre-printed stationery such as Invoices, Statements, etc. This will allow the firm to use good quality headed stationery but with the computer printing on details of transaction.

— *Tax rates*   Most countries have some form of purchase tax (VAT in the UK); this option allows the firm to enter the appropriate tax rates so that the purchase tax can be automatically calculated on each transaction.

— *Alter user table*   This is a vital option and is used to prevent unauthorised access to the program. The firm can designate authorised users and provide them with passwords by using this option. Good packages will not only restrict use of the program to those people listed in the user table but can also restrict which parts of the program that person can use. Therefore the manager can authorise an employee to enter transaction details but not allow that user to create accounts.

The above options are found in virtually all packages and are applicable to all of the ledgers. It is essential that these options are processed to ensure that the system is properly configured before it is used. There are also some characteristics of computer accounts packages that are similar to all of the ledgers which apply when the system is in use. These relate to the audit trail.

Exercises

190A Why do firms still use separate ledger packages instead of just using integrated packages including sales, purchases and nominal ledgers?

191A Why is it necessary to configure a package, and what would the configuration involve?

192 Show in a diagrammatic form an integrated accounting system.

193 Most Commercial Accounting packages will include a "Systems Configuration" option.

    (i)   Briefly explain why this option is necessary.   (3 marks)
    (ii)   Identify 6 typical "Systems Configuration" options.   (12 marks)
                                                           (Mar 91)

194A Show in diagrammatic form the components, and the links between them, of a Computerised Integrated Accounting system (the diagram should show documents produced).

195 (a) Show in the form of a diagram the sequence used in the "Division of the Ledger" in a manually based accounting system.
    (b) Explain why the same Ledgers are still used in a computerised system.

5.3   AUDIT TRAILS

Audit trails were mentioned in Part 3 as a means by which the auditor can follow the documentation of a transaction from source document to profit and loss account. The use of computers can present difficulties in following this "trail", so most software houses have built in options that are designed to assist the auditor and internal management.

One of the main problems is that it may not be possible to ascertain who entered a particular transaction or who altered the details in an account. In a manual system this is usually possible by examining the handwriting, but unfortunately it is not possible to identify users in this way in a computerised system. What most packages do is keep a logbook of users which lists all of the activities carried out by that user whilst they were "logged on". At the end of each day, or week, the logbook is printed out and can be retained to sort out any queries, or can be kept for the auditor to inspect. A sample logbook is shown in Figure 5.4.

ABC Limited Special operations logbook 07-DEC-89 page1			
01-DEC-89	TYRE	User logged on	
01-DEC-89	TYRE	Account created	001/123/3333
01-DEC-89	TYRE	Account created	001/123/3334
02-DEC-89	GBTE	User logged on	
02-DEC-89	GBTE	Account examined	010/122/2155
02-DEC-89	GBTE	Account deleted	021/121/4122
04-DEC-89	TYRE	User logged on	
04-DEC-89	TYRE	User table altered	New user 5: HOSD
06-DEC-89	HOSD	User logged on	
06-DEC-89	HOSD	Account examined	012/123/3312
06-DEC-89	HOSD	Account examined	012/123/3310

Figure 5.4 A sample special operations logbook

The special operations logbook, as it is usually known, does not normally list all of the transactions entered as there would be far too many entries and this information is already recorded elsewhere.

The other problem associated with the audit trail is that the data may have been deleted from the account if the transaction that the auditor is checking is six or seven months old. This problem is solved by the production of "daybooks". These again are used in all ledger packages and list every transaction entered in the ledger in date order. A typical daybook is shown in Figure 5.5. The daybook shows the date of each transactions, the reference for each transaction, the source document, the amount, and the transaction number. The transaction number is "carried" with the transaction into the account and enables the auditor to follow the trail from the daybook into the account.

Many daybooks will also include additional columns which will show which transaction number was the next transaction in a particular account. If the auditor is concentrating on checking one specific account, then this facility obviously streamlines the process.

Exercises

196 Which printouts are needed for the audit trail, and what do they contain?

197A Why do computers cause the auditor problems when following the audit trail?

5.4 NOMINAL (GENERAL) LEDGER

The nominal ledger package is still used to record details of nominal accounts, but firms that do not need a sales or purchases ledger package can use the nominal ledger to store small numbers of accounts for debtors and creditors. The facilities for analysis in the nominal ledger are far less than in other packages such as sales and purchases, the reason being that there is rarely any use served by analysing expenses any further than the obvious analysis which is to produce profit and loss accounts and balance sheets. Most nominal ledger packages will produce trial balances and printouts for individual accounts, but other than this there are few other uses for the ledger.

A typical daybook

Entered/Aged Date	Account	Reference	Entry	Debit	Credit	VAT	VC	Nom/Bank	Alloc	Number
1-Sep-92 1-Aug-92	AECLTD		BrF	382.03		—	—	0000000000	—	1
1-Aug-92	ALPART		BrF	1784.75		—	—	0000000000	—	2
1-Aug-92	BROMAC		BrF	2935.00		—	—	0000000000	—	3
1-Aug-92	DUPONT		BrF	1100.45		—	—	0000000000	—	4
1-Aug-92	FORD		BrF	21114.57		—	—	0000000000	—	5
1-Aug-92	JONES		BrF	2649.42		—	—	0000000000	—	6
1-Aug-92	TESCO		BrF	5126.99		—	—	0000000000	—	7
1-Aug-92	WALLIS		BrF	2317;65		—	—	0000000000	—	8
1-Sep-92	JONES	1100123001	Inv	45.70		5.97dr	1	0000000000	—	9
1-Sep-92	TESCO	1156123002	Inv	10000.00		130.44dr	1	0000000000	—	10
1-Sep-92	WALLIS	1156123002	Paym		100.00	—	—	0000000000	—	11
30-Aug-92	ALPART	1209120003	Paym		250.00	—	—	0000000000	—	12
27-Aug-92	APEX	1204120001	Cred		15.95	2.09cr	1	0000000000	—	13
1-Sep-92	DUPONT	1200123001	Inv	575.65		73.45dr	1	0000000000	—	14
1-Sep-92	DUPONT	1200123001	Inv	498.27		63.57dr	1	0000000000	—	15
1-Sep-92	DUPONT	1200123001	Inv			62.52dr	1	0000000000	—	16
1-Sep-92	DUPONT	1200123001	Inv	1176.05		150.05dr	1	0000000000	—	17
1-Sep-92	DUPONT	1200123001	Inv	676.49		86.31dr	1	0000000000	—	18
1-Sep-92	JONES	0002001102	Inv	7.74		0.99dr	1	0000000000	—	19
1-Sep-92	JONES	0002001102	Inv	46.42		5.92dr	1	0000000000	—	20
1-Sep-92	FORD	0001NWEHJG	Inv	143.14		18.26dr	1	0000000000	—	21
1-Sep-92	FORD	0001NWEHJG	Inv	249.63		31.85dr	1	0000000000	—	22
1-Sep-92	COOPER	1234123432	Inv	235.75		30.75dr	1	0000000000	—	23
1-Sep-92	DUPONT	2000102340	Inv	1000.00		130.44dr	1	0000000000	—	24
1-Sep-92	COOPER	1234123432	Inv	143.14		18.26dr	1	0000000000	—	25
1-Sep-92	COOPER	1234123432	Inv	437.93		55.88dr	1	0000000000	—	26
		TOTALS:		44139.93	365.95	862.57dr				

Figure 5.5 A typical daybook

One aspect of computerised accounts that frequently confuses students is that it is necessary to **create** an account before any data can be entered. This should be obvious, really, but as the two actions are normally done as one activity in a manual system then it sometimes causes confusion when the two are split up. However, the advantage of doing this is that it puts the theory of the "Division of Duties" into practice. By careful selection of passwords it is possible to authorise the supervisor to create accounts and the clerks to input data only.

For this reason most packages will have an opening menu that has "Entering Data" and "Updating Accounts" as two separate options. Before any data can be entered the account must created.

A typical MAIN MENU for a Nominal Ledger package would include the following items.

```
NOMINAL LEDGER                                          MAIN MENU
    1  Transaction Processing
    2  Update Account Codes
    3  End Period
    4  Nominal Ledger reports
    5  Configure system
    6  Quit
```

Figure 5.6   Nominal ledger — main menu

Normally accounts will be created by allocating a code — careful thought needs to be given to the choice of codes as it should be remembered that printouts will also be set out by code, therefore all fixed assets need to be in a similar group, current assets in a different group, and so on.

Some commercially available packages will already have specified codes for some of the more commonly used accounts (eg Bank, Cash, or will contain prompts to ensure that a code is allocated. This will often apply to the Control Codes for Debtors and Creditors as well, as these accounts are vital in an integrated system because they form the link with the other packages.

As already mentioned the main advantage over manual systems is that profit and loss accounts and balance sheets can be produced as frequently as required. One other benefit is that by careful designation of account codes it is possible to produce a profit and loss account that relates just to part of the business, such as selecting only certain products. Most nominal ledgers allow the user to select his or her own account codes and partition them in the way required. For example, the operational configuration may allow nine characters in the nominal ledger account codes. The user may decide to use the first four as the main account reference (eg 1000 refers to sales accounts) and the remaining five as the subdivisions (eg 1000/100001 refers to sales group 1 and 1000/100002 refers to sales group 2). These divisions can be included or left out of the profit and loss account as required.

The Main Menu option of "Update Account Codes" will usually produce a sub-menu which could contain options such as those shown in Figure 5.7 below.

```
NOMINAL LEDGER                   UPDATE ACCOUNT CODES MENU
    1  Create General Ledger Codes
    2  Amend General Ledger Code Details
    3  Rename General Ledge Code Details
    4  Delete General Ledger Code Details
    5  List General Ledger Code Details
```

Figure 5.7 Nominal general ledger — sub-menu

Most good packages will prevent the user from deleting an account which has an uncleared balance; this applies even more so with the Sales and Purchase Ledgers.

Every Nominal Ledger package should refuse to accept "single-entries" but it is common practice to allow the user to enter transactions in batches (especially in the sales and purchase ledger), therefore as most nominal ledger transactions will affect the cash or bank account it is usually possible to enter a number of transactions all debit entries and just one credit entry after to balance the batch.

Figure 5.8 is a sample screen layout for posting of transactions in a nominal ledger; it should be noted that this is an example only and all packages will differ slightly.

Nominal Ledger Postings				Date 170991	
Reference	Nominal Code	Details	Tax	Dr	Cr
WR2345	300/101	Cash sales	T1	300.00	
S346	120/010	Postage	T0		12.50
1209	400/099	Motor Expenses			210.50
TER39	011/900	Wages	T0		150.00
239091	1005001	Bank	T0	73.00	
Batch total must be equal before exit				373.00	373.00

Figure 5.8

The printouts that are normally available from a nominal ledger package include:

— profit and loss account,
— balance sheets,
— trial balance,
— examination of account details,
— list of accounts,
— daybooks/journal,
— special operations logbook.

All of these printouts, with the exception of the special operations logbook, contain virtually the same information as would be obtained from a manual system. A computerised nominal ledger does in fact provide greater detail as it can analyse the profit and loss account, but other than that it cannot be said to provide much greater information than a manual system. The main benefit of the computerised system is that it can provide the information more quickly and frequently.

The List of Accounts printout will show the names and account numbers of all accounts but may also show whether the account is currently included in the profit/loss account and balance sheet.

The profit/loss account and balance sheet printouts can usually be configured in accordance with the codes used to designate the different accounts. Therefore it is possible to produce a full profit/loss account or simplified versions relating to just one type or model of product. Another option often included for printouts of the profit/loss account and balance sheet is the ability to print to "disk" rather than a printer. The reason for this is that a printout from the accounts package will normally be in the standard draft printer mode, as the presentation of these two accounts is important. The "disk" output option can be used to output the final accounts in a format that can then be loaded by a word-processor or spread-sheet. This will then enable the user to take advantage of the various facilities for improving print quality.

Code	Account	Included in: Profit/Loss	Balance Sheet
100 001	Sales: Jugs	Y	N
100 002	Sales: Cups	Y	N
110 001	Purchases: Jugs	Y	N
110 002	Purchases: Cups	Y	N
200 010	Premises	N	Y
200 020	Motor Vehicles	N	Y
200 030	Office Equipment	N	Y
300 001	Stationery	Y	N
300 002	Postage	Y	N
300 100	Wages: Staff	Y	N
300 101	Wages: Factory	Y	N
001 001	Cash	N	Y
001 002	Bank	N	Y

Figure 5.9   List of accounts

If the package does enable the firm to produce selective profit/loss accounts and balance sheets then there will usually be an additional option on the profit/loss accounts reports menu to printout a list of account group names included in the different profit/loss printouts.

Profit/loss account group names for report in sort group A	
Code	Group name
100 099	SALES
110 199	PURCHASES
300 099	EXPENSES
300 199	WAGES and SALARIES

Figure 5.10   Profit/loss sort codes

When a firm is considering purchasing or devising its own nominal ledger program it would need to consider its requirements very carefully as there are a wide range of options available, some of which apply to all ledgers. Some of the more common options include:

— *Number of Accounts*   In order to conserve disk space it is usual to designate the maximum number of accounts required in the program. This option will generally apply to all parts of the package and not just the Nominal Ledger.

If the firm is buying an "off the shelf" package then they will have to consider how many accounts they think they will require *before* starting to evaluate the different packages available.

— *Maximum transaction value* This will be the largest sum acceptable to the system, and the number of decimal places allowed. The firm should consider what is the largest transaction it is likely to be involved with.

Example: 8 characters and two decimal places (£99,999,999.99)

— *Maximum balance value* This will be the largest value allowable for the balance on an account, this should be larger than a transaction value.

Example: 11 characters and two decimal places (£99,999,999,999.99).

— *Account type* Are accounts to be open item or balance b/f/ or both (see Part 2)? Most firms will prefer a mixture of the two methods so should include an option for designating account type.

— *Menus* The vast majority of accounting packages are "menu driven", some "off the shelf" packages contain a user customisation option which allows the user to alter the menu style to suit their own requirements.

— *Help* Some packages contain additional Help screens to those used in word processing, spreadsheets and database packages. These can be referred to by operators as "memory joggers" and may be useful where certain parts of the program are used less frequently.

— *Passwords* Good programs will have Password protection to prevent unauthorised access. Top quality programs will have different levels of security and each user for whom a password is created will be limited to accessing only those parts of the program that are necessary for the performance of their duties. This means that a purchase ledger clerk may only be allowed to enter transaction details and that the accounts office supervisor will be responsible for creating all accounts and producing printouts, the chief accountant will probably be allowed to access all parts of the program.

— *Budgets* More advanced programs can be linked with the cost accounting function by including budgets as part of the ledgers, this will enable firms to calculate variances much quicker and with greater accuracy.

— *Number of companies* Very large firms will often have subsidiary companies, the individual companies may keep their own accounting records or they could be part of the main firm's records. If the main firm is keeping all records then it will need some way of sub-dividing the records of the different companies so that each one can be analysed separately.

— *Reports* The main report from the nominal ledger will be the profit/loss account and balance sheet. A good program will allow the user to alter the report format to include various items so that a range of different reports can be produced. Many firms would want to produce profit/loss accounts that include the data for just one individual subsidiary company or perhaps just one product.

— *Integration*   Obviously, the nominal ledger program should integrate with the sales and purchase ledger programs, even if the intention is not to acquire/write these programs at the same time as the nominal ledger is set up. But, the firm should ensure that other programs that may be required in the future will also integrate with one another, common examples would be payroll, stock control and order processing packages. In addition, the firm may want to consider the possibility of integrating data from the accounts programs with other types of packages such as spreadsheets, databases or word processors. A number of commercially available packages will integrate with other packages, especially spreadsheets. This will give the firm the opportunity to transfer accounting data to a spreadsheet designed for complicated budgeting techniques or even just to take advantage of the improved graphics presentations available on most modern spreadsheets.

— *Back-ups*   The problems caused by loss of data are so great that all packages should not only include an option for making back-ups but good packages should automatically create a back-up at regular intervals, such as when the daybook is printed or when the option to Quit is selected.

— *Repeat entries*   Some items that will be included in the nominal ledger will be "repeat entries" that recur every month, eg loan repayments, standing orders for light/heat and rent. If these entries have to be made each month then the chances are that they will easily be missed out, some packages now include an option whereby these payments can be automatically set.

Exercises

198   What printouts would normally be produced from a nominal ledger package? What is special about the profit and loss account as compared to a manual system?

199   (a)   A company uses the following codes in its nominal ledger program:

001/200/8 – refers to sales of computers in India
002/200/5 – refers to purchases of computers in Malaysia
001/300/7 – refers to sales of printers in Hong Kong
002/400/6 – refers to purchases of diskdrives in Singapore

What would the code be for *sales of diskdrives* in Malaysia and *purchases of printers* in India?

(b)   Briefly suggest what benefits can be derived from this type of coding in a computer system.   (Sep 89)

200A   What "options" should be considered when acquiring a nominal ledger package?

201   Most Computerised Systems will include a provision for the printout of a Daybook from the Nominal Ledger. Design a suitable printout for a Nominal Ledger Daybook and include some sample data.   (12 marks)
                                                                          (Mar 92)

202A   Design a menu for a nominal ledger for "Update Account details".

5.5 SALES LEDGER

The real advantages of computerised systems only come into being when the other ledgers such as sales and purchases are used. The computerised system provides the same information as a manual system but much more as well.

A typical MAIN MENU for a Sales Ledger package has already been shown in Figure 5.1, the other options available from this menu should include.

Enter transaction details: This will allow the user to enter details of:

— Sales Invoices
— Credit Notes
— Payments received

and an extra option to make adjustments. The first three items will be used to enter details of sales, returns inwards and cash received from debtors. The fourth option is a safety device so that various adjustments can be made this could include provision for discounts or simply to rectify errors.

Some packages will allow the user to design the screen used for data entry, the purpose of this is that it can enable the firm to design a data entry screen that is similar in layout to the source document being used. This obviously makes data entry much easier.

A number of software houses have removed the need for a sub-menu of options for "Ledger Processing" as all of the various transactions are entered on the same screen and differentiated by codes to distinguish the different transactions (eg I for Invoice, C for Credit Note, etc). This makes it easier for users to learn the system but may affect the division of duties unless passwords restrict users from entering certain types of transactions.

Update account details: This will allow the user to create accounts for customers and enter various items such as customer name and address, delivery address (if different), credit rating, credit level, credit period, name of contact at customers company, sales representative handling firm, etc.

A typical screen layout would look like the illustration in Figure 5.11.

SALES LEDGER	CUSTOMER DETAILS
ACCOUNT NAME: [ ]	CUSTOMER NAME: [ ]
CREDIT LIMIT: [ ]	CUSTOMER ADDRESS:
CREDIT PERIOD: [ ]	
CONTACT AT COMPANY: [ ]	
SALES REPRESENTATIVE: [ ]	
OPEN ITEM/BAL B/F: [ ]	CURRENT BALANCE: [ ]
LAST TRANSACTION DATE: [ ]	

Figure 5.11

Sales ledger reports: This will generally produce a sub-menu that will include some or all of the printouts listed in Figure 5.12. Access to this menu will usually be restricted by Password level. Although a good system will have different password levels so that users can be allowed to produce some of the reports if it is desirable.

```
SALES LEDGER REPORTS MENU
  1   daybooks
  2   special operations logbook
  3   statements of accounts
  4   examination of customer account
  5   VAT analysis
  6   sales analysis
  7   list of customers' accounts
  8   mailing lists of customers
  9   aged debtor analysis
 10   invoice production
```

Figure 5.12

End of period: This option will balance off all accounts at the end of a period, this is usually done on a monthly basis but certainly once a year. If the accounts are "Open Item" this option will not appear to be quite so relevant but it will still be necessary to ensure that the Aged Debtors reports is calculated correctly.

System configuration: This option will generally contain similar items to those shown in Section 1.6. The major difference with this ledger is that it will normally have a different transaction reference coding from the nominal ledger. A transaction reference is the code used to identify each individual transaction and will often be a code that is subdivided into different sections or partitions. The types of codes mentioned in Section 1.7 will be applied here.

Most firms will try to set transaction codes in such a way that the transactions can be analysed in groups (eg all sales for a particular product type or sales representative) and still have a unique reference number so that each transaction can be separately identified by the auditor when following the audit trail. For example the transaction code JUKE/120/JIM/19029 could refer to a transaction for the sale of a product JUKE model 120 sold by a sales representative JIM with the unique invoice number of 19029 to distinguish this invoice from all other invoices.

The options that should be considered in designing the Sales and Purchase Ledgers are basically the same and would normally include options as follows:

— *Foreign currency*   If the firm has any trading with foreign countries then it will certainly be making/receiving payments in a foreign currency.

— *Reports*   The full range of possible reports have already been mentioned above, but it may desirable to incorporate an option to redesign the layout of the reports so that the firm can make more efficient use of new printers or pre-printed stationery.

— *Labels/letters*   Many packages will allow the user to produce labels (as defined in reports) but some will also allow the user to create short letters for use as a mail shot. The letters would normally be individually addressed by merging the "labels" option with the standard letter.

— *Allocating items*   When payments are received (or made) it is necessary to allocate the receipt/payment to a particular transaction if an open item system is being used. It may be desirable to allow "split" payments so that payments can be spread over a number of transactions.

— *Credit limits*   All debtors accounts should have a credit limit allocated to ensure that the risk of bad debts is kept to a minimum.

The other options described for the nominal ledger will usually be applicable to the sales and purchase ledgers as well.

The Sales Ledger has a large variety of printouts on offer, the functions of these printouts are as follows:

Daybooks   These have already been discussed and serve as a means of keeping track of all items entered in the accounts (Figure 5.5). Most daybooks will include columns to identify the Date, Account(s) involved, Transaction reference

	ABC SUPPLIES PLC
	THE BROADWAY
	DUDLEY
	WESTMIDLANDS

FORD MOTOR CO.   Turnover 7.13cr
HALEWOOD   Credit Limit 25000.00dr
MERSEY SIDE   Credit Period 62 days
               Last Entry   30-Aug-92
               Last Payment 30-Aug-92

G.EVANS   NORTH WEST   192068
Examination of Sales Account   FORD   30-Aug-92   Page 1

AL	Date	Ref	Entry	Debit	Credit	VC	VAT	Entry
	1-Jul-92		Adj	6742.32				12
	1-Aug-92		Adj	12874.23				13
	1-Aug-92	0001NWEGKE	Inv	721.44		1	94.11	23
	29-Jul-92	CHQ.	Pay		3560.21			27
	29-Jul-92	001NWEGKE	CrN		2519.73	1	328.67	32
	30-Aug-92	1156NWEGKE	Inv	1790.10		1	233.50	57
	30-Aug-92	CHQ.	Pay		1120.00			61
	30-Aug-92	CHQ.	Adj		180.40			64

    Balance of Account   14747.75dr

    Current period 1-Aug-92   14085.37dr
       period from   1-Jul-92   622.38dr
       period from   1-Jan-92   0.00dr
       period from 1-May-92   0.00dr
      period before 1-May-92   0.00dr

        Total Outstanding   14747.75dr

Figure 5.13   Sales ledger printout (1)

(eg invoice number), Type of transaction (eg source document type), Debit and Credit entries, Tax, Code for Nominal Ledger account (if applicable) and the individual transaction reference number for the audit trail.

Special operations logbook   This has also already been discussed and serves as a check on who has done what in the accounts (Figure 5.4).

Statement of account   This is sent to customers at the end of each month to inform them how much they owe and detailing all of the transactions currently held in the account.

Examination of customer account   This is basically the same as the customer statement of account but is for internal use only. Management may request a copy of a customer's account for the purpose of checking some details. A sample report is shown in Figure 5.12. Notice that the report shows details of all recent transactions and also general information such as that relating to credit terms and an aged analysis of the account.

VAT analysis   This is only really applicable if the government uses different rates of purchase tax and the firm is selling a variety of goods that are taxed at different rates. This printout will show how much tax has been paid at each of the rates.

Sales analysis   This printout enables firms to analyse their sales in any way that they choose, providing that the method of analysis was stipulated when the system was configured. The most common methods of analysis involve analysing sales by area, product, customer, or sales representative. Most firms will create separate accounts for the different products or countries so the Sales Analysis will be an examination of certain accounts only, eg an Analysis of accounts 3000/09/10 and 3000/09/11 may include details of the sales for products sold in Europe and Asia only. A more common way of analysing sales is to incorporate suitable codes into the transaction codes, an example analysis of the sales ledger where the sales have been analysed by sales representatives is shown in Figure 5.14. The initials refer to the names of the different sales representatives.

Sales ledger	
Sales ledger analysis	
ABC Limited	07-DEC-89 Page 1
Sales rep	Sales invoices
ANK	1,200.65
HGF	398.40
JDF	1,560.25
KNA	128.95
ERD	2,100.40
WIW	281.40
Total sales	5,670.05

Figure 5.14   Sales ledger analysis by sales representative

This analysis is usually achieved by means of the "transaction reference" given to each transaction. If each transaction is given a reference which contains ten characters, the characters can be partitioned so that the first four refer to the area, the next three to the product and the last three to the sales representative. For example, a transaction reference such as NORW/123/WIW means that the sale was in the north-west area (NORW), the product was widgets (123) and the sales representative was William White (WIW). The ledger can be subsequently analysed to categorise sales by either area, product or sales representative as in Figure 5.14.

List of customers' accounts   This is a summary of all debtors' accounts held in the ledger. What makes the printout even more useful is that it is normally possible to select on the account which have exceeded their credit limit or only those which have a turnover in excess of £10,000. Such printouts are normally used by management as a means of obtaining information relating to doubtful debts or just for statistical data on customers. Such a printout might look like Figure 5.15 (the printout has been requested so that only customers who exceeded their limits are included).

Sales Ledger		A Summary List of Customer Accounts		
Accounts exceeding Credit Limit at 31st September 1989				
Account	Customer	Credit Limit	Current Bal	Credit Period
ICON	Icon Trading Ltd	2,000.00	2,100.00	31 days
ABTA	A & B Traders Assoc	4,500.00	6,120.75	62 days
FINA	Fina Plc	500.00	725.56	31 days
DOMI	Dominion Ltd	3,000.00	3,890.35	93 days

Figure 5.15   Customer account printout

Mailing lists of customers   This printout will produce labels containing the names and addresses of customers. This option is particularly useful if the firm wants to do a mailshot to customers, perhaps to advertise some items on offer at a reduced price. A lot of organisations keep mailing lists on a database package, but a mailing list produced from the sales ledger is much better as it is updated whenever a new account is created - mailing lists kept purely as mailing lists tend to only get updated at irregular intervals. Also, on better packages the mailing list produced can be selective so that only customers with a turnover in excess of, say, £10,000 are included. More advanced packages will include some very basic word-processing facilities so that simple messages can be devised and merged with the mailing list. This is especially useful for producing letters informing customers that their account is overdue or their credit limit has been exceeded.

Aged debtor analysis   This printout is one that is extremely useful and also very difficult to produce in manual systems. The program analyses each debtor's account and produces a printout which shows not only the current balance outstanding but also how old that balance is. It will usually break down the balance in the amount owing from this month, last month, two months ago, three months ago, etc. This information is vital for effective credit control and to give advance notice of possible bad debts. Figure 5.16 shows the usual style of printout.

A/C No	Name	A/C Balance	On A/C	Current	Period 1	Period 2	Period 3	Period 4
A0001	Andreas test account Contact Andrea Tel 0270 763967	22366.39	0.00	19322.11	1068.35	1000.00	407.10	558.83
A0002	Susan Lorraine Jones Contact Sue Tel 00270 589191	12718.85	0.00	12718.85	0.00	0.00	0.00	0.00
C0001	Consulsoft Limited Contact J Broadhurst Tel: 0606 77099	4790.89	0.00	4217.69	66.75	0.00	100.00	406.45
E0001	E.R.F. Limited Contact Tel: 0270 763223	2718.94	0.00	0.00	92.00	0.00	1610.00	1016.94
F0001	Foden Trucks Limited Contact Tel 0270 763244	1944.16	113.19	690.00	1150.00	140.30	77.05	0.00
M0001	Midshires Computer Centre Ltd Contact J B Kilgariff Tel 0270 589191	2858.34	0.00	989.00	654.35	1214.99	0.00	0.00
Totals		47397.57	113.19	37947.65 79.87%	3031.45 6.38%	2355.29 4.62%	2194.15 4.62%	1982.22 4.17%

Figure 5.16　Sales ledger printouts (2)

Invoice production   Some packages will include an option to produce an invoice. This is a fairly simple operation but should not strictly speaking be included in sales ledger packages as the sales ledger's purpose is to record transactions, not to originate transactions. However, the facility is sometimes included as the actual sale may take place over the telephone and the invoice is produced as the written confirmation of the transaction.

Exercises

203   What printouts would be obtained from a sales ledger package and what do they contain?

204   Design a suitable printout for the Sales Ledger to show full "Customer Account Details", include some sample data.   (12 marks)   (Mar 91)

205   Design a suitable layout for a *printout* of the *Sales Daybook* for a *sales ledger package*, include a few lines of sample data.   (Dec 88)

206A Design a "screen" suitable for entering account details in a sales ledger program.

207   Devise a suitable layout for a printout to show an Aged Debtors listing and include some sample data.   (8 marks)   (Sep 91)

208A Identify and describe three options/variables that should be considered when devising/buying a sales ledger program.

5.6   PURCHASE LEDGER

This is probably the easiest program to write for an accounting package, provided the sales ledger has been written first, the reason being that the purchases ledger is identical to the sales ledger with one exception. This is that all the transactions are entered on the opposite side of the account. Therefore, for a sales ledger program to become a purchases ledger program, it does not require a programming genius to make the few alterations necessary in the menus and in the general wording used. In fact, many software houses produce a combined manual for the sales and purchases ledgers.

Having said this, it should be apparent that the printouts obtained from a purchases ledger package will be virtually the same as those from a sales ledger package; these are:

— daybooks,
— special operations logbook,
— remittance advices,
— examination of supplier account,
— VAT analysis,
— purchases analysis,
— list of suppliers' accounts,
— mailing list of suppliers,
— aged creditor analysis.

The only "new" printout obtained, as compared to the sales ledger, is remittance advices. These are used to accompany payments to suppliers and would normally be as shown in Figure 5.17.

S & T Supplies Ltd	ABC Limited
The Building	New Yard
Old Town	New Town
31/11/89	
Account no: 2311/1234	Your ref: ABC/1029
Payment enclosed for . . .	£850.75

Figure 5.17 A remittance advice

One additional item that should be included in the password protection is the ability to limit the amount of cheques that users can authorise. Cheques in excess of certain amounts should require clearance by more senior staff to safeguard against fraud.

If accounts in either the sales or purchase ledgers have been designated as "open item" then an additional function needs to be included in the ledger transaction processing part of the program so that the operator can "allocate" payments to specific transactions, this activity is sometimes referred to as "matching". The program should also ensure that any one payment/receipt can be allocated to more than one transaction as most firms will simply write a cheque to pay off the total balance on their account. This may involve a number of different transactions.

It may also be desirable, from the auditors' point of view, to produce daybooks that contain only one type of transaction, therefore when requesting a printout of the daybook there may be an option asking if all transactions should be included or just invoices or just debit notes or just payments. These simplified daybooks make it easier for the auditor to follow particular transactions.

The option for a list of suppliers accounts will normally contain the same information as that provided by the sales ledger. The example given in the previous section showed a sample printout for customers who had exceeded their credit limit; both packages would usually contain an option for a more detailed printout of customers/suppliers accounts and an example of this is given in Figure 5.18.

A number of the reports available on both the sales and purchases ledgers are only required for quick reference purposes, consequently it may not be necessary to obtain a printout and some packages will include an alternative whereby the "report" can be displayed on the screen only.

A less commonly used package that can be integrated with the purchase ledger is a job costing system (see Section 5.9); this will generally be used by manufacturing firms that undertake large scale, long-term operations (eg the construction industry). The procedures for recording costs against specific contracts can be quite involved and there are a number of job costing programs offered by software houses to assist in this recording procedure. However, as most costs will involve the purchase of materials from suppliers on credit, it is quite usual to integrate the job costing program with the purchase ledger.

ABC Suppliers Ltd   Detailed List of Accounts   4-Sep-89   Page 2

SCOTCH Credit 5,000.00cr 31 days
Turnover 335.43cr
                SCOTCH PROD PLC.
                SCOTH HOUSE,
                LEWIS AVENUE,
                NOTTINGHAM.
                        8BK.

SHARP Credit 10,000.00cr 62 days
Turnover 695.65cr
                SHARP PLC.
                SHARP HOUSE,
                SHARP ROAD,
                MILTON KEYNES.
                        4EZ MKB.

SMITHS Credit 500.00cr 31 days
Turnover 347.82cr
                WH SMITHS PLC.
                STATIONERY HOUSE,
                COLMORE ROWE,
                BIRMINGHAM.
                        8QT BY6.

Balance Brought Forward

Balance Brought Forward

Balance Brought Forward
TRIUMPH Credit 10,000.00 62
                        days
Turnover 12,626.94cr
                TRIUMPH EQUIP. PLC.
                210 OXFORD ROAD,
                HOUNSLOW,
                MIDDLESEX,
                        8BY M56.

Figure 5.18 Purchase ledger printout

All of the other printouts and advantages of purchases ledgers have already been described under the heading of the sales ledger. But it should be said that programmers writing a sales ledger package need to think carefully as to how they approach the task, as with a little forethought they could also produce a purchases ledger package.

Exercises

209   In what ways do the printouts from a purchases ledger package differ from those of a sales ledger package?

210   Specify five printouts that a purchases ledger package would be expected to produce and describe the contents of each printout.

211   Describe the items that would normally be included in a "Detailed List of Accounts" printout.

5.7 STOCK CONTROL

These packages would normally record all adjustments to stock and therefore are best served by online systems so that an accurate and up-to-date record is constantly available.

A typical MAIN MENU encountered in a Stock Control program would be as follows:

```
STOCK CONTROL PROGRAM                    MAIN MENU
    1   Make Stock Entries
    2   Report on Stock
    3   Maintain Stock Details
    4   End of Period
    5   Set System Constants
    6   Exit
```

Figure 5.19

The options numbered 4 to 6 perform the same functions as in the other packages (Set System Constants is the same as System configuration).

As with the other packages it is first necessary to designate details for stock items (option 3) before stock entries can be made. This is especially important for stock as there are a number of variables involved.

STOCK CONTROL PROGRAM		ENTER STOCK DETAILS MENU			
Stock reference	Description				Short title
Analysis Code	Cost code	units	Max Qty	Min Qty	Reorder Level
Cost price	Selling prices:	1	2	3	4
	Discount codes:	1	2	3	4

Figure 5.20

The "stock reference" will be the code used to identify the particular item of stock. The "description" will give a description of the nature/use of the item and the "short title" is the usual name by which it is referred to.

The "analysis code" will be used to determine which stock reports it will be included in and efforts should be taken to ensure that all similar stock items are groups in similar codes. The "cost code" may be used if the intent is to analyse stock as part of an overall analysis of costs. The "units" simply states the nature that the item comes in (eg litres, metres, etc). The quantities and reorder levels are part of the inventory control procedures mentioned in section 4.4.1; these figures can either be entered or in some cases will calculated by the computer program.

In most cases there will be more than one selling price or level of discount, good customers will usually get the lower prices whilst small orders will be sold at the higher prices.

The actual entries for stock are usually quite straightforward, although some firms will want an option to record items that are currently on order or have been reserved for a particular user.

STOCK CONTROL PROGRAM	STOCK ENTRIES MENU
1 Stock received	
2 Stock issued	
3 Stock ordered	
4 Stock reserved	
5 Cancel order/reserved stock	
6 Return to MAIN MENU	

Figure 5.21

The printouts of information from such a package would normally include:

STOCK CONTROL PROGRAM	STOCK REPORTS MENU
1 Stock Daybook,	
2 Stock lists,	
3 Stock movements report,	
4 Stock levels and availability,	
5 Stock price list,	
6 Stock valuation,	
7 Special operations daybook,	
8 Outstanding orders report	
9 Reorder report,	
10 Return to MAIN MENU	

Figure 5.22

The special operations daybook has already been discussed in previous sections; the other reports are as follows:

Stock daybook   This is similar in principle to the daybooks produced by the ledger packages and shows details of all items of stock issued, ordered, reserved and received during the period. The printout will show stock items, action, quantity and value.

Stock lists   This printout will give a list of all items currently stocked, together with any description of each item; it may also show the prices of each item or analysis codes. Most packages should be able to produce a stock list for certain items only by selecting an appropriate analysis code.

ABC SUPPLIES LTD	Stock List		Monday 25-Oct-92	Page 1
Stock Key				
APPLEII	COMPUTER	62K		
APPLEIIE	COMPUTER	62K	TD	
APPLELISA	COMPUTER	62K	TD	
APPLEMAC	COMPUTER	128K	TD	
APPLEMACH	COMPUTER	128K	HD	
DIABLO	PRINTER	DAIS	200	
DYSAN	FIDISK	DS	DD	
EPSONFX80	PRINTER	DOTM	160	
EPSONRX80	PRINTER	DOTM	100	
IBMPC	COMPUTER	128K	SD	
IBMPCH	COMPUTER	128K	HD	
MAXELL2	FLDISK	SS	SD	
MAXELLI	FLDISK	DS	DD	
QUME9/55	PRINTER	DAIS	200	
RANK1	COPIER	MK1		
RANK2	COPIER	MK2	COL	
SCOTCH	COPIER			
SHARP	COPIER		COL	
TRIUMPH	FILECAB	4DR	GRY	

Figure 5.23   Stock list report

Stock movements report This is one of the more important printouts from the stock control package and is used to show what quantity of stock for each item has been received and issued, often over a three-month period. This enable management to identify slow-moving stock and, as many packages analyse the movements and produce projected movements for the next month, it enables management to identify future stock requirements.

Once again, careful use of analysis codes should enable the firm to obtain a report on one type of stock only, so that it would be possible to obtain a report on movement of all computers only or even Apple computers only.

Stock levels and availability   This printout shows the current levels of stock for each item and usually shows how many items are currently reserved, on order, or are available, and sales so far this period. It often shows the minimum level required for each item and where the stock has fallen below the minimum level.

ABC SUPPLIES LTD   Stock Movements Report   Monday 25-Oct-82   Page 1

Stock Key				Current		-1 Period		-2 Period		Projected Current	
				In	Out	In	Out	In	Out	In	Out
APPLEII	COMPUTER	62K		5	0	10	15	15	0	12	7
APPLEIIE	COMPUTER	62K	TD	5	8	0	3	10	0	5	1
APPLELISA	COMPUTER	62K	TD	4	6	0	7	15	0	7	3
APPLEMAC	COMPUTER	128K	TD	0	0	5	5	30	0	17	2
APPLEMACH	COMPUTER	128K	HD	0	11	3	3	25	0	14	1
DIABLO	PRINTER	DAIS	20	0	3	18	0	0	0	9	0
DYSAN	FIDISK	DS	DD	25	70	300	0	0	0	150	0
EPSONFX80	PRINTER	DOTM	160	0	2	35	1	0	0	17	0
EPSONRX80	PRINTER	DOTM	100	10	6	25	4	0	0	12	2
IBMPC	COMPUTER	128K	SD	5	10	15	13	40	0	27	6
IBMPCH	COMPUTER	128K	HD	5	10	0	12	25	0	12	6
MAXELL2	FIDISK	SS	SD	50	0	400	28	0	0	200	14
MACELLI	FIDISK	DS	DD	70	295	400	36	0	0	200	18
QUME9/55	PRINTER	DAIS	200	0	3	10	0	0	0	5	0
RANK1	COPIER	MK1		0	5	3	1	10	0	6	0
RANK2	COPIER	MK2	COL	6	1	0	1	6	0	3	0
SCOTCH	COPIER			20	7	35	7	0	0	17	3
SHARP	COPIER		COL	10	3	20	4	0	0	10	2
TRIUMPH	FILECAB	4DR	GRY	15	17	45	12	0	0	22	6

Figure 5.24   Stock control printouts (2)

Stock Key				Suppliers One	Two	Order	Alloc	Level	Avail	Min Lev	Short Sales Period	Sales this	Projected Sales
APPLEII	COMPUTER	62K		APPLE	MICROM	15	0	15	15	10	0	0	7
APPLEIIE	COMPUTER	62K	TD	APPLE	MICROM	0	0	4	4	5	-1	8	1
APPLELISA	COMPUTER	62K	TD	APPLE	MICROM	0	0	6	6	10	-4	6	3
APPLEMAC	COMPUTER	128K	TD	APPLE	MICROM	0	0	30	30	20	0	0	2
APPLEMACH	COMPUTER	128K	HD	APPLE	MICROM	2	0	14	14	15	-1	11	1
DIABLO	PRINTER	DAIS	20	INTOM	MANCOS	0	0	15	15	10	0	3	0
DYSAN	FIDISK	DS	DD	MOCCOM	MICROD	0	0	255	255	100	0	70	0
EPSONFX80	PRINTER	DOTM	160	EPSON	MICROF	0	0	32	32	25	0	2	0
EPSONRX80	PRINTER	DOTM	100	EPSON	MICROF	0	0	25	25	18	0	6	2
IBMPC	COMPUTER	128K	SD	IBM		0	0	37	37	30	0	10	6
IBMPCH	COMPUTER	128K	HD	IBM		4	0	8	8	15	-7	10	6
MAXELL2	FLDISK	SS	SD	MICCOM	MICROD	0	0	422	422	200	0	0	14
MACELLI	FLDISK	KS	DD	MICCOM	MICROD	0	0	139	139	200	-61	295	18
QUME9/55	PRINTER	DAIS	200	INTCOM	MANCOS	0	0	7	7	5	0	3	0
RANK1	COPIER	MK1		RANK	OFFEQP	0	0	7	7	4	0	5	0
RANK2	COPIER	MK2	COL	RANK	OFFEQP	0	0	10	10	2	0	1	0
SCOTCH	COPIER			SCOTCH	OEM	0	0	41	41	25	0	7	3
SHARP	COPIER		COL	SHARP	OFFEQP	0	0	23	23	5	0	3	2
TRIUMPH	FILECAB	4DR	GRY	TRIUMP	OEN	0	0	31	31	15	0	17	6

ABC SUPPLIES LTD   Stock Price List   Monday 25-Oct-82   Page 1

Figure 5.25   Stock control printouts (3)

As with the full stock movements report many packages will also include a column to show projected sales.

Stock price list   Prices are shown against each item of stock so that a price list can be sent to customers. Many packages allow more than one price so that discounts can be offered to trade customers or for export prices. In some instances it is possible to produce a printout showing one price level only; this means that the printout could then be used as a price list.

ABC SUPPLIES LTD		Stock Price List		Monday 25-Oct-92	Page 1
Stock Key				Price Two	Price Three
APPLEII	COMPUTER	62K		635.000	700.000
APPLEIIE	COMPUTER	62K	TD	1175.000	1250.000
APPLELISA	COMPUTER	62K	TD	2550.000	2650.000
APPLEMAC	COMPUTER	128K	TD	2685.000	2785.000
APPLEMACH	COMPUTER	128K	HD	2895.000	2995.000
DIABLO	PRINTER	DAIS	20	1635.000	1695.000
DYSAN	FIDISK	DS	DD	1.950	2.150
EPSONFX80	PRINTER	DOTM	160	325.000	358.000
EPSONRX80	PRINTER	DOTM	100	195.000	225.000
IBMPC	COMPUTER	128K	SD	2700.000	2750.000
IBMPCH	COMPUTER	128K	HD	2950.000	2990.000
MAXELL2	FLDISK	SS	SD	2.050	2.200
MAXELLI	FLDISK	DS	DD	2.250	2.400
QUME9/55	PRINTER	DAIS	200	1810.000	1850.000
RANK1	COPIER	MK1		5900.000	6050.000
RANK2	COPIER	MK2	COL	8955.000	9155.000
SCOTCH	COPIER			350.000	375.000
SHARP	COPIER		COL	5215.000	5350.000
TRIUMPH	FILECAB	4DR	GRY	110.000	125.000

Figure 5.26   Stock price list

Stock valuation   This report will show the total value for each item held in stock and also the total value of all stock. As the cost of each item will usually increase during the year, many packages have adopted one of the methods of accounting for materials mentioned in Part 4.

This type of stock control package is often quite sophisticated and is really only of any benefit to firms that have a large range of stock items. Options that need to be considered with this type of program are:

Stock code length   Careful thought needs to be given to this option as most stock control packages are analysed by reference to the stock code. It may be desirable to include "break-points" so that certain groups of stock can be reported on. eg IBM would report on all IBM items whereas IBMPRIN would only report on IBM Printers).

Costing method   Some "off the shelf" packages will offer alternative methods for costing stock. The most frequently used methods with computer programs are FIFO and Weighted Average. The choice of method may well be dependent upon which method is acceptable for Taxation purposes.

Stock description   The stock record for each item will normally contain a very brief description of the stock but the amount of space allocated for these descriptions will vary according to the technical complexity of the product, some items may need a number of lines to record details adequately.

Exercises

212A Describe five printouts that could be obtained from a stock control package.

213 Design a sample printout from a *stock control package*, including sample data, to show a *stock movements report*.   (Sept 88)

214 Identify and describe, briefly, *five computer printouts* that would normally be produced by a *stock control package*.   (Dec 88)

215A Design a *main menu* for a stock control program.

216 Design a suitable printout to show Stock Movements, include some sample data.   (8 marks)
                                                                       (Sep 91)

217A Design a suitable screen layout for making stock entries in a stock control program.

5.8 PAYROLL

This is a very common, commercially available package, for the simple reason that it not only calculates wages but also usually calculates income tax for employees. As governments specify the way in which tax is to be calculated, it means that such programs are easily transferable between different firms as all firms must use the same methods to calculate tax.

A typical MAIN MENU for a Payroll program will include those items shown in Figure 5.27.

```
PAYROLL PROGRAM                MAIN NEMU
        1)  Payroll Processing
        2)  Payroll
        3)  Payroll Reports
        4)  Employee Details
        5)  Exit
```

Figure 5.27

As with the other packages it is not possible to enter details of hours worked for an employee until a record has been devised, so the item for Employee Details will have to be selected to set up a payroll record for each employee first.

The details required by each system will vary but standard items included as part of employee details will usually include those shown in the sample screen layout in Figure 5.28.

The principal requirements will be the employee's name and employee number or employee code. Most of the other items will determine what deductions are made from wages for tax or insurance or where payment is to be sent if wages are paid direct to the employee's bank account.

The COST CENTRE is included for the purposes of payroll analysis so that managers can ascertain the total cost of wages in each section. If the employee has only recently started with the firm then there are likely to be earnings from a previous job. In many countries taxation of income from employment is done on a cumulative basis, and therefore the pay and tax from previous employment will have to be included in future tax calculations.

```
PAYROLL PROGRAM          EMPLOYEE DETAILS

EMPLOYEE    CODE        NAME                 SEX      BIRTH
NUMBER:     NO.                                       DATE
[        ]  [     ]     [             ]      [ ]      [      ]

GRADE       SALARY LEVEL  NEXT INCREMENT
[     ]     [       ]      [       ]

COST        TAX   INSURANCE  INSURANCE  PREVIOUS  PREVIOUS
CENTRE      CODE  CODE       NUMBER     PAY       TAX
[     ]     [  ]  [  ]       [      ]   [     ]   [      ]

BANK DETAILS: BANK          BRANCH        ACCOUNT
[             ]             [         ]   [              ]
```

Figure 5.28

The MAIN MENU option for payroll processing will be used to enter details of overtime worked and additional payments or deductions required. If staff are paid a salary or set weekly wage then there shouldn't need to be many entries in this option, as most payments and deductions will be standard and can be included

```
PAYROLL PROGRAM                  PAYROLL PROCESSING

EMPLOYEE CODE: [     ]     EMPLOYEE: [            ]

HOURS WORKED:  [     ]     OVERTIME HOURS: Grade 1 [    ]

                                          Grade 2 [    ]

RATE OF PAY:  [     ]      BONUS:    [     ]

COMMISSION:   [     ]      EXPENSES: [        ]

DECUCTIONS:   [     ]
```

Figure 5.29

as part of the weekly/monthly payment via the Employee Details option. The payroll processing option should only need to be used for the unusual or infrequent items.

However, if staff are paid according to hours worked or output then details of hours or quantities will be entered in this option.

The payroll calculation option is the option that actually makes the program calculate wages or salary due. This option will normally require good password protection as once the password has been entered the only other entry normally required will be the period number. The program will then proceed to calculate pay, and will often automatically printout cheques and payslips.

The printouts normally obtained from such packages would include:

```
PAYROLL PROGRAM      REPORTS MENU
    1)  Payslips,
    2)  Cheques
    3)  Summary of pay,
    4)  End of year documents,
    5)  Taxation documents,
    6)  Coin analysis,
    7)  Employee details
    8)  Special operations daybook.
    9)  Exit
```

Figure 5.30

Payslips   It should be fairly obvious that one of the main benefits of having a payroll program is that it should print out employees' payslips. Most programs will allow the user to configure the contents of the payslip print-out to include various items which will usually include some or all of the following:

> Gross Pay for the week
> Overtime payments
> Travel Expenses
> Bonus payments
> Additional allowances
> Total pay to date for the current year
> Tax deducted
> Deductions for State Pension, Health care
> Deductions for Company Pensions
> Deductions for voluntary contributions (eg payments to charities)
> Deductions for Private Health care schemes

Some programs will include options so that a variety of messages can be included on the payslip. This enables employers to inform staff of items that are of interest, this should be a useful means of passing information onto employees as most will pay great attention to their payslip.

The payslip is usually in one of two styles. These styles have developed because of the large quantity of data that may be needed on a payslip. The first style uses code numbers to refer to the individual items of additional payments or deductions. An explanation of the codes can be pre-printed on the reverse of the payslip. This enables payslips to be produced more quickly and cheaply as there is less information to be printed on each payslip. More recent programs are more likely to take advantage of improvements in printer technology and will print all details in full; modern printers will print the full information just as quickly and probably at as low a cost as the old printers took to print information in coded form.

Summary of payments   This is a list of employees showing the pay received by each, together with details of deductions for tax, health insurance, union fees, etc. It enables the firm to keep a weekly or monthly record of all payments made so that any queries can be dealt with. This list of information saves the firm from having to sort throught copies of payslips in order to find details relating to a single employee. It also has the advantage that a copy of the payslips is not needed.

Payroll summary		To date for Dep: A1		Page 1	
Emp No	Name	Tax Code	Gross Pay	Tax	Insurance
120	J Smith	210	156.75	23.23	10.10
122	K Evans	340	230.98	34.70	12.35
123	D Jones	244	187.90	29.70	13.50
128	H Clive	201	340.50	67.90	12.50
129	F Singh	255	285.70	34.00	12.35
Total department:			1201.83	189.53	60.80

Figure 5.31   Payroll summary report

The payroll summary can usually be printed to show details for one department only or for the firm as a whole.

End of year documents   In most countries it is accepted practice that employees be given a statement at the end of each year showing their total pay and deductions for the year. The firm also generally has a printout showing similar information in list form.

Taxation documents   The taxation authorities will normally require the firm to supply them with information at the end of each year to show how much each employee was paid and how much tax was deducted.

Coin analysis   This is used where employees are paid in cash and shows the firm how much of each type of coin is needed to make up the pay packets.

Options to be considered when devising a Payroll program include:

— *Payments and deductions:* A good program will give scope for a reasonable number of payment and deduction types. These should be capable of being set as permanent or temporary payments/deductions and as taxable/non taxable.

— *Enquiries:* This will allow the user to examine on-screen enquiries about various aspects of the payroll details. The most common example is the option to examine employee details.

— *Nominal analysis:* As the payroll calculates the entries for wages it should be possible to integrate this package with the nominal ledger so that the wages account is automatically updated.

— *Job costing integration:* Some software houses will include a job costing program as part of their range, it may be useful to integrate the job costing and payroll packages. This will usually involve the automatic transfer of time sheet data from the job costing program to update the payroll details.

— *Personnel records:* Many firms will now have details of personnel records held on computer, as much of the basic data concerning each employee is the same as the payroll program it may be an advantage to have "new employee" details transferred from the one program to the other automatically. This facility will also be useful for upgraded staff and leavers.

— *Report design:* This option will usually be found as part of the system configuration and enables the user to design the layout of reports; as with the other packages this option will then allow the user to use pre-printed stationery.

Exercises

218   Describe five printouts that could be obtained from a payroll package.

219A (a)   Design a suggested layout for a Sales Ledger printout to show Aged Debtors, including one line of sample data.

(b)   Design a suggested layout for a Payroll package printout to show Coin Analysis.

220A Identify and describe three items that should be considered when buying/writing a Payroll program.

221A Design a *MAIN MENU* suitable for a Payroll program.

5.9   OTHER COMPUTER PACKAGES

Figure 5.2 should give some idea of the other types of packages available for use in an accounting system.

Probably the most common package of those not already covered is that of Invoicers or Order Processing. Many software houses will supply these two packages as one single module although there is a slight difference between them.

In most cases an invoicer is used primarily for the production of invoices. They are often found in on-line systems and enable staff to take orders over a counter or the telephone. The invoicer will normally be linked to the stock control and sales ledger programs. On receipt of an order the operator can enter order details into the invoicer program which will check with the stock control program to ensure that the goods required are in stock. If they are available then the required number of items can be allocated to the current order and the details transferred onto an invoice which is then printed off for the customer's benefit. In addition, the invoicer will also usually update the sales ledger to post the transaction to the customers account and eventually to the sales account.

Integration with both the sales ledger and stock control package is also necessary so that details such as the customers address, credit rating (sales ledger) and discounts, prices, stock levels (stock control) can be checked/transferred from the appropriate package.

Most invoicer packages will also produce debit and/or credit notes to record and update stock and customer records for goods returned. Although they can be used by any firm, they are probably most useful in on-line systems as they allow for greater speed and accuracy.

Order Processing packages are used to determine selling prices on orders received and ensure that the products ordered are manufactured. This type of package would only be used by organisations that are manufacturing or supplying fairly complex products/services, or where there are a wide range of selling prices and discounts. The principal report from this sort of package would also be an invoice; some less sophisticated versions of order processing packages may still be referred to as invoicing programs.

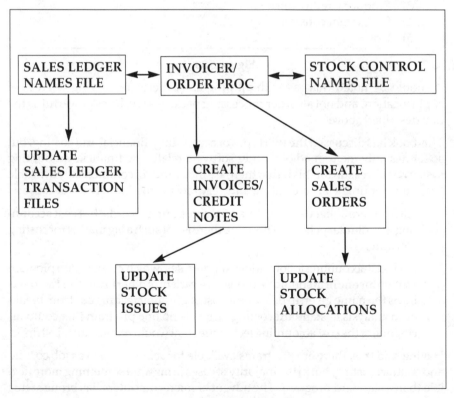

Figure 5.32

The main difference between a proper order processing and invoicing program is that the invoicer merely allocates stock to sales whereas the order processing package will ensure that all stages from ordering raw materials through the manufacture of the product and finally to the delivery of the product are recorded and scheduled through production. This will involve linking with the stock control package (for raw materials and finished goods records), the purchase ledger (for recording details of materials bought), the sales ledger (for recording details of products sold) and the nominal ledger (for recording wages, purchases, sales, etc).

Figure 5.32 shows how an invoicer program would integrate with both a sales ledger and stock control programs.

In some packages it is possible to amend details of stock items for the stock control program or add new customers for the sales ledger through entries in the invoicer program.

A Main Menu for a simple invoicer program is shown in Figure 5.33.

```
INVOICER PROGRAM                    MAIN MENU
1)  Produce Invoices
2)  Produce Delivery Notes
3)  Produce Credit Notes
4)  Set System constants
5)  Exit
```

Figure 5.33

It should be noted that, as with all programs, there are varying degrees of sophistication, and not all order processing packages will be as powerful as the one described above.

This book has discussed the two types of accounting, financial and costing, but so far has only mentioned computer software relating to financial accounting systems. The reason for this is that there are thousands of commercially available programs for financial accounting and very few for costing. This is because:

— All firms are obliged to keep financial accounting records, but cost accounting is a voluntary choice. Therefore there is not such a big market for costing software.

— Financial accounting follows a few, simple rules, which means that a program written for one firm should be usable by a variety of other firms. Cost accounting is the name given to describe a host of different techniques from break-even analysis to standard costing. There is no one program that could include all of the cost accounting techniques that would be relevant for all firms.

Having said this, there are programs available for activities such as job costing and contract costing, but in the majority of cases firms want something more flexible than a standard program. The advent of microcomputers has brought this flexibility in the form of spreadsheet packages.

Job costing programs follow the principles outlined in section 4.7 but can be, and usually are, integrated with the financial accounting records. This can be a complicated aspect of book-keeping for many firms, especially if they are involved in "jobs" that are long-term contracts (eg most construction work). It is essential that the firm maintains proper financial accounting records of work done, but it will also want to keep the records for each job separate so that it can tell if there is still going to be a profit on the job.

Most job costing programs will record details for each specific job but can transfer total details to the relevant accounts in the nominal ledger — this will involve transferring costs to the accounts for purchases (materials), wages (labour costs), sales (income from job) and various expense accounts. It is also possible in some systems to fully integrate the job costing program so that items can be transferred between the purchases ledger (suppliers accounts), sales ledger (customers accounts) and the stock control program (materials issued). This will generally require careful thought before allocating transaction codes so that each job will have a unique code.

JOB COSTING PROGRAM   MAIN MENU

1) Job Cost processing
2) Update Job file
3) Job Cost reports
4) Set System constants
5) Exit

Figure 5.34

The Job File will contain the basic details of each job and may include items such as:

Job number
Job Clients name and address
Job Description
Budgeted cost
Completion date
Open item or balance b/fwd
Completed indicator

This would be summary information only and is primarily to designate a file to which costs can be allocated. The "Description" in particular is likely to be a major simplification as the contracts for many jobs can run to a number of pages of details.

JOB COSTING PROGRAM   JOB PROCESSING MENU

1) Material costs
2) Labour costs
3) Overhead costs
4) Income
5) Exit

Figure 5.35

The actual data for each job will be entered from the job processing menu, once the job number has been entered a sub-menu such as that shown in Figure 5.34 will appear.

Each entry will require a code so that all cost items can be analysed and integrated with the other ledgers. So even items such as wages can have a number of different codes to differentiate between wages paid for unskilled staff, semi-skilled, skilled staff, supervisors, and managers.

As the majority of jobs will continue over a period of time most of the reports produced by this program will be concerned with reporting on the state of progress and cost items to date.

```
JOB COSTING PROGRAM
  1)  Job List
  2)  Cost type list
  3)  Transaction list
  4)  Job Cost
  5)  Job cost summary
  6)  Exit
```

Figure 5.36

The *Job list* report will include the job numbers, descriptions, budgeted cost and completion date for all current jobs.

The *Cost type* list will include for all cost codes the current rates per hours/quantity and percentage mark-ups for overheads.

The *Transaction list* acts like a daybook and will print all transactions in date order showing the job number concerned, date, cost type, cost code, amounts and quantities and possibly a brief description.

The *Job cost* report shows all costs incurred so far on a specified job; the costs are again usually categorised by code, date amount and a brief description.

The *Job cost* summary will include details from all jobs and will generally have headings for job number, budgeted cost, cost to date, cost including a percentage for overheads and an indicator as to whether the job is completed or not.

Exercises

222A Design a MAIN MENU suitable for an Invoicer program.

223A Describe the usual reports produced by a Job Costing program.

224A Show, with the aid of a flowchart how the Invoicer program is integrated with the Sales Ledger and Stock Control program.

225A Describe the main contents of a Job file in a Job Costing program.

5.10 SPREADSHEETS

These are programs which have been written with the intention of being as flexible as the user wants them to be. A spreadsheet was the name originally given to very large pieces of paper which were divided into columns. These sheets were used by engineers and accountants for carrying out long-winded and complex calculations. The sheets had to be large in order to include all of the necessary calculations.

Some programmers saw that it would be possible to duplicate this system on microcomputers by storing the entire spreadsheet in the computer's memory and "scrolling" around the spreadsheet so that only small sections of it were on screen at any one time. A spreadsheet would normally include a number of columns and rows, with each row being given a number and each column a letter. This means that there are "cells" formed, as shown in Figure 5.37.

The cursor <> is currently in cell A1 (column A and row 1); it is possible to move the cursor to any position within the spreadsheet and to show other parts of the spreadsheet by scrolling.

The advantages of spreadsheets are that numbers, text and formulae can be entered into a cell. If a formula is entered, the spreadsheet will carry out any calculations contained within the formula. If cell A1 contained the number two and cell A2 contained the number four then if the formula A1 + A2 were entered in cell A3, cell A3 would show the answer (six). If the numbers in cells A1 or A2 were to be altered, the figure in cell A3 would be automatically recalculated. This is known as the "what if?" function of spreadsheets.

```
    :   A : B : C : D : E : F : G
 1:    < >
 2:
 3:
 4:
 5:
 6:
 7:
 8:
 9:
10:
11:
12:
```

Figure 5.37   A spreadsheet format

The ability to accept formulae and to automatically recalculate when figures are adjusted makes spreadsheet packages ideal for planning applications such as those used in cost accounting. In fact, it would appear that every software house that has written a spreadsheet package has included a cash budget as an example in their manual. Such an example is given in Figure 5.38.

The advantages of using a spreadsheet for this type of application are that most formulae only need to be entered once (in column B) and can then be copied to all of the other cells and automatically incremented by the spreadsheet, and also that any of the figures can be adjusted and the spreadsheet will automatically recalculate the new answers.

:	A :	B :	C :	D :	E :	F :
1:		JAN	FEB	MAR	APR	MAY
2:						
3: SALES		1000	1000	1100	1200	1300
4: Less						
5: PURCHASES		200	200	300	400	400
6: EXPENSES		400	300	300	400	400
7:						
8: TOTAL		600	500	600	800	800
9:						
10: PROFIT		400	500	500	400	500
11:						

Figure 5.38

The formula used in such an application would be as shown in Figure 5.38;

:	A :	B :	C :	D :	E :	F :
1:		JAN	FEB	MAR	APR	MAY
2:						
3: SALES		1000	1000	1100	1200	1300
4: Less						
5: PURCHASES		200	200	300	400	400
6: EXPENSES		400	300	300	400	400
7:						
8: TOTAL		b5+b6	c5+c6	d5+d6	e5+e6	f5+f6
9:						
10: PROFIT		b3-b8	c3-c8	d3-d8	e3-e8	f3-f8

Figure 5.39 Cash budget example in a spreadsheet package

Spreadsheets can be used for any application that the user requires (providing the user has the necessary skill with the package) but are most often used for budgeting, forecasting, stock control, job costing, contract costing, forecasting and variance analysis. Whilst programs can be obtained or written to perform any one of these functions, the spreadsheet has the benefit of being able to perform as many applications as the user is capable of designing a spreadsheet for.

The facilities provided by spreadsheet packages has improved drastically in the last few years and most now include some extremely sophisticated graphics capabilities. These functions are especially useful for management presentations. A major problem with accounting data is that it is often only understood by accountants, but if the same data is shown in graph format, then it becomes much clearer to a wider audience.

One disadvantage with spreadsheets in the past was the need to possess a good understanding of their commands in order to make effective use of them. This is not always as straight-forward as it sounds, as most spreadsheets packages have a larger range of commands than some high level languages. This problem has been largely overcome by the increased sophistication of the macro commands in most spreadsheets.

Macros capture certain key-strokes and can then be recalled by simply typing in the name of the macro or a predetermined command. What this means in practice is that someone who is competent in the use of a particular spreadsheet package can devise a layout and enter the appropriate command sequence to perform a particular function, for example a simple stock control program. Then, by saving the sequence of commands as a macro, they can be recalled and data entered by any member of staff who knows what the macro name is. This enables staff who are not trained in the use of the package to operate a particular application without having the need to learn all of the spreadsheet commands — in effect macros perform the same function as any high level language in that they allow non-computer staff to take advantage of the benefits available by using computerised applications.

Exercises

226 What are the main application areas of spreadsheet packages?

227 A spreadsheet has been partly set up to calculate the Cash budget for the coming 4 months, the data entered so far is:

	A	B	C	D	E
1		July	Aug	Sept	Oct
2	Sales (Units)	1000	1500	1500	1500
3	Revenue				
4					
5	Purchases	350			
6	Labour				
7	Variable costs				
8	Overheads				
9	Total				
10	Surplus				
11	Opening bal	200			
12	Closing bal				

Each unit is sold for $12 and customers pay in the same month as the sale, raw material purchases are paid for one month after the units have been sold and cost $3.00 per unit. Labour costs $3.50 per unit and is paid in the same month as the units are sold, variable costs are $2 per unit and paid in the month *before* the units are sold. Overheads are $300 per month.

REQUIRED:
Show what formulae would be necessary to complete the spreadsheet (NB: the actual figures are NOT required).   (10 marks)
(Sep 91)

228 Which type of *commercial software package* would be most useful for *cost accounting* applications, suggest two possible areas where it could be used.

229 Give examples of formula suitable for Spreadsheet packages formula for the following:

   (i)   To add cells B1 and B2
   (ii) To add all cells in between B1 and B6
   (iii) To calculate the Average of all cells between B1 and B6
   (iv) To calculate an increase of 5% of the value in cell B1

(6 marks)
(Mar 92)

Appendix 1

Answers to selected questions

CHAPTER 1

1 See text : Section 1.1.

4 See text : Section 1.2.

5

Profit	Liquidity
Owner	Banks
Shareholders	Loan Companies
Employees	Debtors
Investors	Creditors
Stockbrokers	Government
Directors	
Managers	

6 See text : Section 1.2.

7 Shareholders, directors, Government, suppliers, customers, managers, employees.

8

TAXATION	Firms will have to pay tax on profits.
EMPLOYMENT	The Government will try to keep unemployment low.
POLLUTION	The Government will try to make firms take steps to reduce pollution.
SOCIAL SECURITY	The firm may have to pay social security costs for employees.
INDUSTRY	The Government will try to encourage investment in industry and in research and development.
INFLATION	The Government may try to stop firms increasing wages/prices as a means of controlling inflation.
FREE TRADE	Most Governments have some policies to stop the formation of monopolies.

9 SHAREHOLDERS/OWNERS - concerned with obtaining a good return on investment, mainly judged by amount of profit.

DIRECTORS - decide how much profit can be paid as dividends, mainly interested in profit.

MANAGERS - higher profits should mean increased salaries, but size of department will also affect salary.

BANKS/LOAN COMPANIES - profit will be important but cashflow is more significant as it determines firms ability to repay loan. Also, will consider assets.

EMPLOYEES - profit will be important as employees will want to be sure that they are getting a fair share of profits.

SUPPLIERS/CREDITORS - most firms operate on a credit basis so suppliers will want to be sure that the firm can pay its debts. May also want to consider possibility of takeover.

CUSTOMERS/DEBTORS - will want to ensure that firm is not going to go bankrupt and leave it without a supplier. May also want to consider possibility of takeover.

STOCKBROKERS/INVESTORS - concerned with amount of profit made and growth of firm, as this will indicate dividends payable in future years.

GOVERNMENT - many interests, including taxation on profits, safeguarding employee's jobs, preventing pollution, social security payments, inflation, free trade.

13 See text : Section 1.4.

14 (i) Prudence (Conservatism) Convention
(ii) Materiality Convention
(iii) Money Measurement Concept
(iv) Business Entity Concept
(v) Dual Aspect Concept   1 mark each = 5 marks

15 a. i Accruals Concept

ii Cost Concept

iii Conservatism/Prudence Convention

iv Business Entity Concept

v Materiality Convention

vi Money Measurement Concept

viii Concept of Duality

ix Going Concern Concept

x Consistency Convention

16 (a)
(i) Cost Concept –
all items are recorded at their purchase price   [1]
this is only value that everyone agrees with   [1]

(ii) Prudence Convention –
   Future losses anticipated but not future profits   [1]
   Always take the figure that will show lowest profit   [1]
(iii) Realisation Concept
   Profit arises when goods change hands   [1]
   Profit recorded in the year of "sale"   [1]
(iv) Materiality Convention
   Items of small value should be recorded as expenses   [1]
   No need to waste time searching for small errors   [1]
(b)
(i) Fixed Assets
         recorded at original cost (Cost Concept)   [3]
         also depreciated to find true value (Prudence convention)   [3]
(ii) Stationery
         value should be carried forward to next year   [3]
            (Realisation concept)
         not significant value and therefore written off   [3]
            (Materiality Convention)

17

	Assets	Liabilities	Capital
Bought a car on credit	Increase	Increase	—
Bought stock paying by cheque	Increase (stock) & Decrease (bank)	—	—
Owner invests money in the firm's bank account	Increase	—	Increase
Pay a creditor in cash	Decrease	Decrease	—
Buy office equipment on credit	Increase	Increase	—
Receive cash from a Debtor	Increase (cash) & Decrease (Debtor)	—	—
Sell stock on credit	Decrease (stock) & Increase (Debtor)	—	—

18

Assets	Liabilities	Capital
£	£	£
19,000	12,000	7,000
30,500	7,500	23,000
16,200	4,400	11,800
31,700	10,300	21,400
17,600	6,400	11,200
8,500	3,900	4,600

19 FIXED ASSET EXAMPLES - premises, fixtures and fittings, machinery, motor vehicles, etc.

   CURRENT ASSET EXAMPLES - stock, cash in hand, cash at bank, debtors.

21

Balance Sheet

	£		£
Fixed Assets		Capital	
Premises	20,000	Capital	26,950
Office Equipment	1,200		
Machinery	3,400		
	24,600		
Current Assets	£	Liabilities	
Stock	4,500	Creditors	4,250
Cash in hand	50		
Cash at bank	500		
Debtors	1,550 6,600		
	31,200		31,200

22

Balance Sheet

	£		£
Fixed Assets		Capital	
Premises	10,000	Capital	25,400
Motor Vehicles	5,000	Add Profit	6,100
			31,500
Machinery	6,100		
Office Equipment	1,600	Less Drawings	5,500
	22,700		26,000
Current Assets	£	Liabilities	
Stock	3,200	Creditors	6,200
Cash in hand	200		
Debtors	4,600		
Cash at bank	1,500 9,500		
	32,200		32,200

23 Because liabilities represent the amount owed to creditors and capital represents the amount ''owed'' to the owner of the business (see Business Entity concept).

24

Balance Sheet

	£		£
Fixed Assets		**Capital**	
Premises	120,000	Capital	164,000
Motor Vehicles	50,000	Add Profit	12,400
Fixtures & Fittings	10,300		176,400
Machinery	5,200	Less Drawings	4,800
	185,500		171,600
Current Assets	£	**Liabilities**	
Stock	12,000	Creditors	16,500
Cash	750	Bank Loan	25,00
Bank	2,100		
Debtors	12,750 27,600		
	213,100		213,100

26 00/1/400/5
002/300/8

Benefits: quicker and easier analysis of data, improved cost control.

27 LX500/9DM/80
LQ850/24DM/132
EP/LSR/A4
LC10/9DM/80
NL10/9DM/80

29 (i) 100/005/008
(ii) 210/006/007
(iii) 210/008/102 (or 100)
(iv) 100/104/204 (or 201)
(v) 210/007/204 (or 201)   [2 marks each]

30 See text : Section 1.8.

CHAPTER 2

33

CASH ACCOUNT		Dr	Cr
Jan 1	Balance b/d	120.00	
Jan 2	Wages		75.00
Jan 3	Rent		25.00
Jan 4	Sales	28.70	
Jan 5	Insurance	50.00	
Jan 6	Carriage Inwards		12.75
Jan 7	Commission received	120.20	
Jan 8	Balance c/d		205.65
		318.90	318.90
Jan 8	Balance b/d	205.65	

1 mark per item = 8 marks

34

B   Transferred 500 from Cash to Bank

Cash			Bank	
	Bank 500		Cash 500	

C   Sold stock 1,000 on credit

Stock			Debtors	
	Debtors 1,000		Stock 1,000	

D   Received payment of 2,000 from Debtors by cheque

Debtors			Bank	
	Bank 2,000		Debtors 2,000	

E   Bought Stock on credit 2,000

Stock			Creditors	
Creditors 2,000			Stock 2,000	

F   Bought additional premises with mortgage of 10,000

Premises			Bank	
Morgage 10,000			Premises 10,000	

G   Bought Motor Van on credit 2,000

Motor Van			Creditors	
Creditors 2,000			Motor Van 2,000	

H   Took drawings of 500 from Cash
Also took drawings of 500 in Stock

Drawings			Cash	
Cash 500			Drawings 500	
Stock 500				

			Stock	
			Drawings 500	

I   (1)   Invested additional 1,000 Capital in Cash

Capital			Cash	
	Cash 1,000		Capital 1,000	

OR (2) Re-invested Net profit in Cash

Capital			Cash	
	Profit 1,000		Capital 1,000	

35   See text: section 2.4.

36

Capital A/c	Dr	Cr		Bank A/c	Dr	Cr
June 1 Bank		12,000		June 1 Capital	12,000	
June 1 Motor				June 2 Rent		1,000
Vehicle		8,000		June 4 Equipment		2,500
June 1 Cash		500		June 10 Cash	400	

Cash A/c	Dr	Cr		June 10 Motor		
June 1 Capital	500			Vehicles		5,000
June 5 Advertising		250		June 14 Sales	450	
June 6 Sales	600			June 18 Cash		1,300
June 10 Bank		400		June 20 H Kelly	750	
June 18 Bank	1,300			June 21 AC Limited		2,000
June 18 Wages		1,300				

Rent A/c	Dr	Cr		Motor Vehicle A/c	Dr	Cr
June 2 Bank	1,000			June 1 Capital	8,000	
				June 10 Bank	5,000	

Purchases A/c	Dr	Cr		AC Limited A/c	Dr	Cr
June 3 AC Limited	3,000			June 3 Purchases		3,000
June 17 AC Limited	1,500			June 17 Purchases		1,700
				June 21 Bank	2,000	

Equipment A/c	Dr	Cr		Advertising A/c	Dr	Cr
June 4 Bank	2,500			June 5 Cash	250	

Sales A/c	Dr	Cr		H Kelly A/c	Dr	Cr
June 6 H Kelley		750		June 6 Sales	750	
June 6 Cash		600		June 20 Bank		750
June 10 D Miles		300				
June 14 Bank		450		D Miles A/c	Dr	Cr
				June 10 Sales	300	

Wages A/c	Dr	Cr
June 18 Cash	1,300	

37

BANK ACCOUNT

Dec 1st Bal b/d	2,400	Dec 3rd Office		
Dec 2nd Capital	12,000	Equipment	7,500	
Dec 6th Sales	3,000	Dec 4th Purchases	1,100	
		Dec 5th Rent	300	
		Dec 7th Bal c/d	8,500	
	17,400		17,400	
Dec 7th Bal b/d	8,500			

38 *Capital*

(a)(d)(g)(i)(j)(m)(p)

Revenue

(b)(c)(e)(f)(h)(k)(l)(n)(o)(q)(r)

40 (a)

	£
List price (less 10% discount)	12,150
Stereo	180
Tinted window	90
Upholstery	125
Number Plates	48
	12,593

Comments

List price — discount must be deducted
Stereo — included as presumably a permanent fixture
Tinted window — as above
Upholstery — as above
Number plates — essential for vehicle to be roadworthy

Warranty — revenue, not a permanent increase in value
Road tax — revenue, only valid for one year
Insurance — as above
Petrol — revenue
Map — revenue

(b)

(1)   Revenue — replacement not improvement

(2)   Capital — presumed to be permanent fixture and increase value

(3)   Capital — permanent fixture, not a replacement

(4)   Revenue — replacement

(5)   Capital — capital item in its own right

(6)   Capital — permanent fixture, increasing value

(7)   Revenue — replacement

(8)   Capital — permanent, enhancing value of asset to the business

(9)   Revenue — not a permanent improvement

(10) Revenue — not a fixture

41

Capital A/c	Dr	Cr
Jan 3 Bank		10,000

Bank A/c	Dr	Cr
Jan 1 Capital	10,000	
Jan 2 Purchases		350
Jan 3 Insurance		100
Jan 3 Stationery		35
Jan 3 Motor Expenses		15
Jan 4 Rent		300
Jan 5 Cash		200

Purchases A/c	Dr	Cr
Jan 2 Bank	350	
Jan 2 H Cully	1,000	
Jan 6 Worthy Ltd	350	

Motor Vehicle A/c	Dr	Cr
Jan 1 ABC Garages	3,500	

ABC Garages A/c	Dr	Cr
Jan 1 Motor Vehicle		3,500

H Cully A/c	Dr	Cr
Jan 2 Purchases		1,000

Insurances A/c	Dr	Cr
Jan 3 Bank	100	

Motor Expenses A/c	Dr	Cr
Jan 3 Bank	15	

Stationery A/c	Dr	Cr
Jan 3 Bank	35	

Rent A/c	Dr	Cr
Jan 4 Bank	300	

Cash A/c	Dr	Cr
Jan 5 Bank	200	
Jan 6 Wages		50

Sales A/c	Dr	Cr
Jan 4 D Watkins		455

Worthy Ltd A/c	Dr	Cr
Jan 6 Purchases		350

Wages A/c	Dr	Cr
Jan 6 Cash	50	

D Watkins A/c	Dr	Cr
Jan 4 Sales	455	

42

Capital A/c	Dr	Cr
May 1 Bank		5,500
May 1 Motor Vehicle		3,000
May 6 Balance		8,500

Bank Account	Dr	Cr
May 1 Capital	5,500	
May 2 Premises		4,000
May 3 Loan	1,250	
May 5 Rates		200
May 5 Insurance		80
May 5 Stationery		15
May 5 Motor Exps.		75
May 5 Cash		120
May 6 F Goodby		450
May 6 W Young		120
May 6 J Singh	750	
May 6 H Jones	200	
May 6 K Patel	425	
	8,125	5,060
May 6 Balance	3,065	

Motor Vehicle A/c	Dr	Cr
May 1 Capital	3,000	

Premises A/c	Dr	Cr
May 2 Bank	4,000	

Purchases A/c	Dr	Cr
May 2 F Goodby	450	
May 2 J Oates	1,000	
May 2 W Young	120	
May 2 G Mistry	245	
May 6 Balance	1,815	

F Goodby A/c	Dr	Cr
May 2 Purchases		450
May 6 Bank	450	
	450	450

J Oates A/c	Dr	Cr
May 2 Purchases		1,000
May 6 Returns Out	120	
	120	1,000
May 6 Balance		880

W Young A/c	Dr	Cr
May 2 Purchases		120
May 6 Bank	120	
	120	120

G Mistry A/c	Dr	Cr
May 2 Purchases		245

Loan A/c	Dr	Cr
May 3 Fixtures & Fittings		750
May 3 Bank		1,250
May 6 Balance		2,000

K Sung A/c	Dr	Cr
May 4 Sales	1,200	

K Patel A/c	Dr	Cr
May 4 Sales	450	
May 6 Bank		425
May 6 Returns In		25
	450	450

Rates A/c	Dr	Cr
May 5 Bank	200	

Insurance A/c	Dr	Cr
May 5 Bank	80	

Fixtures & Fittings A/c	Dr	Cr
May 3 Loan	750	

Sales A/c	Dr	Cr
May 4 J Singh		750
May 4 H Jones		300
May 4 K Sung		1,200
May 4 K Patel		450
May 6 Balance		2,700

J Singh A/c	Dr	Cr
May 4 Sales	750	
May 6 Bank		750
	750	750

H Jones A/c	Dr	Cr
May 4 Sales	300	
May 6 Bank		200
	300	200
May 6 Balance	100	

Stationery Account	Dr	Cr
May 5 Bank	15	

Motor Expenses A/c	Dr	Cr
May 5 Bank	75	

Cash A/c	Dr	Cr
May 5 Bank	120	
May 5 Wages		120
	120	120

Wages Account	Dr	Cr
May 5 Cash	120	

Returns Out A/c	Dr	Cr
May 6 J Oates		120

Returns In A/c	Dr	Cr
May 6 K Patel	25	

Trial Balance at May 6

	Dr	Cr
Capital		8,500
Bank	3,065	
Motor Vehicles	4,000	
Premises	4,000	
Purchases	1,815	

J Oates		880	
G Mistry		245	
Loan		2,000	
Fixtures & Fittings	750		
Sales		2,700	
H Jones	100		
K Sung	1,200		
Rates	200		
Insurance	80		
Stationery	15		
Motor Expenses	75		
Wages	120		
Returns Out		120	
Returns In		25	
		14,445	14,445

43

	Dr	Cr
Capital		34,927
Drawings	10,465	
Bank	4,196	
Cash	500	
Debtors	8,500	
Creditors		4,040
Wages	15,500	
General Expenses	25,850	
Carriage Inwards	650	
Carriage Outwards	1,540	
Purchase Returns		761
Sales Returns	531	
Discounts Allowed	1,150	
Discounts Received		2,324
Sales		107,266
Purchases	50,754	
Motor Vehicles	38,420	
Stock at 1st March 1990	5,830	
Accumulated Depreciation		14,568
	163,886	163,886

½ mark per item + ½ marks for totals = 10 marks

44

	Dr	Cr
Wages	20,500	
Capital		172,380
Motor Vehicles	78,900	
Insurance	2,100	
Debtors	17,500	
Light & Heat	900	
Returns In	1,110	

Creditors		13,400
Sales		65,800
Purchases	45,320	
Returns Out		850
Premises	98,200	
Discounts Received		1,200
Cash	800	
Bank	3,200	
Accumulated Depreciation		12,900
Rent & Rates	4,000	
Bank Loan		6,000
	272,530	272,530

46

any FIVE ONLY from:
Error of omission – stamping source documents
Error of commission – use of unique account numbers
Error of principle – well-trained and capable staff
Error of original entry – well-trained and capable staff
Error of reversal – correct programming (eg: No Dr's in Sales)
Compensating errors – program refuses to accept single entries

2 marks each = 10 marks

48 (i) Principle
(ii) Correct (Capital Expenditure)
(iii) Reversal
(iv) Correct (Business Entity)
(v) Commission
(vi) Correct (Cost Concept)
(vii) Original Entry
(viii) Correct (Materiality)   [1] Mark each

49

The errors are:

i.   Black & Co was debited with sales of $350 instead of C Black.
ii. Furnishings for the managing director's house were posted to the Fixtures & Fittings Account.
iii. An invoice from Jones Ltd for $10 was never entered into the books.
iv. Collins invoiced the firm with goods for $66 but this was recorded as $56. Grahams also sent in an invoice for $544 but this was transcribed as $554.
v.   Peters paid the firm $89 but was recorded in the books as $98.

52

Cost — disposal value	=	£18,000—£6,000
Number of years		4
	=	£3,000 per annum.

53

| | Year 1: | Cost | £18,000 |
| | | Less depr: | £4,500 |

| | Year 2: | NBV | £13,500 |
| | | Less depr: | £3,375 |

| | Year 3: | NBV | £10,125 |
| | | Less depr: | £2,531 |

	Year 4:	NBV	£7,594
		Less depr:	£1,898
		NBV	£5,696

54

Capital A/c	Dr	Cr	Loan A/c	Dr	Cr
Nov 1 Balance		15,500	Nov 1 Balance		500

P Parkes A/c	Dr	Cr	D Parkin A/c	Dr	Cr
Nov 1 Balance		770	Nov 1 Balance		120

G Taylor A/c	Dr	Cr	G Palmer A/c	Dr	Cr
Nov 1 Balance		350	Nov 1 Balance		1000

Sales A/c	Dr	Cr	Returns In A/c	Dr	Cr
Nov 1 Balance		9,500	Nov 1 Balance	250	

Premises A/c	Dr	Cr	Motor Vehicles A/c	Dr	Cr
Nov 1 Balance	6,500		Nov 1 Balance	3,500	

Fixtures & Fittings A/c	Dr	Cr	Bank A/c	Dr	Cr
Nov 1 Balance	1,000		Nov 1 Balance	2,000	

Stock A/c	Dr	Cr	Cash A/c	Dr	Cr
Nov 1 Balance	5,500		Nov 1 Balance	300	

D Wagstaffe A/c	Dr	Cr	P Knowles A/c	Dr	Cr
Nov 1 Balance	355		Nov 1 Balance	710	

J McAlliog A/c	Dr	Cr	D Dougan A/c	Dr	Cr
Nov 1 Balance	200		Nov 1 Balance	800	

S Kindon A/c	Dr	Cr	Purchases A/c	Dr	Cr
Nov 1 Balance	300		Nov 1 Balance	4,500	

Returns Out A/c	Dr	Cr	Carriage In A/c	Dr	Cr
Nov 1 Balance		115	Nov 1 Balance	500	

Wages A/c	Dr	Cr	Motor Expenses A/c	Dr	Cr
Nov 1 Balance	500		Nov 1 Balance	250	

Insurance A/c	Dr	Cr	Advertising A/c	Dr	Cr
Nov 1 Balance	70		Nov 1 Balance	90	

Rates A/c	Dr	Cr	Lighting & Heating A/c	Dr	Cr
Nov 1 Balance	230		Nov 1 Balance	300	

Trial Balance as at Nov 1

	Dr	Cr
Capital		15,000
Loan		500
P Parkes		770
D Parkin		120
G Taylor		350
G Palmer		1,000
Sales		9,500
Returns In	250	
Premises	6,500	
Motor Vehicles	3,500	
Fixtures & Fittings	1,000	
Bank	2,000	
Stock	5,500	
Cash	300	
D Wagstaffe	355	
P Knowles	710	
J McAlliog	200	
D Dougan	800	
S Kindon	300	
Purchases	4,500	
Returns Out		115
Carriage In	500	
Wages	500	
Motor Expenses	250	
Insurance	70	
Advertising	90	
Rates	230	
Lighting & Heating	300	
	27,855	27,855

Bank A/c

	Dr	Cr
Nov 1 Balance	2,000	
Nov 1 P Parkes		120
Nov 1 G Taylor		200
Nov 1 G Palmer		450
Nov 3 D Dougan	350	
Nov 3 S Kindon	150	
Nov 3 J McAlliog	200	
Nov 3 Rates		60
Nov 8 S Kindon	50	
Nov 12 Fixtures & Fittings		300
Nov 25 Drawings		500
Nov 30 Advertising		20
	2,750	1,650
Balance	1,100	

Cash A/c

	Dr	Cr
Nov 1 Balance	300	
Nov 2 Advertising		50
Nov 2 Sales	250	
Nov 5 Carriage In		15
Nov 14 Wages		50
Nov 19 Stationery		25
Nov 23 Wages		50
Nov 25 Drawings		200
Nov 29 Lighting & Heating		40
Nov 29 Sales	110	
	660	430
Balance	230	

Sales A/c

	Dr	Cr
Nov 1 Balance		9,500
Nov 2 Cash		250
Nov 16 D Dougan		120
Nov 16 P Knowles		200
Nov 16 H Curran		150
Nov 29 Cash		110
	nil	10,330

J McAlliog A/c

	Dr	Cr
Nov 1 Balance	200	
Nov 3 Bank		200
	200	200

P Parkes A/c

	Dr	Cr
Nov 1 Balance		770
Nov 1 Bank	120	
	120	770
Balance		650

G Taylor A/c

	Dr	Cr
Nov 1 Balance		350
Nov 1 Bank	200	
	200	350
Balance		150

G Palmer A/c

	Dr	Cr
Nov 1 Balance		1,000
Nov 1 Bank	450	
	450	1,000
Balance		550

Advertising A/c

	Dr	Cr
Nov 1 Balance	90	
Nov 2 Cash	50	
Nov 30 Bank	20	
	160	nil

D Dougan A/c

	Dr	Cr
Nov 1 Balance	800	
Nov 3 Bank		350
Nov 16 Sales	120	
	920	350
Balance	570	

S Kindon A/c

	Dr	Cr
Nov 1 Balance	300	
Nov 3 Bank		150
Nov 8 Bank		50
Nov 8 Bad Debts		100
	300	300

Rates A/c	Dr	Cr
Nov 1 Balance	230	
Nov 3 Bank	60	
	290	nil

D Parkin A/c	Dr	Cr
Nov 1 Balance		120
Nov 5 Purchases		300
	nil	420

M Bailey A/c	Dr	Cr
Nov 5 Purchases		750

Fixtures & Fittings A/c	Dr	Cr
Nov 1 Balance	1,000	
Nov 12 Bank	300	
	1,300	nil

P Knowles A/c	Dr	Cr
Nov 1 Balance	710	
Nov 16 Sales	200	
Nov 27 Returns In		30
	910	30
Balance	880	

Stationery A/c	Dr	Cr
Nov 19 Cash	25	

Returns In A/c	Dr	Cr
Nov 1 Balance	250	
Nov 27 P Knowles	30	
	280	nil

Purchases A/c	Dr	Cr
Nov 1 Balance	4,500	
Nov 5 D Parkin	300	
Nov 5 M Bailey	750	
	5,550	nil

Carriage In A/c	Dr	Cr
Nov 1 Balance	500	
Nov 5 Cash	15	
	515	nil

Bad Debts A/c	Dr	Cr
Nov 8 S Kindon	100	

Wages A/c	Dr	Cr
Nov 1 Balance	500	
Nov 14 Cash	50	
Nov 23 Cash	50	
	600	nil

H Curran A/c	Dr	Cr
Nov 16 Sales	150	

Drawings A/c	Dr	Cr
Nov 25 Cash	200	
Nov 25 Bank	500	
	700	nil

Lighting & Heating A/c	Dr	Cr
Nov 1 Balance	300	
Nov 29 Cash	40	
	340	nil

Capital A/c	Dr	Cr
Nov 1 Balance		15,500

Premises A/c	Dr	Cr
Nov 1 Balance	6,500	

Stock A/c	Dr	Cr
Nov 1 Balance	5,500	

Returns Out A/c	Dr	Cr
Nov 1 Balance	115	

Insurance A/c	Dr	Cr
Nov 1 Balance	70	

Loan A/c	Dr	Cr
Nov 1 Balance		500

Motor Vehicles A/c	Dr	Cr
Nov 1 Balance	3,500	

D Wagstaffe A/c	Dr	Cr
Nov 1 Balance		355

Motor Expenses A/c	Dr	Cr
Nov 1 Balance	250	

Trial Balance as at Dec 1

	Dr	Cr
Capital		15,500
Loan		500
P Parkes		650
D Parkin		420
G Taylor		150
G Palmer		550
M Bailey		750
Sales		10,330
Returns In	280	
Premises	6,500	
Motor Vehicles	3,500	
Fixtures & Fittings	1,300	
Bank	1,100	
Stock	5,500	
Cash	230	
D Wagstaffe	355	
P Knowles	880	
H Curran	150	
D Dougan	570	
Purchases	5,550	
Returns Out		115
Carriage In	515	
Wages	600	
Motor Expenses	250	
Insurance	70	
Advertising	160	
Rates	290	
Lighting & Heating	340	
Bad Debts	100	
Stationery	25	
Drawings	700	
	28,965	28,965

Trading & Profit/Loss A/c for y/e 30 Nov

	£	£	£
Sales			10,330
less Returns In			280
			10,050
Opening Stock		5,500	
Purchases	5,550		
Carriage In	515		
	6,065		
less Returns Out	115	5,950	
		11,450	
less Closing Stock		5,700	
Cost of Goods Sold		5,750	
Gross Profit c/d		4,300	
		10,050	10,050
Gross Profit b/d			4,300
Wages	600		
Rates	290		
Lighting & Heating	340		
Insurance	70		
Advertising	160		
Motor Expenses	250		
Stationery	25		
Bad Debts	100		
Depreciation: Fixtures	325		
Depreciation: Motor Vehicles	875		
Net Profit	1,265		
	4,300		4,300

Balance Sheet as at 31 Dec

Fixed Assets	Cost	Ac Dep	NBV
Premises	6,500	—	6,500
Motor Vehicles	3,500	875	2,625
Fixtures & Fittings	1,300	325	975
	11,300	1,200	10,100
Current Assets			
Stock		5,700	

Debtors		1,955	
Cash		230	
Bank		1,100	
		8,985	

Current Liabilities

Loan		500	
Creditors		2,520	3,020
Net Assets Employed			16,065

Financed by:

Capital as at 1 Nov	15,500	
Add Profit	1,265	
	16,765	
less Drawings	700	16,065

55

	Cost	Acc Dep	NBV	Profit/loss A/c
	£	£	£	£
Year 1 Office Equipment	5,000	1,000	4,000	1,000
Year 2 Office Equipment	5,000	1,800	3,200	800
Year 3 Office Equipment	5,000	2,440	2,560	640
Year 4 Office Equipment	5,000	2,952	2,048	512

Heading (first two columns) | Balance Sheet / Profit/loss A/c

56

(a) (i)   Straight Line Method

Cost Price — Disposal Value $= (8,000-2,000)/3 = 2,000$
        Years in Use

(a) (ii)   Reducing Balance Method (at 25%)

1st Year   25% of 8,000 =   2,000
2nd Year   25% of 6,000 =   1,500
3rd Year   25% of 4,500 =   1,125

(b)   Motor Vehicles Account

Date	Details	Dr	Cr
1 Jan 19.	Bank	8,000	

Prov. for Dep. Acc.

Date	Details	Dr	Cr
31 Dec 19.	Profit/Loss		2,000

			Nil	**2,000**
1 Jan 19.	Bal at this date			2,000
31 Dec 19.	Profit/Loss A/c			1,500
			Nil	**3,500**
1 Jan 19.	Bal at this date			3,500
31 Dec 19.	Profit/Loss			1,125
			Nil	**4,625**

PROFIT/LOSS ACCOUNT EXTRACTS

Prov. for Dep. (Year 2)	2,000
Prov. for Dep. (Year 2)	1,500
Prov. for Dep. (Year 3)	1,125

BALANCE SHEET EXTRACT

		COST	ACC.	DEP NBV
	Motor Vehicle	COST	ACC.	DEP NBV
YEAR 1	Motor Vehicle	8,000	2,000	6,000
YEAR 2	Motor Vehicle	8,000	3,500	4,500
YEAR 3	Motor Vehicle	8,000	4,625	3,375

57

(a) PROFIT & LOSS A/C FOR THE YEAR

	$	$	$
Sales			425,100
Opening Stock		18,390	
Add Purchases		280,900	
Less Closing Stock		16,300	
Cost of Goods Sold		282,990	282,990
GROSS PROFIT			142,110
Wages/Salaries	42,350		
Rent/Rates	18,100		
Light/Heat	17,500		
Depreciation	9,400		
Loan Interest	2,900		
Accrued	150	3,050	
		90,400	90,400
NET PROFIT			51,710

BALANCE SHEET AS AT 31.8.88

	Cost £	Acc Dep £	NBV £
FIXED ASSETS			
Equipment	94,000	37,600	56,400
CURRENT ASSETS			
Stock	16,300		
Debtors	64,340		
Bank	11,760		
Cash	2,100		
	94,500		
CURRENT LIABILITIES			
Creditors	38,900		
Accurals	150		
	39,050		
WORKING CAPITAL		55,450	
NET ASSETS EMPLOYED			111,850
FINANCED BY:			
Capital	45,540		
less drawings	15,400		
	30,140		
Add Net Profit	51,710	81,850	
Long Term Liabilities			
Loan	30,000		111,850

58
    (a) Wear and Tear
    (b) Economic Factors
    (c) Time Factor
    (d) Depletion

  (B) (i) Depletion
      (ii) Economic Factors — alhtough does not usually depreciate
      (iii) Wear and Tear
      (iv) Economic Factors (Obsolete)
      (v) Time Factor
      (vi) Time Factor

61

A Nelson

Trading & Profit/Loss A/c for y/e 31 December

	£	£	£
Sales			52,000
Opening Stock		4,750	
Purchases	30,000		
less Returns Out	400	29,600	
		34,350	
less Closing Stock		5,700	
Cost of Goods Sold		28,650	
Gross Profit c/d		23,350	
		52,000	52,000
Gross Profit b/d			23,350
Discounts received			1,000
			24,350
Insurance		750	
Motor Vehicle Expenses		600	
Sundry Expenses		375	
Lighting & Heating		450	
Rent & Rates		1,000	
Wages & Salaries		8,500	
Bad Debts		400	
Depr: Motor Vehicles		937	
Depr: Furniture & Fittings		750	
Net Profit		10,588	
		24,350	24,350

Balance Sheet as at 31 December

	Cost	Acc Dep	NBV
Fixed Assets			
Premises	15,000	—	15,000
Furniture & Fittings	4,000	1,750	2,250
Motor Vehicles	5,000	2,187	2,813
	24,000	2,937	20,063
Current Assets			
Stock		5,700	
Debtors	7,600		
less Bad Debts	400	7,200	
Cash		400	
Bank		1,100	
		14,400	

Current Liabilities

Creditors		6,125	
Working Capital		8,275	8,275
Net Assets Employed			28,338
Financed by:			
Capital		17,750	
Add Profit		10,588	
		28,338	28,338

62 Trading and Profit/Loss Account

	$	$
Sales		107,266
Less Returns In		531 [1]
Opening Stock	5,830	106,735
Purchases	50,754	
Carriage Inwards	650 [1]	
	57,234	
Less Returns Out	761 [1]	
	56,473	
Less Closing Stock	6,200	
Cost of Goods sold	50,273	50,273
Gross Profit		56,462
Discount received		2,324 [1]
		58,786 [1]
Discounts allowed		1,150
Salaries and Wages	15,500	
Accrued	250 [1]	15,750
Depreciation		7,684
General expenses	25,850	
Prepaid	(180) [1]	25,670
Carriage Outwards		1,540
Provision for Bad Debts		170 [1]	51,964
NET PROFIT		6,882 [2]

Balance Sheet

Fixed Assets	Cost	Acc dep	NBV
Motor Vehicles	38,420	22,252	16,168 [1]
Current Assets			
Stock		6,200	
Debtors	8,500		
Prov for Bad Debts	170 [1]	8,330	
Prepayments		180 [1]	
Bank		4,196	
Cash		500	
		19,406 [1]	

Current Liabilities				
Creditors	4,040			
Accruals	250 [1]	4,290 [1]	15,116 [1]	
NET ASSETS			31,284 [1]	
Financed by				
Capital				
Opening Capital			34,927	
Net Profit			6,882 [1]	
			41,749	
Drawings			10,465	
			31,284 [1]	

½ marks only if incorrect layout   Total = 20 marks

63   Bad Debts A/c: Records details of Bad Debts that have actually been identified — a specific debtor is involved.

Prov for Bad Debts A/c: Records an estimated amount of Bad Debts. No specific person is involved.

64

BALANCE SHEET

	Cost	Acc Dep	NBV
FIXED ASSETS:			
Premises	56,000		56,000
Fixtures & Fittings	45,200	9,040	36,160
Motor Vehicles	25,000	5,000	20,000
	126,200	14,040	112,160

CURRENT ASSETS:			
Debtors	18,400		
less Prov for Bad Debts	600	17,800	
Bank		11,450	
Cash		1,100	
Stock		13,450	
Prepayments		700	44,500
CURRENT LIABILITIES:			
Creditors		12,500	
Bank Loan		4,300	
Accruals		900	17,700
WORKING CAPITAL			26,800	26,800
NET ASSETS EMPLOYED				138,960
Financed by:			
Capital		103,010	
+ Profit		13,450	
		116,460	
− Drawings		7,500	
		108,960	108,960
LONG TERM LIABILITY			
Mortgage		30,000	30,000
			138,960

65

	$	$
Sales		138,430
less Returns In		780
		137,650
Opening Stock	18,300	
Purchases	78,405	
	96,705	
less Returns Out	900	
	95,805	
less Closing Stock	20,080	
Cost of Goods Sold	75,725	75,725
GROSS PROFIT		61,925
Discounts received		1,100
		63,025
Wages	17,410	
+ Accrued	450	17,860
Rent & Rates	3,200	
− Prepaid	45	3,155
Light & Heat		8,422
Insurance	1,300	
+ Accrued	120	1,420
Motor Vehicle Expenses		2,545
Depr: Motor Vehicle		550
Depr: Fittings		2,162
Increase in Prov for bad debts		140
Discounts allowed		950
Loan Interest		1,450	38,654
NET PROFIT		24,371

66

Trading & Profit and Loss Account for the year ended 31st December 1989

Sales		300,000
Purchases	190,000	
Add Opening Stock	10,000	
	200,000	
less Closing Stock	15,000	
Cost of Sales		185,000
GROSS PROFIT		115,000
Distribution in Expenses:		
Motor Expenses	8,000	
Depr: Motor Vehicles	4,000	
	12,000	
Administrative Costs:		
Rent & Rates	4,000	
Heat & Light	3,000	
Bad Debts Written-off	500	
Discounts Allowed	2,000	
Depr: Machinery	1,500	
	11,000	
		23,000
Net Trading Profit		92,000
Other Operating Income:		
Discounts Received		500
Net Operating Profit		92,500

Balance Sheet as at 31st December 1989

Fixed Assets		Cost	Dep'n to Date	NBV
Property		192,000	–	192,000
Machinery		23,000	8,000	15,000
Motor Vehicles		26,000	6,000	20,000
TOTAL FIXED ASSETS				227,000
Current Assets				
Stock		15,000		
Debtors	20,000			
less Prov'n	1,000			
		19,000		
		34,000		
Prepayments		5,000		
			39,000	
Current Liabilities				
Creditors		17,000		
Bank Overdraft		11,000		
Accruals		7,500		
			35,500	
Working Capital				3,500
Total Net Assets				230,500
Financed By:				
Capital Account:				
Balance as at 1st Jan 1989			110,000	
Net Profit for Year			92,500	
			202,500	
Drawings			12,000	
				190,500
Loan Capital:				
5 year Loan			50,000	
Less Repaid			10,000	
				40,000
Capital Employed				230,500

67

TRADING & PROFIT/LOSS ACCOUNT FOR THE Y/E 27/2/90

	$	$	$
Sales			96,210
Opening Stock		8,930	
Purchases	53,100		
Carriage Inwards	2,225		
	55,325		
Returns Outwards	1,205	54,120	
		63,050	
Closing Stock		9,205	
Cost of Goods Sold		53,845	53,845

Gross Profit			42,365
Discounts Received			550
Commission Received			8,700
			51,615
Insurance		1,100	
Wages & Salaries	12,500		
less Drawings	2,000	10,500	
Rent & Rates	2,450		
less Prepayments	210	2,240	
Carriage Outwards		3,540	
Motor Vehicle Expenses		5,425	
Light & Heat	1,800		
plus Accrued	455	2,255	
Provision for Bad Debts		228	
Depreciation:			
Motor Vehicles	6,420		
Fixtures & fittings	715	7,135	32,423
NET PROFIT			19,192

69 Balance Sheet

FIXED ASSETS	Cost	Acc Depr	NBV
Premises	90,000		90,000
Motor Vehicles	35,000	14,300	20,700 [2]
Office Equipment	18,400	5,890	12,510 [2]
	143,400	20,190	123,210 [1]
CURRENT ASSETS			
Stock		5,000	
Prepayments		700	
Cash		1,300	
Debtors	31,600		
Less Provn for Bad Debts	1,580	30,020 [2]	
		37,020 [2]	
CURRENT LIABILITIES			
Creditors	24,500		
Overdraft	6,400 [1]		
Accruals	600	31,500 [2]	5,520 [2]
			128,730 [1]
CAPITAL			
Opening Balance	103,730		
+ Profit	20,000		
	123,730		
− Drawings	10,000		113,730 [2]
LONG TERM LIABILITIES			
Loan			15,000 [1]
			128,730

70   See text. Section 2.7.1.

71   See text. Section 2.7.1.

72

(a)

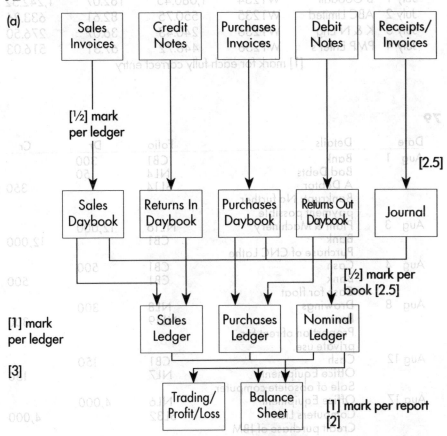

(b)   (i)   Can only have one person entering data in Ledger
Too much data to be entered by only one person
Daybooks enable more people to be employed
Data can be transferred to Ledger when convenient
Daybook clerks don't need much training
[1] mark each item — maximum 5 marks

(ii)   Not strictly needed
Retains historical methods (better understanding)
Improves data for audit trail
Allows greater breakdown/analysis of data
Data entry clerk doesn't need much training
[1] mark each item — maximum 5 marks

75   See Figure 2.46.

76

[1] Date	[1] Account	[1] Invoice	[1] Amount	[1] VAT	[1] Total
July 1	B Goodall	W1234	1,080.45	162.07	1,242.52
July 2	ABC Limited	W1235	550.75	82.61	633.36
July 3	K & N Eng	W1236	240.43	36.07	276.50
July 4	PMP Enter's	W1238	448.72	67.31	516.03

[1] mark for each fully correct entry

79

Date	Details	Folio	Dr	Cr
Aug 1	Bank	CB1	300	
	Bad Debts	NL4	50	
	A Debtor	SL14		350
	Bankrupt: No further payment possible			
Aug 3	Plant & Machinery	NL16	12,000	
	Bank	CB1		12,000
	Purchase of CNC Lathe			
Aug 4	Cash	CB1	500	
	Bank	CB1		500
	Cash for float			
Aug 8	Drawings	NL8	300	
	Rent	NL19		300
	Proportion of rent for private use.			
Aug 12	Cash	CB1	150	
	Office Equipment	NL7		150
	Sale of obsolete computer			
Aug 17	Office Equipment	NL6	4,000	
	Computers Ltd	SL32		4,000
	Credit purchase of IBM micros.			
Aug 21	Cash	CB1	100	
	Commission received	NL12		100
	Received from ABC Ltd			

80

	JOURNAL	Dr	Cr
Mar 1	Drawings	4,500	
	Stock		4,500
	Stock taken for own use		
Mar 2	Bank	110	
	Bank Interest		110
	Interest received paid into Bank		

Mar 3	Bank	1,700	
	Machinery	400	
	Motor Vehicles		2,100
	Motor Van sold in exchange		
	for cheque and machinery		
Mar 4	Bank	100	
	Bad Debts	300	
	XYZ Limited		400
	Final Payment received on		
	liquidation		

[1] mark per item including Narrative

81

JOURNAL

		Dr	Cr
June 1	Shop Fittings	10,000	
	XYZ Ltd		10,000
	Bought Shop fittings on credit		
June 3	Drawings	180	
	Stock		180
	Stock taken for own use		
June 6	Commission paid	200	
	Bank		200
	Commission paid to ABC Ltd		
June 9	Bank	300	
	Bad Debts	900	
	SDT Engineering		1,200
	Final payment received from liquidator		
June 15	Bank	300	
	Cash		300
	Transfer of cash to bank		
June 22	Cash	120	
	Computer		120
	Sale of scrap computer		120
		12,000	12,000

85 See text: Figure 2.46.

90 ABC LIMITED

BUDGETED ACCOUNTS FOR THE YEAR 1990
TRADING & PROFIT/LOSS ACCOUNT

	£		£
Sales			65,000
Opening stock	nil		
Purchases	62,500		
	62,500		
Closing stock	12,500		
Cost of goods sold	50,000		50,000
Gross profit			15,000
Expenses			8,500
Net profit			6,500

BALANCE SHEET

	£	£
Fixed assets		112,000
Current assets		
Bank	2,863	
Stock	12,500	
Debtors	12,637	
	28,000	
Current liabilities		
Creditors	10,000	
Working capital	18,000	18,000
Net asset employed		130,000
Financed by:		
Capital		130,000

CHAPTER 3

94

Sales Ledger Control A/c	Dr	Cr
Dec 31 Balance	4,500	
Sales	248,200	
Receipts		226,200
Bad Debts		4,550
Returns In		11,140
	252,700	241,890
Dec 31 Balance	10,810	

Purchaser Ledger Control	Dr	Cr
Dec 31 Balance		3,120
Purchases		120,500
Payments	94,300	
Discount received	2,480	
Discount received	5,710	
Returns Out	8,340	
Refund		210
	110,830	123,830
Dec 31 Balance		13,000

95

Sales Ledger Control A/c		Dr	Cr
Jan 1	Balance	10,500	
	Sales	91,500	
	Discount Allowed		7,200
	Returns In		2,750
	Dishonoured cheques	150	
	Receipts		82,250
	Bad Debts		650
		102,150	92,850
Feb 1	Balance	9,300	

There is a discrepancy of £200, therefore it will be necessary for the firm to check the debtors accounts in order to trace the error.

96   See Text : Section 3.2.1.

97

Bank Control			
Balance b/fwd	2,600	Purchase Control	78,000
Sales Control	75,600	Returned cheques	300
Balance c/fwd	120	Difference	20
	78,320		78,320

Purchase Control			
Returns Out	400	Creditors b/fwd	28,000
Bank Control	78,000	Purchases	70,400
Disc Received	700		
S. L. Contra	100		
Balance c/fwd	19,200		
	98,400		98,400

Sales Control			
Debtors b/fwd	12,100	Bank Control	75,600
Sales	75,500	Discount Allowed	640
Returned cheques	300	Returns Inward	460
		P. L. Contra	100
		Bad Debts written-off	200
		Balances c/fwd	10,900
	87,900		87,900

98   (a)

SALES LEDGER CONTROL ACCOUNT	Dr	Cr
Bal b/d	10,450	
Bank/cheques		34,892
Sales (Invoices)	36,858	
Discounts Allowed		2,862
Bad Debts		925
Credit Notes		1,105
Contra entry		1,549
Bal c/d		5,975
	47,308	47,308

PURCHASE LEDGER CONTROL ACCOUNT	Dr	Cr
Bal b/d		7,346
Bank/Cheques	29,428	
Discounts Received	1,440	
Debit notes	1,207	
Purchases (invoices)		32,324
Contra entry	1,549	
Bal c/d	6,046	
	39,670	39,670

[1] mark per item = 15 marks

NB: Cash Sales and Increase in Provision for Bad Debts are not included in Control Accounts.

(b) (i)   To check the accuracy of accounting records
To identify which Ledger an error occurs in
To assist the auditor in the checking of accounts

[1] mark per item

(c) (ii)   To provide a "bridge/link" between the different Ledgers
To assist with the checking of accounts

[1] mark per item

99

Suspense Account	Dr	Cr
May 1 Re Trial Balance	211	
Returns In		350
Cash	75	
Cash	30	
T. Jones	18	
	334	350
May 31 Balance		16

100   See text : Section 3.3.

101 (a)

SUSPENSE ACCOUNT	Dr	Cr
Difference per Trial Balance	780	
Motor Expenses		410
Returns Out (Nominal Ledger)	120	
Bank		85
Creditors accounts		305
R Naik		90
Petty Cash		10
	900	900

2 marks per item = 14 marks

(b) Additions and entries more accurate

Reports can be produced more quickly and frequently

Reports not possible in manual systems can be produced

2 marks per item = 6 marks

102 (a)

Suspense Account	Dr	Cr
Jun 1 Balance b/d	586	
Returns In		425
Bank	68	
Cash		270
T. Loo		90
Balance	131	
	785	785

(b)

(i) Employees will be handling the employer's/owner's money and there will need to be very careful controls in respect of fraud.

(ii) The other user groups will be using the accounts as a basis for deciding whether to invest/lend money to the business and therefore there needs to be controls to ensure that the figures in the accounts are accurate.

103 (a)

Suspense A/c			
Returns Out	755	Re Trial Balance	1,050
Cash Sales	35	Motor Vehicles	91
Creditors A/c	126	Petty Cash	25
		Sales	100
Balance c/d	350		
	1,266		1,266

(b) All computerised accounts packages should not allow *"single-entry"*, the program *should not proceed* to enter details of any transaction until the "double-entry" has been recorded.

Also, the Daybook totals will be transferred *automatically,* thereby *eliminating any possibility* of error.

104 See text : Section 3.4.

105 (a) Employing well-motivated, competent personnel.
(b) Physical controls over access to records/equipment.
(c) Adequate supervision.
(d) Adequate standby arrangements.
(e) Insurance cover.
(f) Back up copies of files.

106
(i) Input controls
(ii) Hardware security
(iii) File controls
(iv) Testing and Trials
(v) Division/Segregation of Duties
(vi) Managerial involvement
(vii) Output controls
(viii) Conversion
(ix) Storage controls/Authorisation & Approval
(x) Training
[1] mark each = 10 marks

107
(i) Separation/Division of duties
(ii) Supervisory
(iii) Managerial controls
(iv) Personnel
(v) Authorisation and Approval
(vi) Arithmetic and Accounting
(vii) Organisation structure
(viii) Physical controls
[2] marks each

108 (a) Skilled technician
Proper procedures for issuing/returning files
Good Labelling and Indexing
Adequate protection from dust, humidity, magnetic fields, fire
Procedures for retaining files for minimum legal period
Adequate procedures for file reconstruction
Backup copies of all files
[1] mark each point

(b) No record of amounts owed by debtors
No record of amounts owed to creditors
No record of wages paid/due
No record of expense items already paid
No record of Assets owned
Unable to prepare final accounts
[1] mark each point

110
- (i) Minutes of meetings
- (ii) Letter of confirmation to debtor
- (iii) Physical inspection
- (iv) Systems flowcharts
- (v) Mass media/Minutes of meetings
- (vi) Invoices

[1] mark each

111 Trail should not vanish after, say, three months due to file purging
Source documents to be available to auditor.
Clerk entering data should be identifiable.
Audit trail designed in conjunction with auditors.
Daily or weekly printouts should be produced for audit.

112 Audit Evidence
— any item from the "Audit trail"
— statements from independent third parties (eg: confirming balances with debtors)
— physical inspection of assets
— use of flowcharts to confirm systems of work
— discussions with management and employees
— minutes of meetings
— reports from the mass media.

113 See text : Section 3.6.

114 See text : Section 3.6.

115 See text : Section 3.6.3.

116 See text : Section 3.6.3.

117
- (a) Employing well-motivated, competent personnel.
- (b) Division of duties.
- (c) Authorisation for all amendments to programs.
- (d) Range test on values.
- (e) Feasibility test on quantities.
- (f) Running both manual and computer systems concurrently so that results can be validated.
- (g) Adequate testing of programs.

118 Adequate physical controls over access to computer rooms, possibly by means of sophisticated security procedures governing access to the computer room.

Provision of stand-by facilities and back-up copies of all files to ensure that operations can continue.

119

    (a)   Well defined organisation structure — shows how responsibility and authority are delegated and will enable employees to see what they are responsible for.

              Segregation of duties — no one person should fully record and process a transaction, if not applied then fraud can be quite easily carried out.

              Physical controls — access to assets and records should be restricted to authorised personnel only.

              Authorisation and approval — all transactions over a certain limit should be approved by a manager.

              Personnel — only well-motivated, competent personnel who possess integrity should be employed.

              Supervision — the provision of supervisory procedures will help to reduce errors and fraud.

    (b)   The auditor.

120 SYSTEMS DEVELOPMENT CONTROLS

Standardisation — the use of standards laid down by management for the design and development of the system, this could include the documentation of the system, including flowcharts.

Managerial involvement — the preparation of feasibility studies, use of budgets for capital and revenue expenditure, and regular evaluation of performance to ensure that each project is viable and cost effective.

Testing and trials — thorough testing of programs, involving the use of ''benchmarks'' to determine optimum time to run the program.

Training — training should be provided for staff who will be using the program to ensure that there is a reduction in the risk of errors.

Conversion — running both old and new systems concurrently so that results can be validated.

121 The ability to follow recording of transaction from source document through all subsidiary books through to the final accounts.

122

    (i)   Unable to enter any data — maintenance contract, back-up facilities

    (ii)   Unable to enter any data — back-up disks, file labels

    (iii) Unable to enter any data — restricting access, secure locks, good

supervision, use of competent staff
only
(iv) Fraud/damage to data   — use of passwords, restricting access
(v) Unable to amend program — proper documentation, division of
duties, use of standards

123

(a) — Restriction of access to computer
   — Not allowing unauthorised use of machines
   — Better supervision
   — Restricting use to bona-fide programs

(b) — Improved Library facilities
   — Employing a librarian to issue/store disks
   — Proper labelling of disks to prevent accidental erasure
   — Additional back-up copies held on a different site

(c) — Prepare full documentation for all programs
   — Use of standards in preparing documentation
   — Use of flowcharts
   — Use of well-trained programmers

(d) — Through testing and trials for new systems
   — Use of validation tests: check digit verification, consistency of
field, range tests, feasibility tests on quantities

124

Procedure Controls

Input Controls

— Serial numbering of documents, validation checks on documents, batching documents and noting batch totals, and authorisation procedures.

— Also vetting batches to ensure they are complete and accurate.
Secheduling work to meet arranged deadlines, and checks on the data
conversion methods.

Processing Controls

— Validation checks including check digit verification, size of field/record,
mode of field, consistency of field, range test on numbers or values,
feasibility test on quantities, 'hash' totals for batches, control/record total
checks.

Output Controls

— Vetting of output to ensure input and output are consistent.

Storage Controls

— No unauthorised amendments to the program file or accidental destruc-
tion to master file.

— Back-up copies should be kept in secure place.

— All amendments etc, must have necessary authority and be fully documented.

— Auditor to check accuracy of records and examine effectiveness of firm's internal controls.

125

(a) Operational Controls — rotation of duties, operations log, duty rostas, positive vetting of personnel. Input controls, storage controls and output controls.

File Controls — restricted access to equipment, handshaking between terminals, secure operations site.

Development controls:

Standardisation — management set standards for system procedures, audit trails, large transaction/file balance alerts.

Testing and Trials — Benchmarks to test for illicit changes in programs.

Training — Reduction in errors (cash difficult to retrieve once sent down line).

Conversion — Parallel running to test system in early stages of operations.

(b) Up-dating of stock records, cost saving on physical stocktaking. Automated stock re-ordering, analysis.
Error reduction at interface with customer, better public image.
More secure system from fraud by "customers".

CHAPTER 4

126

   (a) Semi-variable
   (b) Variable
   (c) Fixed
   (d) Variable
   (e) Fixed (or semi-variable)
   (f) Variable

127

   (i) Sales & Distribution
   (ii) Direct
   (iii) Indirect
   (iv) Administration
   (v) Administration

   (vi) Administration
   (vii) 0.5 Indirect, 0.25 Admin, 0.25 S & D
   (viii) Finance
   (ix) Direct
   (x) Indirect

[1] mark each point

128
- (i) Factory Indirect costs
- (ii) Administrative costs
- (iii) Direct Costs
- (iv) Selling & Distribution costs
- (v) Factory Indirect costs

130

		£
Revenue		221,350
Direct Materials		58,000
Direct Labour		45,500
Direct Expenses		2,300
PRIME COST		105,800
		£
Foremens wages	12,200	
Depreciation	3,500	
Light & Heat	5,050	
Rent & Rates	7,350	28,100
MANUFACTURING COST		133,900
ADMINISTRATION COST		
Depreciation	1,500	
Salaries	27,780	
Light & Heat	3,100	
Rent & Rates	2,100	34,480
S & D COST		
Depreciation : vans	2,500	
Depreciation : fittings	1,000	
Advertising	12,000	
Salaries	12,450	
Light & Heat	2,150	
Rent & Rates	1,550	31,650
FINANCE COST		
Audit fees	2,000	2,000
TOTAL COST		202,030
PROFIT		19,320

131

	£
Revenue	221,300
Direct Materials	63,870
Direct Labour	42,000
Direct Expenses	12,662
PRIME COST	119,512

	£	
Factory foremen	14,000	
Depr: Machinery	2,000	16,000
MANUFACTURING COST		135,512
ADMINISTRATION COST		
Office staff salaries	24,500	
Rent & Rates	8,000	
Light & Heat	5,000	
Depr: Office equip.	1,300	
Insurance	600	39,400
S & D COST		
Salesmens Salaries	19,000	
Depr: Delivery Vans	4,010	
Depr: Shop Fittings	890	23,900
FINANCE COST		
Loan Interest	3,120	3,120
TOTAL COST		201,932
NET PROFIT		19,368

132

OPERATING STATEMENT

Revenue	$	$
		185,900
Direct Materials	13,500	
Direct Labour	40,000	
Direct Expense	1,000	
Prime Cost	54,500	
Indirect Materials	12,000	
Indirect Labour	16,000	
Lighting/Heating	2,000	
Rent/Rates	4,000	
Depreciation Costs (M/c)	3,000	
	91,500	91,500
Administration Cost:		
Wages/Salaries	14,000	
Light/Heat	1,500	
Rent/Rates	2,000	
Depreciation (Equipment)	1,000	18,500
Selling/Distribution:		
Wages/Salaries	13,000	
Lighting/Heating	1,500	
Rent/Rates	2,000	

Advertising	2,500	
Depreciation (Shop Ftgs)	2,000	21,000
TOTAL COSTS	131,000	131,000
PROFIT		54,900

133

(a) FIFO

	Receipts			Issues			Balance		
	Units	£	£	Units	£	£	Units	£	£
Jan	20	1	20.00				20	1	20.00
Feb				12	1	12	8	1	8.00
Mar	10	1.05	10.50				8	1	8.00
							10	1.05	10.50
							18		18.50
Apr				6	1	6	2	1	2.00
							10	1.05	10.50
							12		12.50
May	15	1.05	16.50				2	1	2.00
							10	1.05	10.50
							15	1.10	16.50
							27		29.00
June				2	1	2	1	1.05	1.05
				9	1.05	9.45	15	1.10	16.50
							16		17.55
July				1	1.05	1.05			
				3	1.10	3.30	12	1.10	13.20
Aug				5	1.10	5.50	7	1.10	7.70
Sept	25	1.20	30.00				7	1.10	7.70
							25	1.20	30.00
							32		37.70
Oct				7	1.10	7.70			
				3	1.20	3.60	22	1.20	26.40
Dec				8	1.20	9.60	14	1.20	16.80

(b) LIFO

	Receipts			Issues			Balance		
Jan	10	1.00	20.00				20	1.00	20.00
Feb				12	1.00	12.00	8	1.00	8.00
Mar	10	1.05	10.50				8	1.00	8.00
							10	1.05	10.50
							18		18.50

	Issues			Balance		
Apr	6	1.05	6.30	8	1.00	8.00
				4	1.05	4.20
				12		12.20
May	15	1.10	16.50	8	1.00	8.00
				4	1.05	4.20
				15	1.10	16.50
				27		28.70
June	11	1.10	12.10	8	1.00	8.00
				4	1.05	4.20
				4	1.10	4.40
				16		16.60
July	4	1.10	4.40	8	1.00	8.00
				4	1.05	4.20
				12		12.20
Aug	1	1.00	1.00			
	4	1.05	4.20	7	1.00	7.00
Sept	25	1.20	30.00	7	1.00	7.00
				25	1.20	30.00
				32		37.00
Oct	10	1.20	12.00	7	1.00	7.00
				15	1.20	18.00
				22		25.00
Dec	8	1.20	9.60	7	1.00	7.00
				7	1.20	8.40
				14		15.40

(c) Average Cost

	Receipts			Issues			Balance		
	Units	£	£	Units	£	£	Units	£	Av. Cost
Jan	20	1	20.00				20	20	1.00
Feb				12	1	12.00	8	8	1.00
Mar	10	1.05	10.50				18	18.50	1.03
Apr				6	1.03	6.18	12	12.32	1.03
May	15	1.10	16.50				27	28.82	1.07
June				11	1.07	11.77	16	17.05	1.07
July				4	1.07	4.28	12	12.77	1.07
Aug				5	1.07	5.35	7	7.42	1.06
Sept	25		1.20	30.00			32	37.42	1.17
Oct				10	1.17	11.70	22	25.72	1.17
Dec				8	1.17	9.36	14	16.36	1.17

134

	(a)	FIFO	(b)	LIFO	(c)	Average Cost
		£		£		£
Sales		84.00		84.00		84.00
Cost of issues		60.20		61.60		60.64
Profit		23.80		22.40		23.36

135

(a) FIFO method

	Receipts			Issues			Balance		
	Units	£	£	Units	£	£	Units	£	£
Jan	8	10.00	80.00				8	10.00	80.00
Feb	8	10.20	81.60				8	10.00	80.00
							8	10.20	81.60
							16		161.60
Mar				6	10.00	60.00	2	10.00	20.00
							8	10.20	81.60
							10		101.60
Apr	5	10.30	51.50				2	10.00	20.00
							8	10.20	81.60
							5	10.30	51.50
							15		153.10
May				2	10.00	20.00	3	10.30	30.90
				8	10.20	81.60			
				2	10.30	20.60			
June	8	10.50	84.00				3	10.30	30.90
							8	10.50	84.00
							11		114.90
Jul	4	10.60	42.40				3	10.30	30.90
							8	10.50	84.00
							4	10.60	42.40
							15		157.30
Aug				3	10.30	30.90	1	10.50	10.50
				7	10.50	73.50	4	10.60	42.40
							5		52.90
Sept	10	11.00	110.00				1	10.50	10.50
							4	10.60	42.40
							10	11.00	110.00
							15		162.90

	Receipts Units	£	£	Issues Units	£	£	Balance Units	£	£
Oct				1	10.50	10.50	9	11.00	99.00
				4	10.60	42.40			
				1	11.00	11.00			
Nov	8	11.10	88.80				9	11.00	99.00
							8	11.10	88.80
							17		187.80
Dec				9	11.00	99.00	5	11.10	55.50
				3	11.10	33.30			

Total cost of goods issued = £482.80

(b) LIFO method

	Receipts Units	£	£	Issues Units	£	£	Balance Units	£	£
Jan	8	10.00	80.00				8	10.00	80.00
Feb	8	10.20	81.60				8	10.00	80.00
							8	10.20	81.60
							16		161.60
Mar				6	10.20	61.20	8	10.00	80.00
							2	10.20	20.40
							10		100.40
Apr	5	10.30	51.50				8	10.00	80.00
							2	10.20	20.40
							5	10.30	51.50
							15		151.90
May				5	10.30	51.50	3	10.00	30.00
				2	10.20	20.40			
				5	10.00	50.00			
June	8	10.50	84.00				3	10.00	30.00
							8	10.50	84.00
							11		114.00
Jul	4	10.60	42.40				3	10.00	30.00
							8	10.50	84.00
							4	10.60	42.40
							15		156.40
Aug				4	10.60	42.40	3	10.00	30.00
				6	10.50	63.00	2	10.50	21.00
							5		51.00
Sept	10	11.00	110.00				3	10.00	30.00
							2	10.50	21.00
							10	11.00	110.00
							15		161.00

	Receipts			Issues			Balance		
	Units	£	£	Units	£	£	Units	£	£
Oct				6	11.00	66.00	3	10.00	30.00
							2	10.50	21.00
							4	11.00	44.00
							9		95.00
Nov	8	11.10	88.80				3	10.00	30.00
							2	10.50	21.00
							4	11.00	44.00
							8	11.10	88.88
							17		183.80
Dec				8	11.10	88.80	3	10.00	30.00
				4	11.00	44.00	2	10.50	21.00
							5		51.00

Total cost of goods issued = £487.30

(c) Average Cost

	Receipts			Issues			Balance		
	Units	£	£	Units	£	£	Units	£	Av. Cost
Jan	8	10.00	80.00				8	80.00	10.00
Feb	8	10.20	81.60				16	161.60	10.10
Mar				6	10.10	60.60	10	101.00	10.10
Apr	5	10.30	51.50				15	152.20	10.16
May				12	10.16	121.93	3	30.58	10.19
Jun	8	10.50	84.00				11	114.58	10.42
Jul	4	10.60	42.40				15	159.98	10.66
Aug				10	10.66	106.60	5	53.38	10.67
Sept	10	11.00	110.00				15	163.38	10.89
Oct				6	10.89	65.34	9	98.04	10.89
Nov	8	11.10	88.80				17	186.84	10.99
Dec				12	10.89	131.88	5	54.96	10.99

Total cost of goods issued = £486.34

	FIFO	LIFO	Average Cost
	£	£	£
Sales	920.00	920.00	920.00
Cost of goods issued	482.00	487.30	486.34
Profit	437.20	432.70	433.66

136 (a) LAST IN FIRST OUT (LIFO) [1]

(b) *Note: One method only to be marked*

Using FIFO method

Date	Receipts			Issues			Balance			
	Qty	$	$	Qty	$	$	Qty	$	$	
1 Jun	10	5.00	50.00				10	5.00	50.00	[1]
2 Jun	5	5.10	25.00				10	5.00	50.00	
							5	5.10	25.00	
							15		75.50	[1]
3 Jun				4	5.00	20.00	6	5.00	30.00	
							5	5.10	25.10	
							11		55.10	[1]
4 Jun	10	5.20	52.00				6	5.00	30.00	
							5	5.10	25.10	
							10	5.20	52.00	
							21		107.10	[1]
5 Jun				6	5.00	30.00	4	5.20	20.80	
				5	5.10	25.10				
				6	5.20	31.20				[1]

Plus [1] for layout

or AVERAGE COST method

Date	Receipts			Issues			Balance			
	Qty	$	$	Qty	$	$	Qty	Ave	Total	
1 Jun	10	5.00	50.00				10	5.00	50.00	[1]
2 Jun	5	5.10	25.50				15	5.03	75.50	[1]
3 Jun				4	5.03	20.13	11	5.03	55.36	[1]
4 Jun	10	5.20	52.00				21	5.11	107.36	[1]
5 Jun				17	5.11	86.91	4	5.11	20.44	[1]

Plus [1] for layout

(c)

	LIFO	FIFO	or	Average Cost
	$	$		$
Sales (21 × $10)	210	210		210
Cost of issues	107.5	106.7		107.4
Gross Profit	102.5	103.3		102.6
	[3]	[2]	or	[2]

141

Date	Receipts	Issues	Balance		
			No.	Amount	Average Price
Jan	100 @ £12.10		100	1,210.00	12.10
Feb	60 @ £12.50		160	1,960.00	12.25
Mar		120 @ £12.25 = $1470	40	490.00	12.25
May	210 @ £13.00		250	3,220.00	12.88

Jul	190 @ £12.88 = 2447.2	60	772.80	12.88
Aug	60 @ £13.60	120	1,588.80	13.24
Sept	40 @ £13.24 = £529.6	80	1,059.20	13.24
Nov	80 @ £13.90	160	2,171.20	13.57
Dec	125 @ £13.57 = 1696.25	35	474.95	13.57

Cost of goods issued: £6,143.05

Trading Account

Sales (475 x £22)	£10,450.00
Cost of goods sold	£6,143.05
Gross Profit	£4,306.95

143

Section		A	B	C	TOTAL
Item:	Basis:	£	£	£	£
Rent & Rates	Floor area	3,000	6,000	3,000	12,000
Indirect Wages	Indirect Employees	7,620	10,160	7,620	25,400
Depr: Equipment	Cost of m/c	7,000	2,500	500	10,000
Insurance	Cost of m/c	700	250	50	1,000
Maintenance	Use of m/c's	11,000	2,000	2,000	15,000
Light & Heat	Floor area	1,000	2,000	1,000	4,000
Canteen	Number of Employees	780	3,240	1,980	6,000
	Total	31,100	26,150	16,150	73,400

Absorption rates

Machine hours		31,000	26,150	16,150
		33,000	6,000	6,000
	=	£0.94	£4.36	£2.69
Labour hours		31,100	26,150	16,150
		15,000	80,000	45,000
	=	£2.07	£0.33	£0.36

144

Total Costs	£551,900
30% mark-up	£165,570
	£717,470

$$\text{hourly charge} = \frac{£717,470}{60,000 \text{ hrs}} = £11.96 \text{ per hour}$$

145

Item	Basis	Assembly	Painting	Finishing	Total
Rent	Floor area	4,500	3,100	2,400	10,000
Rates	Floor area	3,600	2,480	1,920	8,000
Fuel	Machine hours	15,238	19,047	5,715	40,000
Depr: Equip.	Cost of Machines	18,000	5,000	7,000	30,000
Foremen's wages	Foremen	70,000	20,000	30,000	120,000
Canteen	Foremen + Employees	13,970	4,412	6,618	25,000
Insurance(m/c)	Cost of Machines	1,800	500	700	3,000
Heating	Cubic Capacity	2,141	1,407	1,452	5,000
		129,249	55,946	55,805	241,000

(a)   Machine hour basis

	£129,249	£55,946	£55,805
	40,000	50,000	15,000
	= £3.23	= £1.12	= £3.72

(b)   Labour hour basis

	£129,249	£55,946	£55,805
	96,000	31,000	46,000
	= £1.35	= £1.80	= £1.21

148

	$	$	
Direct Materials:			
Disks	2.20		
Photocopying, etc	3.50	5.70	[1]
Direct Labour:			
5 hours × $7.50		37.50	[1]
Overheads:			
3 hours × $5.00		15.00	[1]
Total costs		58.20	
+ 25% mark-up		14.55	
Charge for job		72.75	[1]

149

Item	Basis	Systems Analysis	Programming Dept		
Rent/Rates	Floor Area	22,000	33,000	[3]	1 for
Depr of equip	Cost of equip	15,000	65,000	[3]	each
Insurance	Cost of equip	3,750	16,250	[3]	figure and
Labour	Staff	166,667	83,333	[3]	1 for
		207,417	197,583		basis

Absorption rate:		207,417	197,583	
		40,000	90,000	
=		$5.185	$2.195	[2] 1 each
		per machine hour		

150

Job Number 129

		$	$
Materials		15.40	15.40
Labour			
Assembly:	3 x $2.30	6.90	
Refining:	2 x $1.60	3.20	
Finishing:	3 x $3.10	9.30	19.40
Overheads			
Assembly:	3 x $3.50	10.50	
Refining:	4 x $4.75	19.00	
Finishing:	3 x $6.10	18.30	47.80
TOTAL COST:			82.60

151

	Basis	Programming $	Systems $
Wages & Salaries	Employees	56,000	84,000
Rent & Rates	Floor Area	8,000	4,000
Light & Heat	Volume	5,000	4,000
Equipment Maintenance	Cost of Equip	13,500	4,500
Travelling	Mileage	1,000	4,000
Canteen	Employees	2,800	4,200
Administration	Employees	5,600	8,400
TOTAL		91,900	113,100

(b) Labour hours:

		Programming	Systems
40 hrs x 47 weeks = 1,880 hrs/employee			
	Employees	8	12
	Total hours	15,040	22,560

Overhead Absorption rates:

	Programming	Systems
Overheads	$91,900	$113,100
Labour hours	15,040	22,560
Rates per hour	$6.11	$5.01

(c)

	$	$
Direct Materials		25.00
Direct Labour:		
Programming: 100 hrs @ $3.50	350	
Systems: 175 hrs @ $4.20	735	1,085.00
Overheads:		
Programming: 100 hrs @ $6.11	611	
Systems: 175 hrs @ $5.01	876.75	1,487.75
		2,597.75
Mark-up (30%)		779.32
Price		3,377.07

154

(a) $\dfrac{\text{Fixed Costs}}{\text{Contribution}} = \dfrac{£30,000}{£20}$ = 1,500 units

(b) No, as they can only sell 1,400 units and therefore do not achieve the break-even point.

(c) $\dfrac{\text{Fixed Costs}}{\text{Contribution}} = \dfrac{£30,000}{£10}$ = 3,000 units

(d) $\dfrac{\text{Fixed Costs + Profit}}{\text{Contribution}} = \dfrac{£30,000 + £10,000}{£10}$ = 4,000 units

155

(a) break-even in units:

$\dfrac{\text{Fixed Costs}}{\text{Contribution}} = \dfrac{£100,000}{£20 - £12}$

$= \dfrac{£100,000}{£8} = $ 12,500 units

(b) break-even in £s:

12,500 x £20 = £250,000

(c) $\dfrac{\text{Fixed costs + Profit}}{\text{Contribution}} = \dfrac{£130,000}{£8}$

= 16,250 units

(d) 16,250 x £20 = £325,000

(e) $\dfrac{\text{Fixed Costs}}{\text{Contribution}} = \dfrac{£100,000}{£20 - £13}$

$= \dfrac{£100,000}{£7} = $ 14,286 units

160

(i) Fixed Costs $190,000
Selling price - Variable cost $25 - $11.50
= 14,074(5) units

(ii) Sales (17,000 x $25) $425,000
Direct costs (17,000 x $11.50) £195,500
Contribution $229,500
Admin costs $120,000
S & D Costs $70,000
$190,000
Net Profit $39,500

(iii) New Contract:
Selling Price - Variable costs = $20 - $11.50
= $8.50

Contribution from new contract = 4,000 x $8.50
= $34,000

As all Fixed Costs are covered by existing sales then the contribution from the new contract will be additional profit.

Therefore this contract should be accepted.

(iv) Fixed Costs $190,000
Selling price - Variable cost $25 - $12.50
= 15,200 units

(v) Sales (20,000 x $25) £500,000
Direct costs (20,000 x £12.50) £250,000
Contribution £250,000
Admin costs £120,000
S & D Costs £70,000 £190,000
Net Profit £60,000

161

(a) Direct Materials $4
Direct Labour $7
Direct Expenses $1
$12
Mark-up (50%) $6
Selling Price $18

(b) $$\frac{\text{Fixed Cost}}{\text{Selling price - Variable cost}} = \text{Break-even point}$$

$$\frac{\$50,000}{\$18 - \$12} = 8,333.33 \ (8,334) \text{ units}$$

(c)   Contribution = $6
    Required sales   11,000
    Break-even point   8,334
                      2,666 x $6 = $15,996

(d) $\dfrac{\text{Fixed Cost + ROCE}}{\text{Selling price - Variable cost}}$ = Sales to achieve ROCE

    $\dfrac{\$50,000 + \$12,500}{\$18 - \$12}$ = 10,416.66 (10,417) units

(e) $\dfrac{\text{Fixed Cost + Profit}}{\text{Selling price - Variable cost}}$ x $18 = Required sales

    $\dfrac{\$50,000 + \$10,000}{\$18 - \$12}$ x $18 = $180,000

(f) $\dfrac{\$50,000}{\$18 - \$13}$ = 10,000 units

(g) $\dfrac{\text{Fixed Cost}}{\text{Selling price - buy-in cost}}$ = New break-even point

    $\dfrac{\$20,000}{\$18 - \$15}$ = 6,666.66 (6,667)

As this break-even point is lower than if the product is manufactured by the firm it would be more beneficial to "buy-in" the product.

However, the firm would need to be sure that the figure for Fixed Costs is correct and that there were no other hidden costs.

163

Debtors Budget	Jan	Feb	Mar	Apr	May	Jun
2 months previous	750	875	625	625	750	875
1 month previous	875	625	625	750	875	875
	1,625	1,500	1,250	1,375	1,625	1,750

Creditors Budget	Jan	Feb	Mar	Apr	May	Jun
	750	500	750	750	625	625

Cash Budget	Jan	Feb	Mar	Apr	May	Jun
Sales	1,625	1,500	1,250	1,375	1,625	1,750
Purchases	750	500	750	750	625	625
Wages	300	300	300	300	300	300
Rent	400			400		
Light & Heat			1,000			
Other Overheads	100	100	100	100	100	100
Total Cost	1,550	900	2,150	1,550	1,025	1,025
Surplus	-75	600	-900	-175	600	725
Opening Balance	200	275	875	-25	-200	400
Balance c/f	275	875	-25	-200	400	1,125

164

	Jan	Feb	Mar	Apr	May	Jun
Sales	-	-	2,400	2,400	2,400	2,400
Purchases	-	600	600	600	600	600
Wages	600	600	600	600	600	600
Rent	1,000			1,000		
Sundry Expenses	300	300	100	100	100	100
Equipment	1,000					
Total Cost	2,900	1,500	1,300	2,300	1,300	1,300
Surplus	(2,900)	(1,500)	1,100	100	1,100	1,100
Opening bal.	-	(2,900)	(4,400)	(3,300)	(3,200)	(2,100)
Balance c/f	(2,900)	(4,400)	(3,300)	(3,200)	(2,100)	(1,100)

Maximum overdraft required = £4,400.

165

Sales Budget

	Dec	Jan	Feb	Mar	Apr	May	Jun
Units	1,000	1,000	1,000	1,000	1,500	1,500	1,500
Receipts:							
Cash	-	500	500	500	750	750	750
Credit	-	4,500	4,500	4,500	4,500	6,750	6,750
		5,000	5,000	5,000	5,250	7,500	7,500

Purchases Budget

	Nov	Dec	Jan	Feb	Mar	Apr	May	Jun
Units:	2,000	2,000	500	500	500	1,000	1,000	1,000
Payments	-	-	3,000	3,000	750	750	750	1,500

Cash Budget

	Jan	Feb	Mar	Apr	May	Jun
Sales	5,000	5,000	5,000	5,250	7,500	7,500
Purchases	3,000	3,000	750	750	750	1,500
Wages	300	300	300	300	300	300
Rent	200			200		
Rates		1,000			1,000	
Machinery			1,000	1,000	1,000	
Sundries	150	150	150	150	150	150
Total Cost	3,650	4,450	2,200	2,400	3,200	1,950
Surplus	1,350	550	2,800	2,850	4,300	5,550
Opening bal.	7,500	8,850	9,400	12,200	15,050	19,350
Balance c/f	8,850	9,400	12,200	15,050	19,350	24,900

168

Receipts Schedule	Jan	Feb	Mar	Apr	May	Jun	Control Total
Cash from Debtors:							
3 months @ $12	960	1,080	840	1,200	720	1,440	6,240
Sale of Land			5,000				5,000
	960	1,080	5,840	1,200	720	1,440	11,240

Payments Schedule

Raw Materials: @ $4	520	560	600	480	640	680	3,480
Labour: @ $3	300	330	390	420	450	360	2,250
Variable Extras:							
75% x $2	150	165	195	210	225	180	1,125
25% x $2	45	50	55	65	70	75	360
Fixed Extras:							
	100	100	100	100	100	100	600
Motor Van				6,000			6,000
	1,115	1,205	1,340	7,275	1,485	1,395	13,815

Cash Budget

Balance b/f	640	485	360	4,860	(1,215)	(1,980)	640
Receipts	960	1,080	5,840	1,200	720	1,440	11,240
	1,600	1,565	6,200	6,060	(495)	(540)	11,880
Payments	1,115	1,205	1,340	7,275	1,485	1,395	13,815
Balance c/f	485	360	4,860	(1,215)	(1,980)	(1,935)	(1,935)

171

	Budget	Flexible Budget	Actual	
Sales	10,000 units	12,000 units	12,000 units	Variance
	£	£	£	£
Revenue	25,000	30,000	31,000	1,000(F)
Materials	6,000	7,200	7,440	240(A)
Direct Labour	4,500	5,400	5,760	360(A)
Prodtn O'heads	3,000	3,000	2,750	250(F)
S & D O'heads	3,800	3,800	3,800	–
Admin O'heads	4,200	4,200	4,400	200(A)
Finance O'heads	750	750	750	–
Net Profit	2,750	5,650	6,100	450(F)

Comments

(a) Overheads are not specifically identified as being variable and therefore should be classed as Fixed. Consequently, they will not alter in Flexible budget.

(b) *Sales Revenue Variance* — variable is favourable not because of increased sales (the flexible budget should have been at that volume) but because selling price has increased to £2.58. This may be because of inflation, an improvement in the product, less competition resulting in an increased demand for the company's product, etc.

Materials Variance — variance is not due to increased production but because material costs have increased to £0.62 per unit. This could be due to increases in prices of raw materials, greater wastage, using better quality materials, etc.

Direct Labour Variance — again the increase in total costs is because the cost per unit has increased to £0.48. This could be because of a pay rise or less efficiency by the workforce. Products might be taking longer to make because there was an industrial dispute or untrained staff are being used.

Overhead Variances — any variance in respect of all overheads will generally be due to circumstances outside the firm's control, e.g. increases in rent, rates, insurance, lighting and heating costs, etc. However some of the increase might possibly relate to pay increases for staff in the various departments.

173 (i)

	Budget	Flexible Budget	Actual Results	Variance		
Units	20,000	21,500	21,500			
	$	$	$	$		
Sales	80,000	86,000	82,775	3,225	(A)	[2]
Materials	10,000	10,750	11,825	1,075	(A)	[2]
Labour	25,000	26,875	23,650	3,225	(F)	[2]
Var O'heads	5,000	5,375	4,945	430	(F)	[2]
Fixed O'heads	12,000	12,000	12,900	900	(A)	[2]
Profit	28,000	31,000	29,455	1,545	(A)	[2]

(ii) Materials Variance — price increase, increased wastage, better quality materials, etc

[1] mark per reason MAX 2 marks

Labour Variances — Greater efficiency, less skilled staff reduction in overtime, etc

[1] mark per reason MAX 2 marks

174

	Budget	(a) Flexible	Actual	(b) Variance
Sales (units)	100,000	119,000	119,000	
	$	$	$	$
Revenue	850,000	1,011,500	1,029,350	17,850
Materials	210,000	249,900	255,850	5,950(A)
Labour	165,000	196,350	184,450	11,900(F)
Prod O'head	105,000	105,000	113,000	8,000(A)
Selling O'head	45,000	45,000	45,000	
Admin O'head	90,000	90,000	88,000	2,000(F)
Profit	235,000	325,250	343,050	17,800(F)

(c) Sales variance: due to price increase to £8.65

Materials variance: due to increase in waste/scrap, increase in price, use of more expensive materials (with less waste)

Labour variance: increase in productivity, use of less skilled staff (lower wage rate)

Prod Overhead: due to under – estimate of costs, may be some unidentified variable costs
Admin Overhead: due to under – estimate of costs, increase in prices.

(d) Formula could have been entered in column for budget and these could then have been copied to a new column for the flexible budget. The only data to be typed would be the revised quantity.

175

	Budget	(a) Flexible	(b) Actual	(c) Variances
Sales	10,000	11,000	11,000	
Revenue	200,000	222,000	238,650	16,650
Materials	35,000	38,850	40,515	(1,665)A
Labour	40,000	44,400	43,290	1,110 F
Variable				
Overheads	17,500	19,425	16,800	2,625 F
Fixed Overheads	60,000	60,000	63,000	(3,000)A
Net Profit	47,500	59,325	75,045	15,720F

(d)   Reasons for Variances

Revenue	Increase in price Increase in sales volume
Materials	Increase in price (may be better quality)
Labour	May be wage reduction Increased productivity
Variable Overheads	More efficient production
Fixed Overheads	Generally outside of the firm's control

178

(a)   Using Marginal Costing approach:

	A £	B £	C £	Total £
Sales	130,000	50,000	75,000	255,000
Variable Costs	70,000	35,000	45,000	150,000
Contribution	60,000	15,000	30,000	105,000
Fixed Costs				95,000
Profit				10,000

Using this approach product B is contributing £15,000 and, assuming that the production capacity would not be used elsewhere, then product B should not be dropped.

(b)   Operating statement (B dropped)

	A	C	Total
	£	£	£
Sales	130,000	75,000	205,000
Variable Costs	70,000	45,000	115,000
Contribution	60,000	30,000	90,000
Fixed Costs			95,000
Profit			(5,000)

This confirms how important the £15,000 contribution from product B was, the original profit was £10,000 but by deducting the lost contribution (£15,000) this becomes a loss of £5,000.

(c)

	A	C	Total
	£	£	£
Sales	130,000	115,000	245,000
Variable Costs	70,000	69,000	139,000
Contribution	60,000	46,000	106,000
Fixed Costs			95,000
Profit			11,000

* Variable costs need to be increased proportionately.

179

(i)   Marginal (Variable) cost   = £280,000 - £67,500

= £212,500

Unit Marginal cost $= \dfrac{£212,500}{85,000}$ = £2.50

(ii)   Situation without new order:

Sales	£340,000
less Costs	£280,000
Profit	£60,000

The contribution from the existing production covers Fixed Costs, therefore provided that the new contract 'covers' variable costs then additional profit will be made:

(iii)   new order: Selling price   £3.00

Variable cost   £2.50

£0.50

(iv)   Additional profit: Contribution x additional units

£0.50 x 15,000

= £7,500

180 (i)

	Computers	Printers	Software	Total	
Sales	$30,000	$37,000	$50,000	$117,000	
Direct Materials	$10,000	$5,000	$1,000	$16,000	
Direct Labour	$10,000	$12,000	$25,000	$47,000	
Contribution	$10,000	$20,000	$24,000	$54,000	[1]
Fixed Costs				$45,000	[1]
Profit				$9,000	[1]

Computers are still making a positive contribution towards Fixed Costs [2]
and therefore should not be discontinued.　　　　　　Total = 5 marks

(ii)

	Printers	Software	Total	
Sales	$37,000	$50,000	$87,000	
Direct Materials	$5,000	$1,000	$6,000	
Direct Labour	$12,000	$25,000	$37,000	
Contribution	$20,000	$24,000	$44,000	
Fixed Costs			$45,000	[1]
Profit			($1,000)	[2]

Total = 5 marks

182

(a)

Product	A	B	C	D	Total
	$	$	$	$	$
Sales	190,000	250,000	300,000	410,000	1,150,000
Variable costs	125,000	262,500	280,000	320,000	987,500
Contribution	65,000	(12,500)	20,000	90,000	162,500
				Fixed costs	120,000
				Profit	42,500

(b)　Product B should be dropped as it has no contribution
　　　Product C should not be dropped as it has a positive contribution of $20,000
　　　towards Fixed costs.

(c)

Product	A	C	D	Total
	$	$	$	$
Sales	237,500	300,000	512,500	1,050,000
Variable costs	156,250	280,000	400,000	836,250
Contribution	81,250	20,000	112,500	213,750
			Fixed costs	120,000
			Profit	93,750

(d)

Product	A	B	D	Total
	$	$	$	$
Sales	237,500	250,000	512,500	1,000,000

Variable costs	156,250	262,500	400,000	818,750
Contribution	81,250	(12,500)	112,500	181,250
			Fixed costs	120,000
			Profit	61,250

(e)

Product	A	D	Total
	$	$	$
Sales	285,000	615,000	900,000
Variable costs	187,500	480,000	667,500
Contribution	97,500	135,000	232,500
		Fixed costs	120,000
		Profit	112,500

183

a. Marginal Cost = variable cost
    Absorption Cost = total cost

b.

	Fixed Costs	Variable Costs	Total Cost	Notes
Labour	45,626	1,300	46,926	$5 bonus for each PC
Materials	–	44,946	44,946	
Overhead	46,390	260	46,650	$1 power cost per PC
	92,016	46,506	138,522	

$$\text{Absorbed cost} = \frac{138,522}{260}$$

$$= £532.78$$

c. Selling Price = 532.78
    + 20%   106.56
    ─────────────
                   639.34

d. Marginal cost = $\dfrac{46,506}{260}$

$$= £178.87$$

e. Cost of 280 units = 280 × 178.87 =   50,083.60
                                       + 92,016.00
                                       ───────────
                                       $142,099.60

f. Additional Profit = (700 − 178.87) × 20 extra units
                      = $10,422.60

186 (a) Total Fixed Costs = $200 × 10,000 computers

= $2,000,000 [1]

Fixed Costs = $2,000,000

Contribution = $1,000 − $650

= 5,714.28 (5,715) units [1]

(b) (Level of sales − Break-even) × Contribution per unit

(10,000 − 5,715) × $350 [1]

= $1,499,750 [1]

(c) New break-even point: $2,000,000

$900 − $650

= 8,000 units [1]

(Level of sales − Break-even) × Contribution per unit

(11,000 − 8,000) × $250

= $750,000 [1]

(d) New order only:

Selling price	$750
Variable costs	$650
Contribution	$100	[1]

ACCEPT ORDER AS:

Fixed costs already covered by normal orders [1]

Contribution on extra orders will be <u>all profit</u> [1]

Increase in total profit = $100 × 2,000 = $200,000 [1]

(e) OTHER FACTORS:

Will other customers demand same reduced price?

Can production make extra machines?

Are all Fixed Costs really fixed or semi-variable?

Can extra materials/labour be obtained?

Can normal sales be increased by improved advertising?

Any other relevant points

[1] mark for each point − maximum of 5 marks

(f) Fixed costs will presumably not decrease so option with highest contribution is most preferable [1]

	$
Bought-in:	
Selling price	1,000
Cost per unit	750
Contribution	$250	[1]

As this has a lower contribution per unit than self-made products the products should NOT be bought in ready made. [1]

(g) Can spare production be used to produce alternative products?

Is the ready-made product a better specification?

Can Fixed Costs be reduced?

Any other relevant points

[1] mark for each point − maximum of 3 marks

CHAPTER 5

189 (a)   The practice of "splitting" accounts into different books

To enable data to be entered quicker by employing more staff

If all accounts kept in one book then impossible for one person to make all entries

Makes reporting from Ledgers easier by keeping all related accounts together (eg: Credit Control).

2 marks each = 8 marks

(b)   Firm may not need all Ledgers (eg: if all sales for Cash then no need for Sales Ledger)

Restricts opportunity for fraud by dividing duties

Allows more than one person to work on system without "locking" out accounts

Allows production of specialised reports from each Ledger (Sales Ledger reports are different to those from Nominal Ledger)

3 marks each = 12 marks

192   See Figure 5.2.

193   package can be configured for firm's own hardware

package can include firm's own name on printouts

package can be set for number of accounts required

1 mark each = 3 marks

(ii)   Set company name/address

Computer hardware configuration

Printer configuration

Operational configuration (type of codes, No of accounts)

Page format (length of paper, pre-printed forms)

Tax rates

Alter user table (set passwords)

Any SIX ONLY   2 marks each = 12 marks

195

(a)

Source Document	Sales Invoice	Credit Note	Purchase Invoice	Debit Note	Receipts Invoices, etc.
Book of Original Entry	Sales Daybook	Returns In Daybook	Purchases Daybook	Returns Out Daybook	Journal
Ledger	Sales Ledger		Purchase Ledger		Nominal Ledger

Information	Balance Sheet	Profit/ Loss A/c

(b) No credit sales or purchases
For continuity of manual system
Restricts opportunity for fraud
Simplifies data entry where more than one operator is employed
Greater variety/more useful reports can be produced

196 See text: section 5.3.

198 See text: section 5.4.

199 See Question 26.

201   NOMINAL DAYBOOK

[1] Date Entered	[1] Trans Date	[1] Account	[1] Ref	[1] Entry	[1] Dr	[1] Cr	[1] VAT	[1] VAT code	[1] Nom code	[1] Alloc	[1] No
1/9/92	1/8/92	FORD	12345	Inv	75.50		15.50	1	001	N	1
	3/8/92	APEX	12346	CrN		6.75	1.54	1	001	N	2
	5/8/92	JONES	12347	Inv	21.90		9.80	1	002	N	3
	7/8/92	ABC	12348	Paym	9.99		1.50	1	005	Y	4

Allow up to [2] marks for entries, maximum marks = 12

203 See text: section 5.5.

204

[1]
CUSTOMER ACCOUNT DETAILS   Includes: Credit Limit exceeded

[1] Acct Code	[1] Customer	[1] Credit Limited	[1] Turnover	[1] Last Trans	[1] Last Payt	[1] Balance
1200	Evans Builders	1,000	4,500	11/10/90	01/11/90	1,200
1300	G & K Smith Ltd	4,000	10,000	02/02/91	12/02/91	12,450
1401	AJK Limited	2,500	8,120	12/01/91	21/12/90	9,345

Plus maximum of 4 marks for data. Total = 12 marks

205

SALES DAYBOOK   DATE:

No	Type	Date	A/c	N/c	Ref	Amount	Tax
1	SI	10/12/88	SMITH	10000	S123	100.00	15.00
2	CN	12/12/88	JONES	10001	C23	50.00	7.50
3	SI	13/12/88	ROBERTS	10000	S200	200.00	30.00

207

AGED DEBTORS ANALYSIS

REPORT DATED: 31/08/91   ABC Limited

A/c No	Name	A/c Bal	Current Bal	Period 1	Period 2	Period 3
[1]	[1]	[1]	[1]	[1]	[1]	[1]
A001	Andreas	200	180	20		
A002	S Jones	125	75	30	30	
B001	BK Ltd	210	100	60	40	10
C005	Comp Ltd	500	300	100	50	50
Totals:		1035	655	210	120	60

[1] mark for TOTALS

209 Apart from the fact that the headings differ the main different in content is that there is usually a debit balance on Sales Ledger accounts and a credit balance on Purchase Ledger accounts. The different between entries in the Ledger is simply that they are reversed.
The only additional printout is the remittance advice.

210 See text: section 5.6.

211 See text: section 5.7.

213 See Figure 5.24.

214 Stock Control Printouts

Stock Daybook — shows details of all items issued, received, ordered and reserved. Details given include item, quantity and value.

Stock Lists — lists all items currently stocked, includes description of each item.

Stock Movements — shows quantities of stock received over three month period, used for identifying slow moving stock.

Stock Levels & Availability — shows current levels of stock and items reserved, also shows minimum levels for each item.

Stock Price List — used as a price list to send to customers, may allow for more than one price so discount can be included.

Stock Valuation — shows total value of each item of stock and total value of all stock.

216

ABC LIMITED		STOCK MOVEMENTS REPORT				31/08/91	
[1]	[1]	[1]		[1]		[1]	[1]
STOCK KEY	DESCRIPTION	CURRENT – 1 PERIOD		– 2 PERIOD		PROJECTED	
		In	Out	In	Out	In	Out	In	Out
APPLE11	COMPUTER 640K	5	0	10	15	7	10	12	7
IBM	COMPUTER 640K	12	11	5	7	12	6	10	5
EPSOM	PRINTER	4	5	3	8	10	3	6	6
DIABLO	PRINTER	2	6	5	5	0	0	4	3

Columns must include In/Out columns for marks   Plus [2] marks for sample data

218   See text: section 5.8.

226   See text: section 5.10.

227

	A	B	C	D	E	
1		July	Aug	Sept	Oct	
2	Sales (Units)	1000	1500	1500	1500	
3	Revenue	b2×12	c2×12	d2×12	e2×12	[1]
4						
5	Purchases	350	b2×3	c2×3	d2×3	[1]
6	Labour	b2×3.5	c2×3.5	d2×3.5	e2×3.5	[1]
7	Variable costs	c2×2	d2×2	e2×2	f2×2	[1]
8	Overheads	300	300	300	300	[1]
9	Total	sum(b5:b8)	sum(c5:c8)	......	......	[1]
10	Surplus	b3–b9	c3–c9	......	......	[1]
11	Opening bal	200	b12			[2]
12	Closing bal	b10+b11	c10+c11	......	......	[1]

NB: Formula only needs to be entered in column B – except for Opening bal

228   Spreadsheets.

229   (i)   B1+B2   [1]
        (ii)   SUM(B1:B6) or SUM(B1.B6)   [1]
        (iii) AVERAGE (B1:B6 or AVG(B1.B6)   [2]
        (iv)   B1×105% or B1×105/100   [2]

Appendix 2

Examination technique

As the author of this book has also been an examiner for the NCC Joint Diploma since it started running the Accounting subject as an externally assessed subject, and has also been an examiner for other externally set examinations, there are a few points which it may be worthwhile for students to consider when preparing for and sitting examinations.

First, you should remember that the intention of an examination is not to fail students. All examinations will be set at a level whereby the majority of fairly able students can achieve a Pass. Consequently the odds are in the student's favour. All papers should be set in such a way that all students have a reasonable chance of demonstrating their true ability. This is one reason for having a range of questions to answer — a student can (and often does) do badly on one question for one reason or another but can still achieve a Distinction grade. Therefore if you feel that you have mastered all of the topics as they were dealt with on your course and have prepared for the examination properly, then it should not be a problem to obtain at least a Pass grade.

It would appear that most students who obtain a Fail or Refer grade are those that have performed weakly throughout the course and who, in all honesty, would probably be most surprised if they did obtain a Pass. However, there are very large numbers of students who do clearly not achieve the grade of which they are capable. This is generally for one of the following reasons:

(1)   Failing to read the question — this would seem to be a most unlikely error but is undoubtedly the biggest cause of errors in students' papers. Every year, thousands of students will merely glance at a question and identify what they feel is the "key word" and then proceed to write everything they know about that particular topic — this will generally mean reiterating their notes. Unfortunately, a large number of questions will require an "interpretation" and will expect students to "apply" their knowledge to a specific area or problem. Simply repeating notes will often result in no marks being awarded.

Always read the question paper thoroughly before attempting any questions. The paper should have been tested and the examiner will have checked that sufficient time is available; spending an extra five or ten minutes reading the paper through will not mean that you run short of time and will almost certainly mean that you will select those questions that you can answer.

(2) Failing to notice how many marks are awarded — virtually all papers will provide details of the marks available per section. The reason for this is to give students some guidance on how much work is expected. Obviously a section worth two marks will require a lot less work than one worth ten marks. Unfortunately, most students tend to ignore these guides and will feel that every question will require them to write everything they know about a subject. Whilst it is apparent that, in some countries, marks are awarded for length of answer as opposed to content, this is not true of the NCC or any other professional examination.

Take note of the marks available and don't waste time writing half a page for a section worth one or two marks, many questions will only require a one word or one line answer. Any extra work will simply be repeating the answer and no additional marks can be awarded.

(3) Filling the answer book — some students seem to feel that they cannot possibly achieve a Pass unless they completely fill the answer book and a few additional sheets as well. It has already been explained that the marking scheme will be allocating marks on the basis of "content" not "length". The only time that an answer book should need to be filled is if the student's writing is very large.

Avoid the temptation to "waffle"; try and remember that the examiner will be marking many scripts, possibly hundreds. Having to wade through pages of irrelevant material does not put examiners in a generous mood and consequently "waffly" work tends to merit less marks than short, concise answers.

(4) Plan your answers — it is amazing how many students will attempt seven or eight questions when they only have to answer five, or alternatively answer two or three questions only to scrub them out and then re-start all over again. The biggest constraint in an examination should be the time that it takes to write down your answers. If you discover an error and decide to start writing out whole questions all over again, then you are wasting tremendous amounts of time.

Once again, you should consider the effect that your script is going to have on the examiner. Whilst marks cannot be deducted for students who fill their answer book with part completed answers, it is very frustrating for an examiner to try and find where the proper answer is — if the examiner is frustrated with your script, then you are not going to get the benefit of the doubt in any answers. In very severe cases the examiner may become so annoyed that he/she may quite rightly feel that any student incapable of properly planning their work does not deserve a Pass as they would quite clearly not be capable of planning their work in a real job.

(5) Untidy work — most students should have been informed by their lecturers

of the need for neatness in accounts. Untidy figures are very easily misinterpreted and can produce errors in calculations.

In most examinations there will be a certain amount of discretion given to markers in respect of untidy or incorrectly laid out work; this is especially true of accounting examinations. Therefore, even if you have got the correct answer, the marker may still feel that some marks should be deducted because of untidy work.

(6) Inadequate preparation — there will be occasions when students have been unable to prepare properly for the examination. If this is the case, then simply making a note to this effect on the paper will not warrant any special consideration. If you feel that you have valid grounds for special treatment, then inform your lecturers and provide them with any suitable evidence. Always ensure that you have all the necessary equipment with you when you arrive for the examination.

Students who make comments to the effect that they have forgotten to bring a calculator rarely get any special consideration — the object of the examination is to prove to employers that you are capable in a certain area. If students cannot even remember to bring a calculator, then they are not very likely to do well in a computing job!

Appendix 3

Sample paper for new syllabus

NCC INTERNATIONAL DIPLOMA IN COMPUTER STUDIES
COMPUTERISED ACCOUNTING
SAMPLE PAPER
CANDIDATES SHOULD ATTEMPT QUESTIONS ONE AND TWO AND
ANY OTHER THREE QUESTIONS.

All Students should attempt this question.

1(a)
- (i) A cost which varies in direct proportion to output is known as a . . .
- (ii) Acc Dep stands for . . .
- (iii) Entering a transaction in the wrong type of account is known as an error of . . .
- (iv) Variances are usually calculated for Sales, Materials, Labour and . . .
- (v) The Current ratio is calculated by the ratio . . .
- (vi) The type of software package most often used in Cost Accounting applications is a . . .
- (vii) Testing and trials of new programs will often involve the use of . . . to determine the optimum time taken for the program to run.
- (viii) What is the break-even point if Fixed Costs are $12,000, Selling price $10 and Variable Costs $6.
- (ix) The practice of sub-dividing accounts into different books for Sales, Purchases and Nominal is known as the . . .
- (x) An asset costing $10,000 which will be used for 5 years and then sold for $4,000 would have an annual depreciation of $ . . . using the Straight-Line method.
- (xi) If a product costs $8 to make and the firm require a Profit margin of 20%, what would the selling price be.
- (xii) The document sent to customers to show a "history" of their account is known as a . . .
- (xiii) The abbreviation CN in a Daybook printout from a Sales Ledger program is short for . . .
- (xiv) The formula "Maximum usage × Maximum lead time" is used to calculate . . .
- (xv) The simplest way to avoid fraud and prevent errors is to ensure that there is a . . .
- (xvi) Sales Invoices are initially recorded in the . . .

(xvii) The normal Dr entry for the Provision for Bad Debts is in the...
Account.

(xviii) The ruling that all items should be recorded at the amount paid for
them is the...Concept.

(xix) Most commercial accounting packages are... driven to assist the
user.

(xx)   The auditor checks the accounts of a firm by gathering...

(20 marks)

All Students should attempt this question.

2   The balances on a firm's control accounts at 31/12/90 were as follows:
Sales Ledger control account $2,000, Purchases Ledger control
account $1,720. During the year 1991 the following transactions took
place:

	$
Purchases	32,800
Sales (including $350 cash sales)	42,955
Payments to suppliers	26,752
Discounts Received	2,040
Bad Debts written off	5,401
Discounts Allowed	2,308
Goods returned to suppliers	7,320
Refund of customers overpayment	855
Goods returned by customers	3,906
Receipts from customers	29,902

Prepare the Sales and Purchase Ledgers Control Accounts for the
year and calculate the closing balances.   (14 marks)

(b)   Identify 6 possible printouts produced by a Job Costing program.

(6 marks)

Students should attempt any other THREE questions only.

3   (a)   Examine the table shown below and describe what transactions have
taken place between each column.

	A	B	C	D	E	F
Premises	10,000	10,000	10,000	15,000	15,000	15,000
Motor Van	5,000	5,000	3,000	3,000	3,000	3,000
Creditors	1,000	1,000	1,000	1,000	2,500	2,500
Capital	14,000	14,000	14,000	14,000	14,000	11,000
Bank	1,000	3,000	5,000	5,000	5,000	2,000
Stock	2,750	2,750	2,750	2,750	4,250	4,250
Loan	8,000	8,000	8,000	13,000	13,000	13,000
Debtors	4,250	2,250	2,250	2,250	2,250	2,250

(5 marks)

(b)   Draw up the double-entry accounts to record each of the
transactions.   (10 marks)

(c) In a computerised system most of the above transactions would be entered in the Nominal Ledger, design a suitable screen for the UPDATE ACCOUNT DETAILS MENU. (5 marks)

4 Draw up an OPERATING STATEMENT from the following figures:

	$	$
Purchase of raw materials		69,400
Wages and Salaries:		
Direct Labour	83,150	
Factory Foreman	42,600	
Office Staff	38,300	
Salesmen	31,550	195,600
Hire of special machinery		750
Sales		354,200
Rent & Rates:		
Factory	10,200	
Offices	5,400	
Showroom	3,245	18,845
Light & Heat:		
Factory	6,540	
Offices	3,250	
Showroom	2,109	11,907
Depreciation:		
Factory machinery	8,905	
Office equipment	4,555	
Display equipment	1,540	15,000
Insurance:		
Factory	2,400	
Offices	1,200	
Showroom	1,200	4,800
Loan Interest		3,000
Royalties paid		3,542

(20 marks)

5 (a) Design and complete a sales invoice to record the following transaction details:

Goods sold by NCC & Co, New Buildings, Singapore to J. Patel & Sons, 123 Old Calcutta Road, Delhi. Invoice dated 21st January 1992, number K2903. Their order number WR20101, dated 15th December 1991.
10 pairs of Hubs at $15.00 per pair
20 pairs of Rims at $22.00 per pair
15 Levers at $8.50 each
30 Stirrups at $330 per hundred
2 pallets of brackets at $8 per half pallet

Trade discount of 25% is to be given on the total value of the order and a cash discount of 2% is offered for payment within 30 days. Sales tax is charged at 15%. (10 marks)

(b)   Design a suitable printout from a Sales Ledger package to show EXAMINATION OF SALES/CUSTOMER ACCOUNT DETAILS, include some sample data.   (10 marks)

6   (a)   A firm has obtained the following data relating to Stock:

Maximum Stock level	20,000 units
Maximum monthly usage	5,000 units
Minimum monthly usage	2,000 units
Maximum delivery time	60 days
Minimum delivery time	40 days

Calculate the following:
(i)   Reorder level
(ii) Reorder quantity
(iii) Minimum level
(iv) Average Stock held

(8 marks)

(b)   The firm have continually experienced problems with shortages of Stock and pilferage. Suggest how the firm can improve its control of Stock by improving its internal controls. Your answer should use the internal control headings of Organisation Structure, Segregation of Duties, Physical controls, Authorisation and Approval, Personnel and Supervision.   (12 marks)

Sample answers

1   (a)   (i)   Variable/Direct/Product cost
          (ii)   Accumulated Depreciation
          (iii)   Principle
          (iv)   Overheads (or Profit)
          (v)   Current Assets: Current Liabilities
          (vi)   Spreadsheets
          (vii) Benchmarks
          (viii) 3,000
          (ix)   Division of the Ledger
          (x)   1,200
          (xi) $9.60
          (xii) Statement of Account
          (xiii) Credit Note
          (xiv) Reorder level
          (xv) Separation/Division of Duties
          (xvi) Sales Daybook/Journal
          (xvii) Profit/Loss Account
          (xviii) Cost
          (xix) Menu
          (xx) Audit evidence

2   (a)

Sales Ledger Control A/c	Dr	Cr
Balance b/f	2,000	
Credit Sales	42,605	
Bad Debts written off		2,040
Discounts allowed		5,401
Refund of overpayment		855
Sales returns		3,906
Receipts		29,902
Balance c/d		2,501
	44,605	44,605

Purchase Ledger Control A/c	Dr	Cr
Balance b/f		1,720
Purchases		32,800
Payments	26,752	
Discounts received	2,040	
Purchase returns	4,320	
Balance c/d	1,408	
	34,520	34,520

    (b)   Job list, Cost type list, Transaction list, Job cost, Job cost summary, Special operations logbook

3   (a)   B   Debtors paid $2,000 by cheque
C   Sold Motor Van for $2,000, paid by cheque
D   Bought $5,000 Premises using Loan
E   Bought Stock $1,500 on credit
F   Withdrew Capital $3,000 from Bank

(b)

Debtors	Dr	Cr
Bank		2,000

Bank	Dr	Cr
Debtors	2,000	
Motor Van	2,000	
Capital		3,000

Motor Van	Dr	Cr
Bank		2,000

Premises	Dr	Cr
Loan	5,000	

Loan	Dr	Cr
Premises		5,000

Stock	Dr	Cr
Creditors	1,500	

Creditors	Dr	Cr
Stock		1,500

Capital/Drawings	Dr	Cr
Bank	3,000	

(c)

```
NOMINAL LEDGER     UPDATE ACCOUNT CODES MENU

 1  CREATE NOMINAL LEDGER CODES
 2  AMEND NOMINAL LEDGER CODES
 3  RENAME NOMINAL LEDGER CODES
 4  DELETE NOMINAL LEDGER CODES
 5  LIST NOMINAL LEDGER CODES
 6  EXIT
```

4

OPERATING STATEMENT	$	$	$
Sales			354,200
Raw Materials		69,400	
Direct Wages		83,150	
Direct Expenses:			
Hire of machinery	750		
Royalties	3,542	4,292	
PRIME COST		156,842	
FACTORY OVERHEADS			
Foremen	42,600		
Rent & Rates	10,200		
Light & Heat	6,540		
Depreciation	8,905		
Insurance	2,400	70,645	
PRODUCTION COST		227,487	

ADMINISTRATIVE COST

Office staff	38,300	
Rent & Rates	5,400	
Light & Heat	3,250	
Depreciation	4,555	
Insurance	1,200	52,705

SALES & DISTRIBUTION COST

Salesmen	31,550	
Rent & Rates	3,245	
Light & Heat	2,109	
Depreciation	1,540	
Insurance	1,200	39,644

FINANCE COSTS

Loan Interest	3,000	3,000	322,836
PROFIT			31,364

5 (a)

INVOICE	
	Invoice No: K2903
TO: J Patel & Sons	From: NCC & Co
123 Old Calcutta Road	New Buildings
Delhi	Singapore
	Invoice date: 21/01/92

Your order: WR20101   Dated: 15/12/91
Terms: 2% Cash – 30 days   Sales Tax 15%

Quantity	Description	Price	Total	Tax
10	Hubs	15.00	150.00	
20	Rims	22.00	440.00	
15	Levers	8.50	127.50	
30	Stirrups	3.30	99.00	
2	Pallets	16.00	32.00	
			848.50	
	TRADE DISCOUNT		212.13	
			636.37	95.45
E&OE				

(b)

ABC SUPPLIES PLC	FORD MOTOR CO
THE BROADWAY	HALEWOOD
DUDLEY	MERSEYSIDE

Turnover: 7,330 Credit limit: 20,000 Credit Period: 62 days
Last Entry: 30-08-92 Last Payment: 30-08-92

Examination of Sales Account: FORD						30-08-92
Date	Ref	Entry	Debit	Credit	TAX	Entry No
1-07-92	WE7658	Bal	6,432			12
10-07-92	FS9898	Invoice	10,898		1,234	13
20-07-92	H899	Cr Note		980	142	14
01-08-92	J720111	Payment		7,500	1,090	15

Balance of Account: 8,850 Dr

Current Period	1-Aug-92	2,418
period from	1-Jul-92	5,402
period from	1-Jun-92	1,030

6   (a)   (i)   Reorder level

Maximum usage × Maximum lead time

$5,000 \times 2 = 10,000$

(ii)   Reorder Quantity

Maximum Stock − (Reorder level − Min usage in Min time)

$20,000 − (10,000 − [2,000 \times 1.25])$

$20,000 − (10,000 − 2,500) = 12,500$

(iii)   Minimum Level

Reorder level	−	Average usage in average lead time
10,000	−	$([5000+2000/2]\times[2+1.25/2])$
10,000	−	$(3,500 \times 1.625)$
10,000	−	$5,687.5 = 4,312.5$

(iv)   Average Stock held

Minimum level + 1/2 Reorder quantity

4,312.5	+ 1/2 (12,500)
4,312	+ 6,250 = 10,562

(b)   *Organisation control*

Clearly define responsibilities and authority

Who can order stock, issue stock, pay for stock, etc

Segregation of duties

No one person should fully record transaction

Separate requisitions, ordering, issuing, paying functions

Physical Controls

Restrict access to assets

Careful security on warehouse/stores, lock stores

Authorisation and Approval

All transactions to be authorised

Set limits for staff, restrict access to authorised staff

Personnel

Only well-motivated, competent staff employed

Stores staff must be honest and reliable

Supervision

Provision of adequate supervision

Possible use of security cameras in warehouse area

Appendix 4

Short answer questions and answers

Questions

1 (i)   The... concept decrees that profit should not be taken until a sale is made.
   (ii)   Stock is an example of a... asset.
   (iii) One example of an error which is revealed by a trial balance is...
   (iv)   The term LIFO stands for...
   (v)   The... is a person employed by the shareholders to check the accounts.
   (vi)   The book of prime entry in which credit notes received from suppliers are recorded is...
   (vii) Money owed by a customer who has gone out of business would appear in the Profit/Loss account as...
   (viii) Money taken for his own use by the owner of a business is known as...
   (ix)   The... concept demands that there should be both a credit and debit entry for every transaction.
   (x)   The process of setting up the... is necessary to ensure that a commercial package will run on a particular machine.   (10 marks)
                                                                                    (Jun 92)

2 (i)   The Accounting Equation is...
   (ii)   Sales Less Cost of Goods sold = ...
   (iii) A cost which alters in direct relationship to output is known as a...
   (iv)   The document showing customers the current balance on their account and a summary of transactions is the...
   (v)   That part of a program used to set up the package for use on the firm's own equipment is usually referred to as...
   (vi)   FIFO stands for...
   (vii) The Current Ratio is calculated by...
   (viii) A payment made in advance is known as a...
   (ix)   The method of depreciation which uses the same amount each year is the... method
   (x)   The budget which combines all other subsidiary budgets is the...
                                                                                    (10 marks)
                                                                                    (Mar 92)

3   (i)   LIST FOUR types of error not revealed by a trial balance.

   (ii)   IDENTIFY TWO methods of calculating depreciation on fixed assets.

   (iii)   What is the ACCOUNTING EQUATION?

   (iv)   How is CONTRIBUTION calculated?

   (v)   LIST SIX common printouts from computerised payroll packages.

   (vi)   Which of the following would you normally expect to find on the debit side, and which on the credit side, of the trial balance?

      (a)   Discounts allowed

      (b)   Returns Inward

      (c)   Accumulated Depreciation

      (d)   Provision for Bad debts carried forward

      (e)   Sales

      (f)   A Bank overdraft

  (vii)   LIST TWO methods of VERIFYING input data in a computerised accounts system.

  (viii) NAME TWO books of Prime Entry.   (Dec 91)

4   Write on your ANSWER PAPER the missing word or phrase from each of the following statements:-

   (i)   An independent person who checks the accuracy of accounts is known as an...

   (ii)   The method of depreciation which requires the "scrap or disposal value" is the...

   (iii)   A person who owes the firm money in respect of goods bought is known as a...

   (iv)   The statement ASSETS = CAPITAL + LIABILITIES is the...

   (v)   The difference between a Budgeted figure and the Actual amount paid is the...

   (vi)   A computer program that links all of the different Ledgers is known as an... package.

  (vii)   The source document for the Purchases Daybook is the...

  (viii) An account created to take account of expenses arising in the future is known as a...

   (ix)   A cost which remains constant regardless of changes in production/output is a... cost.

   (x)   The "What If?" function is a feature of... packages.   (10 marks)
                                                              (Mar 91)

5   (i)   An expense item not yet paid is recorded as...

   (ii)   An amount owed to the firm that is unlikely to be paid is written off as a...

   (iii)   The book of original entry for recording Sales Invoice details is the...

   (iv)   Selling Price less Variable Cost =...

   (v)   NBV stands for...

   (vi)   In the Purchase Account all purchases should be entered on the... side.

(vii) The concept of... refers to when a manager is running a business on behalf of the owner(s).

(viii) An entry made in the wrong persons account is an error of...

(ix) An account used as a temporary store for errors is the... account.

(x) The difference between budgeted sales and the break-even point is the...

                                                          (10 marks)

                                                            (Sep 91)

Answers

1	(i)	Realisation
	(ii)	Current
	(iii)	Single entry/incorrect addition/incorrect balancing
	(iv)	Last In First Out
	(v)	Auditor
	(vi)	Returns Out/Purchase Returns
	(vii)	Bad Debts
	(viii)	Drawings
	(ix)	Dual Aspect
	(x)	System Configuration [1 mark each = 10]

2 (i) Assets = Capital + Liabilities
   (ii) Gross Profit
   (iii) Direct or Variable or Product cost
   (iv) Statement (of Account)
   (v) System Configuration
   (vi) First In First Out
   (vii) Current Assets: Current Liabilities
   (viii) Prepayment
   (ix) Straight Line
   (x) Master Budget   [1] mark each 1(a)

3 (i) Commission, Principle, Omission, Original Entry, Reversal, or Compensating errors
   (ii) Reducing Balance, Straight Line method
   (iii) Assets = Capital + Liabilities
   (iv) $\dfrac{\text{Fixed Costs}}{\text{Selling Price} - \text{Variable Costs}}$ or Selling Price – Variable Costs
   (v) Payslips, Cheques, Summary of Pay, End of year documents, Taxation documents, Coin Analysis, Employee Details, Special Operations logbook, EPF, Pay cheques
   (vi) (a) Debit (Discounts Allowed)
        (b) Debit (Returns Inwards)
        (c) Credit
        (d) Credit
        (e) Credit
        (f) Credit
   (vii) Serial numbering of documents, validation checks on documents, batch documents, authorisation procedures, check digit verification, Hash Total
   (viii) Journal, Sales/Purchase/Returns In (Sales Returns)/Returns Out (Purchase Returns) Daybooks/Journals, Cashbook

4 (i) Auditor
  (ii) Straight-Line method
  (iii) Debtor
  (iv) Accounting Equation
  (v) Variance
  (vi) Integrated
  (vii) Purchase Invoice
  (viii) Provision
  (ix) Fixed
  (x) Spreadsheet   [1] mark each = 10 marks

5 (i) Accruals
  (ii) Bad Debt
  (iii) Sales Daybook/Journal
  (iv) Contribution/Marginal cost
  (v) Net Book Value
  (vi) Debit
  (vii) Stewardship
  (viii) Commission
  (ix) Suspense
  (x) Margin of Safety   [1] mark each = 10 marks

Index